Shine the Light

Shine the Light

Sexual Abuse and Healing in the Jewish Community

RACHEL LEV

If I am not for myself, then who will be for me?
And if I am only for myself, then what am I?
And if not now, when?

Rabbi Hillel, *Pirkei Avot* (*Ethics of the Fathers*)

You have been telling the people that this is the
Eleventh Hour
now you must go back and tell the people that
this is the Hour . . .
It is time to speak your truth
Create your community
Be good to each other
And do not look outside yourself for the leader . . .
We are the ones we've been waiting for.

Hopi Elder, Hopi Nation, Oraibi, Arizona

Northeastern University Press
Boston

Northeastern University Press 2003

Advisor to Northeastern University Press
Claire Renzetti

Library of Congress Cataloging-in-Publication Data

Lev, Rachel, 1949–
    Shine the Light : sexual abuse and healing in the Jewish
community / Rachel Lev.
        p.   cm.
    Includes bibliographical references and index.
    ISBN 1–55553–534–8 (cloth : alk. paper)
    1. Child sexual abuse—United States—Psychological aspects—
Case studies.   2. Adult child sexual abuse victims—United States.
3. Sexually abused Jewish children—United States.   4. Child sexual
abuse—Religious aspects—Judaism.   I. Title.

    HV6570.2 .L475   2003
    616.85'8369'00899240973—dc21   2002070990

Designed by Janis Owens

Composed in Goudy by Coghill Composition in Richmond, Virginia.
Printed and bound by Thomson-Shore, Inc., in Dexter, Michigan.
The paper is Glatfelter Supple Opaque Recycled, an acid-free sheet.

MANUFACTURED IN THE UNITED STATES OF AMERICA
07   06   05   04   03   5   4   3   2   1

This book is dedicated to those who opened doors I didn't even know were closed and helped the light enter my heart, warm it awake, and remind me how to sing.

This includes those who study and expose evil like Dr. Robert Lifton and Alice Miller as well as those who were personally kind, loving, and generous to me throughout my life—my kindergarten and first grade teachers, my friends, and helpers.

And, to my clients for boldly embracing life and inspiring me.

CONTENTS ↗

B. B. Adams

Dr. Adams wrote her first poem when she was twelve, in imitation of John Masefield's "Sea Fever," because that was her father's favorite poem. She wrote her second poem thirty years later, in graduate school, found a vocation as a writer, and began publishing poems in journals. She also published a book of poems, *Hapax Legomena*, and a chapbook, *Double Solitaire*. She always wanted to write stories, and began writing them as she finished her Ph.D. in English at New York University in 1981. Several of her stories have been published in magazines and anthologies; "Portrait of the Artist's Daughter" won first prize in the 1999 *Negative Capability* fiction contest. Then she wanted to write more directly about herself and published essays in *Psychoanalytic Review*, *Free Associations*, and *Life Stories: A Teaching Case Book* (2001). In the fall of 2000, her first play, *God's Lioness and the Crow: Sylvia Plath and Ted Hughes*, was produced by the Mohonk Mountain Stage Company in New Paltz, New York.

She was a professor of English at Pace University for eighteen years, and recently retired to write poems, stories, essays, and whatever, full-time.

Adrienne Affleck

Adrienne was referred to Shalom Bayit (a Jewish domestic violence agency) by her rabbi. She says, "Shalom Bayit gave me the will to live when I had lost it, and continues to give me the strength and resolve to move beyond survival."

As part of a small committee, she developed the Sukkoth healing service included here (see Appendix E).

Asenath Barzani

Asenath Barzani is a thirty-something Mizrahi woman.[1] A musician, writer, and feminist, she is passionate about the safety and rights of women.

Ellen Bass

Ellen Bass is an award-winning author who has published several volumes of poetry as well as nonfiction books. She began working with survivors in the early 1970s, facilitated *I Never Told Anyone* workshops for survivors for many years, and trained professionals to work with survivors nationally and internationally.

Nonfiction books include the best-selling *The Courage to Heal: A Guide for Women Survivors of Child Sexual Abuse*, which she coauthored with Laura Davis and which has been translated into nine languages (Harper-Collins, 1988, 1994). Other books include *I Never Told Anyone: Writings by Women Survivors of Child Sexual Abuse*, coedited with Louise Thornton (HarperCollins, 1983, 1991); *Beginning to Heal: A First Book for Survivors of Child Sexual Abuse*, coauthored with Laura Davis (HarperCollins, 1993); a children's book, *I like you to make jokes with me, but I don't want you to touch me* (Lollipop Power, 1981; Carolina Wren Press, 1993); and *Free Your Mind: The Book for Gay, Lesbian, and Bisexual Youth—And Their Allies*, coauthored with Kate Kaufman (HarperCollins, 1996).

Ellen has also published several volumes of poetry. A new volume of poetry, *Mules of Love*, is forthcoming in 2002 from BOA Editions.

Zena David

Zena David grew up in the Midwest. At nineteen she spent six months as a volunteer in Israel after the Six-Day War. By the end of 1969 she returned to the States and moved to California, where she married an Israeli she had met in Jerusalem.

In the 1970s Zena began assistant producing and acting in plays for the Northridge Theater Guild located in Hollywood. In 1977, after returning home from a rehearsal, she was raped in her apartment. Friends and family opened their hearts and homes to her until she felt safe living by herself again.

Zena returned to teaching, receiving several grants and a couple of awards for her teaching efforts. Several years ago she wrote a play that was given a reading at Barnsdall Theater and Art Gallery. The topic was a three-part response by the community, the artist, and herself to a sculpture by Ed Massey called *Morality/Mortality*. The three-part sculpture displayed the aftermath of a sexual assault and was shown in storefront windows in five American cities across the United States.

In the play, *Passing Over*, Zena found a creative theatrical vehicle to eulogize her mentor as well as identify and integrate childhood sexual abuse into her psyche.

Rabbi Elliot Dorff

Elliot Dorff was ordained a Conservative rabbi by the Jewish Theological Seminary of America in 1970 and earned his Ph.D. in philosophy from Columbia University in 1971 with a dissertation in moral theory. Since then he has directed the rabbinical and master's programs at the University of Judaism, where he currently is rector and Distinguished Professor of Philosophy. He also teaches a course on Jewish law at UCLA School of Law as a visiting professor.

Rabbi Dorff is a member of the Conservative movement's Committee on Jewish Law and Standards and the editorial committee of the new Torah commentary for the Conservative movement.

In Los Angeles, he is a vice-president of Jewish Family Service, and he is a member of the ethics committees at the Jewish Homes for the Aging and the UCLA Medical Center. He serves as cochair of the Priest-Rabbi Dialogue sponsored by the Los Angeles Archdiocese and the Board of Rabbis of Southern California, and he is a vice-president of the Academy for Jewish, Christian, and Muslim Studies.

Rabbi Dorff's publications include over 150 articles on Jewish thought, law, and ethics, together with eight books. He wrote the responsum, adapted here in chapter 3, approved unanimously by the Conservative movement's Committee on Jewish Law and Standards on Family Violence, a responsum that will appear in his forthcoming book, tentatively titled *Doing the Right and the Good: A Jewish Approach to Social Ethics* (Philadelphia: Jewish Publication Society, 2002).

He was featured in the video *To Save a Life*, on the subject of spouse abuse in the Jewish community, produced by the Center for Prevention of Sexual and Domestic Violence.

Elizabeth

Elizabeth was born in Kharkov, Ukraine. Her family moved to the States when she was thirteen. She started writing poems and stories a year later and believes, "on a purely subconscious level, it was an attempt to compensate for my lack of social and communication skills and for the disabling fear of people that I had developed as a result of years of physical, emotional and sexual abuse." She wrote a column for her college paper and started writing plays in her late twenties. A chef by profession, Elizabeth dreams of having her own restaurant someday. Her hobbies are jewelry design, photography, horseback riding, sailing, and writing horror stories.

Barbara Engel

Barbara Engel has been an activist in the movement to end violence against women for twenty-five years. She was the director of a sexual assault and domestic violence counseling, public policy advocacy, and training center in Chicago. She cofounded both sexual assault and domestic violence city coalitions and has spearheaded institutional advocacy efforts with criminal justice and law enforcement agencies. In 2001 she became a gubernatorial appointee to the board of the Illinois Criminal Justice Information Authority, and an appointee to the mayor's Advisory Council on Women. She has an M.A. in public health from the University of Illinois and a B.S. in humanities from the University of Chicago.

Masha Gladys

Masha Gladys is a volunteer with a Jewish service organization that helps families in trouble. She decided to write under a pseudonym because her children are not public about the incest in their lives, and she did not want to expose this secret for them.

Shauna Green

Shauna is a forty-something artist, therapist, and survivor of ritual abuse, who over the years recovered from a dissociative identity disorder.

Carol Greenfield

Carol Greenfield is a professional writer and college educator.

Hadass G.

Thirty-seven-year-old Hadass G. was born in Israel and spent most of her childhood there. She describes her pictures as "a kind of mirror of my healing process from 'adult-victim' of severe childhood sexual abuse to a survivor. I always drew what I felt, the current mental situation I was in, and exactly dated my pictures. They became a pictorial diary of my healing process."

Hadiyah C.

Hadiyah's healing was rooted in a nontraditional life journey which took her in the 1960s from the middle-class Jewish suburbs of Newark, New Jersey, to the hippie capital of Haight Ashbury, San Francisco. In the 1970s, she juggled the stresses of poverty, single motherhood, and trail-blazing as the first and only female shipyard welder in a small town north of Seattle. The 1980s brought her back East, where she earned her M.S.W. and worked as a policy analyst in urban economic development.

Presently, she continues her healing through the pleasures of hiking, swimming, and biking; facilitating writing workshops; and experiencing the world of childhood through the eyes of her young grandchildren.

Hillary

Born on the East Coast and educated in the Midwest, Hillary is a survivor of both sexual molestation and an ugly divorce during her childhood. She rose above these traumas to pursue successful careers in education (both public and Jewish), sales, administration, social work, and fund-raising.

At the age of thirty-eight, Hillary was forced to deal with the crises of her past, as she was confronted with a barrage of chronic stress-related illnesses. With the love of her husband and two sons, the support of numerous caring friends, and the guidance of dedicated professionals, she moved through the recovery process and is now recreating a life for herself and her family.

Hillary writes, paints, crafts jewelry, and is committed to volunteer work that helps others achieve their full potential, especially Jewish adolescents and young adults. For the past twenty years she has found peace and happiness within her Jewish community.

Jerome

Jerome describes himself as a middle-aged businessman and writer. Although raised in an Orthodox Jewish setting, he now tends toward Conservatism. He is a survivor of maternal sexual abuse that began, as far as he can remember, when he was eight years old. He is grateful for the opportunity to contribute to this book insofar as it helps dispel the myth of "perfect" Jewish families and for the opportunity to help others with their feelings of isolation and anger. What happened to Jerome has had a devastating effect on his life, especially as it relates to issues of trust. As a consequence, he has been and continues to be in therapy.

Rae

Rae is fifty years old with two children—a son, twenty-one, and a daughter, nineteen. Her company is dedicated to building self-esteem, healing the heart, and giving voice to the soul through the arts.

"I was very quiet about the abuse for many years, except to close friends and family. Five years ago I got active in the Silent Witness Initiative (through the National Council of Jewish Women), which works diligently to end domestic violence. At the same time I decided to give my first public talk/slide show on abuse. I was terrified but told myself that if I helped one person it would be worth it. After the presentation a young woman came up to me and said, 'You saved my life.'"

Laurie Suzanne Reiche

Laurie Suzanne Reiche is a forty-something wife, mother, writer, and student of feminism who says, "I consider the fact that I am alive a miracle and every day, every day I am grateful that I was born and survived the brutality of my childhood and I just don't know what else to say at the top of my head like this except that life is astounding. What else is there?"

Briana Rose

Briana has dedicated her life to "truth telling and authentic artistic expression." She started writing seven years ago as a vehicle for self-discovery and healing. Singing and songwriting came more recently as "too amazing to even hope for" by-products of her recovery.

Briana's poems have appeared in *The Healing Woman* newsletter and in *Summer Room*, an anthology of women's poetry and prose published in 1996 by Renegade Press of Mill Valley, California. Through her new company, TRUTHSONG, Briana has recorded *For your safety & mine . . .* , a CD of songs and poems that reveal an incest survivor's healing journey in all its pain and joy. *For your safety & mine . . .* is available through the websites www.truthsong.net or www.foryoursafetyandmine.net.

Sue William Silverman

Sue William Silverman is the author of *Love Sick: One Woman's Journey Through Sexual Addiction* (W. W. Norton). An earlier memoir, *Because I*

Remember Terror, Father, I Remember You, won the Associated Writing Programs Award Series in Creative Nonfiction (University of Georgia Press, paperback). She is a professional speaker on the subjects of incest, family dynamics, and addiction, and received an honorary degree of doctor of humane letters from Aquinas College for her work in literature and child abuse victim advocacy. In addition, she is associate editor of *Fourth Genre: Explorations in Nonfiction*, a literary journal published by Michigan State University Press.

Esta Soler

Esta Soler is the founder and executive director of the San Francisco–based Family Violence Prevention Fund (FVPF), a national organization working to develop innovative responses to the epidemic of domestic violence. Established in 1980, the FVPF is widely respected for its pioneering work. It has created model policy, advocacy, prevention, education, and training programs that have been replicated in all fifty states and many foreign countries.

Esta has served as a consultant and adviser on domestic violence to many private and governmental organizations, including the Department of Justice, the U.S. Department of Health and Human Services, the Centers for Disease Control and Prevention, the Soros Justice Fellowship program, the Ford Foundation/Harvard University Innovations in American Government, and the Aspen Institute. Ms. Soler was appointed to serve on the Presidential Commission on Crime Control and Prevention and the National Advisory Council on Violence Against Women, cochaired by Secretary Donna Shalala and Attorney General Janet Reno. She is coauthor of the book *Ending Domestic Violence: Changing Public Perceptions/Halting the Epidemic.*

Marcia Cohn Spiegel

Marcia Cohn Spiegel received her M.A. in Jewish communal service at Hebrew Union College in 1978. Her thesis, *The Heritage of Noah: Alcoholism in the Jewish Community Today*, was the first documentation of the widespread presence of the disease in the Jewish community. As a result of lectures, workshops, and classes, she heard firsthand stories of other stigmatized behaviors long denied by Jews—incest, sexual abuse, and family violence—and has dedicated her life to bringing the awareness of these problems to the community.

Founder of the Creative Jewish Women's Alliance, a participating founder of Women Writers West, and board member of the Jewish Arts Associates, she has facilitated many conferences and workshops on poetry, arts, creativity, and spirituality. She has collected poetry by over six hundred Jewish women; a small part of the collection is included in *Women Speak to God: The Poems and Prayers of Jewish Women*, which she edited, and in *Sarah's Daughters Sing*, edited by Henny Wenkart.

Currently she serves on the national Jewish task force of the Center for Prevention of Sexual and Domestic Violence, and is actively involved with Project Kesher, an organization working to empower Jewish women of the former Soviet Union by teaching organizational skills, group process, and Judaism.

She has been on the faculties of UCLA Extension and the University of Judaism, and has taught at synagogues and centers across the United States as well as in Russia, Ukraine, London, Jerusalem, and Sydney, Australia. Because of the convergence of her work with dysfunction in the Jewish family, women's studies, spirituality, and the arts, her current work focuses on the impact of changing roles and relationships within the family, particularly on women's lives and self-esteem; helping people to learn "how" and "why" they act as they do, so that they can make intelligent choices in their lives. The culmination of this work is *The Jewish Women's Awareness Guide* (of which she is coauthor), a facilitator's manual for small groups, exploring issues of identity formation as Jews and as women.

ACKNOWLEDGMENTS

I feel very grateful and lucky to have received the support of so many people throughout the creation of this book. Some are friends, others began as total strangers. Some of these strangers became friends. They believed in me. They believed in the importance of this project. They gave of their time and their ideas. Some lent their country homes or screened-in porches for me to write in peace and beauty. Many helped me network and find the resources I needed.

Shalvi, Emunah, and Beth helped begin this journey by letting me interview them as a group. Countless others from around the world generously shared their stories and art. To all those who submitted materials, including those who are not featured here, please know that I was touched by your courage and strength.

I thank those who listened to me read chapters and those who read and gave feedback. It is hard to express how wonderful it was to look up from reading and see someone listening with tears in their eyes, head nodding. One of these was my therapist whose generous light-filled soul often sustained and inspired me.

I am grateful to those whose research, teaching, and/or writing on trauma has helped me heal and be better able to help others. They have refused to deny the existence and long-term impact of evil acts against children. These include Alice Miller, Judith Lewis Herman, Bessel van der Kolk, John Briere, Maurice Shengold, and Andrew Vachss.

I acknowledge the gifts of life and strength I received from my family heritage—from my grandmothers who faced incredible challenges throughout their lives, and from my parents. From my father I learned it's important to take a stand for those in need and for what is right. It feels awkward to acknowledge him as the source of that teaching while relying on it to take a stand against what he did to me. From my mother I continue to learn about friendship, love, resiliency, and staying in the stream of life—no matter what.

I met Marcia Cohn Spiegel via e-mail. A total stranger, she shared her vast knowledge and resources regarding ending violence in Jewish lives. She offered ideas and friendship, and affirmed my work. As I searched for a publisher, she suggested I get in touch with Claire Renzetti, which I did. Claire offered to help, and after reading a draft of my manuscript, handed it to Bill Frohlich of Northeastern University Press, who, thank God, became my publisher! I say "thank God" because (1) I sometimes feared I'd never find one and (2) he has been absolutely wonderful. Working with Bill has been a surprising and delightful addition to my journey. He is thoughtful, compassionate, witty, and patient. He took me and the issues in this book seriously, and he made me laugh. He was very helpful in teaching me, as a new author, things I needed to know about the publishing process and ways to look at my writing from the viewpoint of a broader reading audience. Thank you, Marty, Claire, and Bill!

Thank you all for continuing to shine the light! Together we bear witness to the miracles that can happen when people of good will join together. This is true community.

Grateful acknowledgment is made for the following:

Excerpts from "Surviving Incest in a Holocaust Family" by *Lilith Goldberg* from *Lilith* (winter 1993) are reprinted by permission from *Lilith: The Independent Jewish Women's Magazine.*

Chapter 3 is based on Rabbi Elliot Dorff's rabbinic ruling (*teshuvah*), "Family Violence," approved unanimously by the Conservative movement's Committee on Jewish Law and Standards on September 13, 1995. See *Responsa 1991–2000: The Committee on Jewish Law and Standards of the Conservative Movement*, ed. Kassel Abelson and David J. Fine (New York: Rabbinical Assembly, 2002). Used by permission of Rabbi Dorff.

Excerpts from *The Prophet* by Kahlil Gibran, copyright 1923 by Kahlil Gibran and renewed in 1951 by Administrators C.T.A. of Kahlil Gibran Estate and Mary G. Gibran, are used by permission of Alfred A. Knopf, a division of Random House, Inc., and the Gibran National Committee in Beirut, Lebanon.

"Bubba Esther" by Ruth Whitman Sacks, copyright 1980 by Ruth Whitman Sacks, was first printed in *The Radcliffe Quarterly* and later collected in *Permanent Address: New Poems 1973–1980 by RWS* (Alice James Books). Reprinted by permission of Morton Sacks.

Excerpt from *Because I Remember Terror, Father, I Remember You* by Sue William Silverman, copyright 1996 by Sue William Silverman, is reprinted by permission of the University of Georgia Press and the author.

The High Holy Day Message of the Jewish Theological Seminary for 1992 is copyrighted by JTS and reprinted by permission.

Excerpts from "The thing is" by Ellen Bass, copyright 1997 by Ellen Bass, appeared in *Mules of Love* (Rochester: BOA Editions, 2002) and is reprinted by permission of the author.

The art throughout the book is copyrighted and reprinted by permission of each artist.

INTRODUCTION ॐ

I sit along the lake's edge. The sail of a single boat makes its triangular slash against the sparkling surface of the lake. Another boat comes toward me from the south, its sail invisible, its mast a pencil-thin vertical line atop a darker box, rocking side to side. As I look northeast I see another sailboat, matte gray, its sail full. As the first boat moves farther north, the lake loses its slash. I love light—its myriad shades and influences. The same object moves a few degrees and is transformed by the light. The object has not changed, and yet it is different. The thought comes, "Shine the light and transform what you see."

Incest is there. It has always been. You could not see it because the light was not shining in the right direction, someone was blocking it, or you avoided looking. It is time to shine the light so we transform the lives of children and adult survivors of childhood sexual abuse and incest.

Nobel Peace Prize winner and Holocaust survivor Elie Wiesel said, "Whoever survives a test, whatever it may be, must tell the story. That is his [her] duty."[1]

I survived. This book is a synthesis of my story and the stories of over one hundred Jewish women and men sexually abused or incested as children.[2] It contains the thoughts of those who care about survivors and are committed to prevention of future abuses. As a clinical social worker I am part of this group as well.

The gathering of information for this book began by sending letters to colleagues and survivors I knew, then placing notices in Jewish, survivor, literary, and therapist magazines, and newsletters. As people heard about this project they posted notices on the Internet, at literary workshops, and at professional conferences, social service agencies, and universities.

Survivors range in age from their twenties to their eighties and represent the cities, suburbs, and small towns of every region of the United States. A few survivors' stories came from Canada, Austria, and England. All identify themselves as Jews. A few are my friends, my clients, or my colleagues.

Most are people previously unknown to me. The perpetrators include parents, stepparents, grandparents, brothers, uncles, cousins, rabbis, teachers, youth leaders, and friends of a family member. All perpetrators were identified as Jews. Most perpetrators were described as highly successful, well-respected members of their communities—doctors, lawyers, professionals, businesspeople, directors of Jewish agencies, rabbis, and teachers.[3]

This gets very confusing for most of us—whether survivor or not. How can someone be both well respected and a child molester? We search for ways to describe those who abuse, those who do evil. We want them to be identifiable. Yet, studies of those who have done monstrous things—from Adolf Eichmann to those who molest their children—show that the thing they have most in common is their apparent normality. Eichmann, engineer of unimaginable horrors, was certified by half a dozen psychiatrists as normal.[4] More needs to be understood and communicated about perpetrators. That is beyond the scope of this book.

Our tendency to demonize those who do evil makes the task of stopping the violence harder. How? First we look for monsters rather than wounded men and women. Second, we deny that each human being has the capacity to do evil things. Third, we make it harder for molesters to self-identify.

The term "incest" is generally distinguished from "sexual abuse," with incest referring to molestation by a family member. For the purposes of this book, the terms "incest" and "sexual abuse" are used interchangeably to mean the sexual violation of a minor child by someone in a position of trust and authority. Sometimes both terms will be used. Since most survivors who contacted me were female and their perpetrators were male, the pronoun "she" is used in reference to survivors and "he" for perpetrators. When I speak of "survivors," unless otherwise noted, I'm speaking of Jewish survivors of incest. Each experienced violations that crossed a physical boundary—fondling, kissing, and/or rape. Many also experienced emotional incest—sexual jokes, innuendo, being treated as a surrogate partner (even when nonsexual), and inappropriate comments about their bodies or other forms of emotional and physical abuse as children.

Some lived in homes where their mothers were battered. Some are children of Holocaust survivors. Some were victimized as children and as adults. Together, they represent all affiliations within the Jewish community, including those who consider themselves secular Jews.

My sample is not all-inclusive. While there are men survivors, probably many more than we know about, I heard from only a few men. Survivors included are almost exclusively women. People told mostly of abuse by men. Although molestation by women happens, it seems even more taboo to acknowledge.

Most of the literature and my discussions with other clinicians omit or dismiss women as perpetrators. Studies by Diana Russell and David Finkelhor show that up to 5 percent of those who molest girls and 20 percent of those who molest boys are female.[5] How does gender socialization impact what we see? How does it impact the labeling and reporting of abuse by those who are molested by women? How does a predisposition to think of men as the aggressors and women as victims impact assessment and treatment? These issues need more exploration.[6]

Most of the survivors included here are functioning at very high levels. Many are degreed professionals who work and have relationships that sustain them. Many have the capacity to express their needs and the resiliency and resources to cope well with day-to-day living. This is not true of all survivors. Those who are healing have worked hard and been greatly aided by the support of people, of conscientious community, whether a teacher in grade school or a friend, rabbi, therapist, or self-help network in their adult lives. Without people, without compassionate community, without connection, without help, healing cannot happen.

This book is more than stories. It is about the need to be part of community—to connect or reconnect with our Jewish selves. Many who are seeking ways to be a part of the Jewish community don't feel welcome when they reveal their stories of abuse. Others, uncertain about their desire to connect to Judaism as a religion or to a Jewish community, are exploring their identity as Jews. Some want to help break through the denial within the Jewish community. Some want only to be heard.

Abuses committed within the Jewish community are no different from those committed within any other group. But too many of us think they are. We believe, *"We're different. We don't do such things."* Someone has to say out loud, *"We are not different. We do these things."* For those survivors who want to belong, there is a need to have this issue in the open. From the perspective of families and community, if children are to be safe from molestation, we must talk about it and know about it so we can prevent it.

Incest is a difficult issue for most communities to face. As a minority culture we can too easily dismiss what is true for the general population as not applicable to us. While the stories here are by and about Jews, since the 1970s as a student intern, then therapist, I have seen what is described here in many families, regardless of religion, where cultural identity is strong—from Algerian to Irish to Italian to Israeli to Hispanic to African-American. The similarities are especially true when talking about minorities or oppressed people.

Incest is traumatic whether physical, verbal, or emotional. For some of us who are lucky and willing to work hard, there is hope. Some are so brutalized that there is no way out. These people often end up homeless, addicted, suicidal

I'm grateful to have found my voice. I'm grateful to be recapturing and expanding my capacity for love and joy. This book lets you know how hard a battle it has been and sometimes still is. I hope it will help someone heal. I'd love the stories, rituals, and information in this book to find their way into rabbis' sermons, Jewish curricula for children and adults, and the creation of healing rituals for individuals and groups. And I hope some child will grow up safer because of what someone read here.

To be molested as a child makes you different. Suddenly, you are outside yourself and those around you. Nothing is the same. You are not the person you were the second before it began. To be compelled to keep this secret widens the gap between you and everyone and everything else.

To be a Jewish child makes you different. Already "outside" the dominant culture, we are taught the importance of not drawing attention to our "differences," not to bring shame or danger to our families or community. Whether molested or not, the message is clear: It is not safe to be noticed too much. We learn, often indirectly, a responsibility to reflect positively upon our people. We are taught to respect our parents, teachers, rabbis, and elders. But what are we to do when one of them is molesting us? If we start to tell, who will listen? Without compassionate listeners to believe us and help us, the gap between us and others widens. For a Jewish child to be molested adds to any existing feeling of being alone. Our loneliness is often profound.

When people can't express what was done to them, they can't heal. When people cannot heal within a community, they may physically leave or emotionally withdraw as Dr. Judith Lewis Herman wrote:

> Traumatic events [such as sexual abuse and incest] destroy the sustaining bonds between individual and community. Those who have survived learn that their sense of self, of worth, of humanity, depends upon a feeling of connection to others. The solidarity of a group

provides the strongest protection against terror and despair, and the strongest antidote to traumatic experience. Trauma isolates; the group re-creates a sense of belonging. Trauma shames and stigmatizes; the group bears witness and affirms. Trauma degrades the victim; the group exalts her. Trauma dehumanizes the victim; the group restores her humanity.[7]

The "group" we call the Jewish community has the power to help survivors heal and protect children from the trauma of incest and sexual abuse. First, we must bear witness to the fact that incest happens in Jewish homes and institutions at the hands of family members, neighbors, rabbis, cantors, youth advisers, teachers and school administrators, baby-sitters, and coaches.

We bear witness in part by listening to survivor stories. Then we address the questions: How do we help people heal? What do we do to stop these abuses? Where do we start? Simple answers will not work. Blaming and shaming won't work even though they're tempting. Healing and prevention happen when together we listen to the stories that must be told, then share resources and a commitment to peaceful relationships. Healing comes when we "shine the light" on what is, what was, and what needs to be.

Incest hurts not only during the time it happens. When undiscovered, ignored, discounted, minimized, or disbelieved, it hurts that person throughout her life. Sexual molestation hurts the child, the adult she becomes, and those who love her. Chapter 1 explores the child's experience, while chapter 5 describes how the abuse of so long ago impacts survivors today.

Unresolved trauma of any kind leaves its legacy in future generations. *Lilith Goldberg* (in chapter 2) writes about the parallels and the pain in her father's experience as a Holocaust survivor and her own as someone incested by him.

Human beings are capable of great good and achievements as well as evil. Why, then, do we deny sexual abuse in Jewish lives? Chapter 2, "If It's There, Why Don't We See It?" presents some reasons we deny incest, what denial looks like, and what some of its costs are.

In chapter 3, Rabbi Elliot Dorff reviews Jewish history, law, and tradition regarding abuse.

Some of the family dynamics that make incest more likely to occur and to be hidden are explored in chapter 4, "Honey, I'm Cold. Put on a Sweater."

This book's focus is the impact of sexual abuse and incest on Jewish adult survivors, not the details of the abuse. Because some people, myself included, can be retraumatized by vivid descriptions of the ways people have been molested, I have limited these details. I want this book to be about the long-term consequences of violating a child and about healing.

Specific clinical interventions are not offered here. Content in chapters 8, 10, and 11 on the benefits of expression through art, our Jewish identity, and healing rituals can augment clinical work with survivors. Compassionate listening is essential but not enough for complete healing. Over time, we survivors must be helped to reinhabit our bodies, to integrate our traumatic histories with all of who we are. For many of the survivors included here, the use of art, movement, energy psychology, body-mind integrative techniques, and the like were essential to fully reclaiming our lives. (See Appendices G and H.)

Survivors need the context of a safe relationship in which to tell our stories, express the range of our emotions, and develop our abilities to live our lives. Sexual abuse often shatters our trust in others. A safe therapeutic relationship can make it possible for us to learn to trust again. This, however, takes time. Many current models of treatment and managed health care, with their focus exclusively on brief behavioral and cognitive therapy, do more harm than good with incest survivors. Survivors end up feeling there is something wrong with them when they are not helped by models that emphasize (primarily or only) mind over matter and here-and-now problems. In addition, managing someone's anxiety attacks and/or depression with medication may be essential but often is not enough.

We survivors need therapists, doctors, and rabbis to (1) believe in our wholeness, no matter what, (2) hold the positive possibilities for us until we can hold them for ourselves, (3) be willing to be part of a "team" of helpers we may need, (4) be willing to be creative with us—boundaried, and creative and open to learning, and (5) recognize the power they have to influence us and use it judiciously.

In addition, those who agree to work with survivors must see us as individuals. We need our defenses to be recognized and appreciated for their part in our ability to survive as well as we have. Too many blame us when we use the defenses we developed to enable us to survive.[8] Karen Olio speaks of the need to shift attitudes, when working with trauma survivors, from "What's wrong with her?" to "What happened to her?"[9] Effective and empathic helpers will applaud our rough edges, our controlling behavior, our neediness while helping us heal so we can let go of beliefs and behaviors that no longer serve us. They will also get a great support network for themselves because helping us isn't always easy.

This book presents more than the pain of incest. It also expresses the courage, creativity, and contribution of people who survive traumatic events and are able to move beyond survival to thriving. Dr. Rachel Naomi Remen, in her books *Kitchen Table Wisdom* and *My Grandfather's Blessings,* writes about wounded healers and how they enrich the lives of others. Dr. Remen discusses how having an illness can create a level of empathy and recognition of suffering that enables individuals to relate to others who experience similar and different survival issues. There is nothing good about having been traumatized. Yet, to the extent that people learn and grow from their experiences, they have that knowledge to share with others—and not just with those who have suffered from the same things. As an activist for peace and safety in Jewish lives reminded me, "Survivors who are healing are not just takers, not just depositories for kindness. They are people whose work to heal forces a deepening of who they are. That depth is a gift to the community. Their depth of character and experience can be shared and often is, just by virtue of their being who they are. Communities benefit from survivors because they have survived—not despite the fact."

For those who want to learn more about child sexual abuse, adult survivors of these abuses, as well as research and treatment approaches, there is much already written. For those choosing to work with trauma survivors, specific learning and training must take place. A selected bibliography is in Appendix H.

In addition to our trauma histories, our identity as Jews is likely to play a part in our pain and our healing—whether we are religious or secular Jews. Melanie Kaye/Kantrowitz believes an individual Jew's connection to the community is so profound that any separation from it causes extreme loss.[10] When survivors identify themselves as "Jewish," some exploration is needed of what that means and what they want or need with regard to that identity.

There is no "one" Jewish community. There is much diversity among those of us who call ourselves "Jews." We are Sephardic,[11] Ashkenazi,[12] Mizrahi. For some, Jewish identity is religious; for others it is cultural. For some it is both. This diversity must be understood and respected as part of any exploration of the problems and solutions in healing and preventing incest. Creating *shalom bayit* (peace in the home) requires attention to our different and unique needs as well as sharing resources and information with each other. This book points to the importance of that issue and trusts others with more knowledge of the unique needs of our diverse cultures and religious affiliations to develop materials, programs, and ways of communicating. Some examples of what has been developed are included in chapters 11, 12, and 14.

Writing this was hard. There were times I wondered why I was doing this. I was blessed at those times to get a call or letter from someone who heard what I was doing, who would thank me for writing this while telling me why it mattered so much to them that I was giving voice to their experience. At other times when I voiced my doubts, a colleague or friend would say, "You have to write this. It's important. Don't give up." Their support and valuing of this work sustained and nurtured me. I am grateful, too, for nature's nurturing presence as I wrote. The beauty of the earth and sky, the incredible force and healing presence of lakes, streams, and oceans, the beauty of apricot color sunrises, the wonder of woodpeckers and chickadees were reminders to me that I was not doing this alone and that there is beauty and sustenance in life, not just pain. I am grateful for my ability to laugh and find humor even in the dark, or as a friend says, "to laugh at the face of the abyss."

I am humbled and moved by the generosity and talent of those who have shared their stories with me. Whether their work appears here or not, they are a part of this project and I thank them.

Ultimately, I had to write this—for myself—to say, "Yes, this happened to me"—emphasis on the *past* tense. I need to tell my story so I can move on. I need to reclaim this part of my history so it becomes an integrated part of myself rather than "the" issue that defines me.

Most of the survivor stories I heard came from people who never forgot they'd been abused. Some involved remembering details of the abuse as adults. The process of remembering is agonizing. Most would rather die or go crazy than remember.

The first-person art, poetry, and stories in this book accurately reflect the feelings, experiences, and circumstances expressed by contributors. Identifying details, such as locations, names, and ages, have been changed with the exception of those who have previously made their stories public. Most incest survivors and their family members chose to write anonymously. Anonymity is a way to avoid hurting those we love and, for some, to protect themselves. Some therapists and rabbis chose to remain anonymous to protect their clients' or congregants' identities. In some situations, the decision to disguise people's identities was mine, based on legal advice I received (regarding the handling of stories of abusers and/or family members who were alive and identifiable).

Hadiyah C.'s stories reflect the courage and strength it takes to survive the violations of childhood and adulthood, including the patriarchal power structure,[13] which is more likely to punish and blame the victim than help her. Stories by B. B. Adams and Carol Greenfield reflect the powerful presence of childhood molestation in adulthood. Poetry by Elizabeth, Hillary, and Laurie Suzanne Reiche evoke the feeling states of child victim or adult survivor.

In chapter 6, "A Mother's Story," we read what happened when Masha Gladys's adult daughter, Jenny, told of having been molested by her father. Chapter 7 tells of the survivor's journey, "From Terror to Triumph." Chapter 8, "A Way Out: Healing through Creative Expression," presents the art of Rae, Shauna Green, Hadass G., Asenath Barzani, Shoshana, and myself, an overview of Zena David's play *Passing Over*, as well as discussion of the role creative expression has played in our healing.

We move from the stories of what happened to us, how it affected us, and some of how we're healing, to an exploration of our Jewish identity. Sue William Silverman writes of her belief as a child that it was only Jewish children who were abused. In chapter 9, "My Jewish Journey Home," she explains how she came to that conclusion and her current search for her identity as a Jew. Chapter 10 presents survivors' often ambivalent dance with Jewish identity and connection.

In chapter 11, Marcia ("Marty") Cohn Spiegel describes healing rituals women have found and created within the Jewish community. I am immensely grateful for all the work Rae and Marty have done to raise awareness about domestic violence and for their support of this project and me. A Sukkoth service developed by Adrienne Affleck presents another healing ritual for abuse survivors (see Appendix E).

In chapter 12, Esta Soler, executive director of the Family Violence Prevention Fund, helps define true community. Activist Barbara Engel emphasizes the need for more men to join in the work, in the leadership to stop the violence, and in the need for boys and girls to be taught that being masculine does not mean the domination of others. There are many individuals who are taking action to stop the violence in their communities, in their congregations, and in their lives. Some of their projects are mentioned here.

In chapter 13, Rabbi Elliot N. Dorff writes about "The Role of Rabbis, Cantors, and Educators in Preventing Abuse and Repairing Its Consequences."

In chapter 14, "Hope: Creating Day, Living in the Light," Hadiyah C., Laurie Suzanne Reiche, Elizabeth, and Ellen Bass reflect the sweetness and strength of healing in poetry and story. Chapter 15 focuses on "Building Communities of Hope" as we imagine a world that is safe for children and some of what it will take to create it.

Thank you for reading this, for taking it seriously, for encouraging others to read it, and for figuring out what you and those you know can do to help shine the light—to make peace, safety, and tranquillity possible for Jewish adult survivors of child sexual abuse or incest and to prevent today's children from ever needing our help.

Hope lies in our strength as a community. When we decide there is something we must do, we are terrific at getting it done. I hope through this book to further break the silence within the Jewish community on these issues. Writing helps me make meaning out of events that were cruel and devastating. Writing has helped me reconnect to my soul—to the light. I hope it will help others, too.

Through my work addressing issues of abuse, I became friends with a number of women from all affiliations in the Jewish community. Through them I rediscovered the joy of being Jewish and a memory of connection from long ago—a feeling of connection on which I continue to build.

My Shul
᠕

My *bubby* used to sit upstairs with the other women.[14] That changed when the congregation got so small it cost too much to heat the whole place. Then everyone—women, men, and children—sat together on the first floor. I loved that room—its sights and sounds. The balcony formed a U around the sides and back. The room was long and narrow with slightly faded pastel-colored frescoes on stucco walls. At the very front of the room, on either side of the worn velvet curtains that protected the Torahs, were two golden lions, standing on their hind legs. Instead of a roar coming out of their mouths, there were lightbulbs.

There were three sections of dark wood high-backed benches. In the center was the *bimah*, a raised section where the rabbi, the cantor, and the elders would stand and read the Torah. The *bimah* was covered with a tapestry throw that would slip and slide around and get brought back in line by one of the elders. He was tall and lank and slightly stooped over, with Coke bottle lenses in his glasses and the biggest nose I'd ever seen. When there was too much conversation going on or he wanted our attention, he'd slam the wooden *bimah* with his flat hand and say "Sha!" with great authority. While it didn't get quiet immediately, he'd started a ripple of "sha, sha, sha's" throughout the shul, and eventually it got a little quieter.

I can't decide what was my favorite part. I loved the rabbi—a small man with a scraggly gray-black beard and the sweetest eyes I'd ever seen. He spoke almost no English, but when he looked at me I felt blessed.

One of my favorite memories was being on the ground floor on the side with all the men, sitting next to my dad and playing with the *tsitsis* on his *tallis*.[15] They were silky and soothing. Then there was the parade down the aisles with our apples and candles on what holiday I'm not sure, but I loved it.

I loved listening to the men *davening*, watching them stand, rocking back and forth, gently rolling from heels to toes and back again. Each prayed in his own different and unique key, and none on any scale you could find. There was a melody to their *davening* and h'mmm h'mmming (emphasis on the second h'mmmm), complete with crescendos quickly falling into a more muffled cry to their inner souls. Theirs was the joyous sound of talking to God.

I carry that rhythm within me—of joy with God—of resting in God—of talking to God—of a personal relationship with God—of God being color and sound and movement even though I never understood a word they said.

To rediscover that rhythm has required remembering what happened. Knowing. That's some of the hardest work of all.

"I am afraid this will be too hard for you to see and hear and feel. I am more afraid of silence."
Rachel Lev

Painting by Rae

PART ONE

The Context:
Survivors Then and Now,
Denial, Jewish Law,
and Family Dynamics

Remembering and Telling

*My Journey Back to My Self
and Other People's Stories*

RACHEL LEV
WITH HILLARY,
ELIZABETH, JEROME,
LAURIE SUZANNE REICHE,
AND CAROL GREENFIELD

> *One does not become enlightened by imagining
> figures of light, but by making the darkness
> conscious.*
>
> C. G. Jung, *Alchemical Studies*

The Late 1970s
ॐ

The therapy room was dimly lit. With my feet flat on the floor, I bent my knees and arched backward so my shoulder blades rested on the padded beam of a miniature sawhorse. Body therapists in those days called it "the bench." Clients laughed sardonically and called it "the rack." Mike, my therapist, told me to breathe down to my belly and up into my chest. So, I breathed. It felt good having my chest and belly stretched open by my deep breathing. Suddenly, my breathing changed and a rasping sound came out of my throat. I was gasping, terrified, seeing an image of myself as a child surrounded by white, unable to breathe, unable to move. I saw my small head resting on a white pillow. I looked terribly sad. My therapist said, "Stay with that." I did. The terror got worse, and then it passed. I was exhausted and very, very confused. What had just happened?

As Mike and I talked, he suggested I talk to my mother about whether anything like this had happened to me. What could it be? How could I see myself and this be a memory?

I called my mom that night and asked, "Was there ever a time when I was little, surrounded by white, couldn't breathe and couldn't move?" She said, "I can't believe you'd remember that." I said, "Remember what?" She then proceeded to tell me that when I was three years old, I stopped breathing.

3

My sister found me turning blue and ran for my mother. My mother picked me up, supposedly dislodging something in my throat. I began gasping. The fire department came and took me by ambulance to the local children's hospital, where I was placed in a steam room.

My hospital room had a one-way mirror through which my parents watched me. I *could* see myself! This really was a memory. My parents were not allowed to see me. One of the nurses, writing that I was "uncooperative" in my hospital chart, put me in restraints. I couldn't move! My mom and I were amazed. She said the family had never talked about it after it happened. They were just glad I was alive.

I *was* little, surrounded by white, couldn't breathe and couldn't move.

Years later, different blips and bleeps and explosions of sensations and images came to tell me of other terrifying events in my life.[1] Deciding to tell others that I was molested as a child was a challenge and a risk that came only after I had the courage to tell myself what I had always known. To do that I had to dance with a tornado. It nearly killed me.

As I prepared to read a chapter I'd named "Dancing with a Tornado," a fellow student in a writing class reacted. With eyebrows raised and consternation in her voice, she said, "You can't dance with a tornado. No one in their right mind would dance with a tornado." She was right. No one in her right mind would dance with a tornado, but it was learn to dance with this rapidly twirling, violent maelstrom of energy or fall into its destructive path and die. Her comment angered me, but I didn't say anything. Some people just aren't going to understand. What matters is that I do and that I tell. This is what happened.

Dancing with a Tornado: 1986 to 1950-something to 1999
ॐ

It came from nowhere—storms often do. I stood waiting for the bus on a summery day on a beautiful metropolitan thoroughfare. The bus came in sight. A voice said, "Just step in front of the bus." I started to step forward. Suddenly I realized what I was doing. I stepped back. I was horrified . . . terrified. What was going on? I could have killed myself. That wasn't "me." Had someone pushed me? No. The voice came from within me, and I'd almost obeyed. Stunned and shaking, I got on the bus.

Somehow I got to work and walked into my friend's office. She looked at me and said, "You look so scared." "I am," I said, and proceeded to tell her

Drawing by Hadass G.

what had just happened. She said, "I hope you'll call Hannah." Hannah was the name of a therapist my friend had mentioned to me before. I called Hannah. I don't remember what happened from that moment in my friend's office until I somehow made it to Hannah's. My whole world had unraveled. I was drowning, spinning, lost. Images, bodily tremors, waves of terror and despair flooded me throughout the day, and nightmares were my nightly companions. What was happening to me? Hannah said, "It's a lot but you can swim." My friends, Hannah's respectful distance and compassion gave me something to hang on to while everything else was spinning out of control within me.

I started going to therapy. I went to work. I walked along the lake. I went to therapy some more. I talked to my friends. I don't remember much about what else I was doing in my life in those days. Somehow I kept making it to Hannah's. One day she asked, *"Did you ever get the feeling there was a secret?"* As a shudder tore through me, I knew the answer was yes. But what was it? What could it be? Hannah offered no suggestions or hints.

Sometime later, in therapy, I saw an image of myself as a small child, huddled in the corner of a room, terrified by the whirling, swirling darkness of a tornado that filled the center of the room. The tornado was between me and the door. There was no way out. At times there were three and four tornadoes in the room. I learned that tornadoes can stand stationary or move one hundred feet per second. The sky gets so black at first that you can't see anything. It's like somebody turned out the lights. It's amazing how everything can be destroyed in fifteen to twenty seconds.

Few buildings can withstand the horizontal blasts of tornado winds. And me? Fragmented images, feelings, nightmares, sensations swept through me, touching down here, then there, picking me up without warning, then dumping me out in the middle of nowhere. To get out required that I dance with each tornado, that I become one with each and ride it out. And what a ride it has been. Years of flashbacks, nightmares, depression so bad I had to keep my knives in my car trunk. I wore black all the time but didn't know that then. Everything scared me. That, I knew.

I fought what I was seeing. It couldn't be real, true. I must be crazy. Better to be crazy than to believe this. I would have done anything—and did—to not know this. I almost died in order to keep this secret. From childhood on, I compulsively overate to numb myself. I developed somatic symptoms and focused on my physical health, rather than the events that "made me sick."

My memory is fragmented. The good news is, as I allow myself to know that there was a bogeyman in my closet, the more memories of what was good and pleasant return. It has taken many years of arduous work, tens of thousands of dollars, incredible courage, and the good fortune to have found tenacious, steadfast, knowledgeable, hardy, and loving therapists and friends.

I became suicidal on a beautiful summery day in 1986. I didn't want to know what I knew, to remember what had been done to me.

It began when I was three.

As an adult, much of me thought I should die—kill myself—rather than betray the image—the illusions about my father, family, and childhood.

I adored my father. He was my sun and moon and stars.

He was tall, dark haired, with blue eyes and a hairy chest.

He was dramatic and silly. He made me laugh . . . and then,

he made me cry.

It began as a game suggested as a way to make me feel better on a day when I didn't feel good. It happened over and over for years.

Being sexually abused by my father, whom I loved and on whom I depended, exploded my world and sense of self and safety into a million pieces. Nothing was ever the same. I remember.

I remember pain, being little, all alone, wide-eyed nights. No one there. Getting up after falling asleep only after the light had come. Then to school. In walking to school some of the scales and horrors of the night before fell off while others fell in, onto themselves, going deep, deep within me. Nightmares forgotten for now. Now tiny sparks of hope as school appears. Here, I will be safe. Here, no one will hurt me. Here, people will be kind. I loved my teachers. With them I'd begin to breathe again—to hope.

But oh, the bone-crushing sadness when I wasn't picked for a team until last or the teacher didn't call on me. My slim hold on hope would dwindle, sizzle, and die. The horrors of the night before returned, and I became that little girl again—all alone in the night. Afraid to move. My solution was to push the pain and memories farther away—to pretend everything was all right. I learned to perform perfectly. The lessons of the night transferred to everything. There was no room for error—anywhere. And always, there was fear.

I remember the nights I was so scared I'd leave my warm bed, bare feet on cold, hardwood floors, and go to the door outside my parents' bedroom. I wanted comfort. As I stood outside their closed door, I remembered the joy of some weekend mornings, jumping into bed with my parents, laughing and snuggling and reading the funnies. But that was daytime, light time, not nighttime, not now when bad things could happen. So I sat quietly, afraid, seeking comfort by placing my palm on the door through the night.

Years later, as an adult, I remembered this as I found myself night after night sleeping close to the wall, my palm flat against it. I didn't understand what I was doing, but found comfort in it.

"What did he do to you?" a friend asked after reading the above. "Where are the details? I want to know. I ache to know. If you don't tell what he did, somehow the coercive power of the abuse is winning. If we are to strip the abuse and abusers of their power we must tell—tell out loud—tell without shame." Her telling me this reminded me of my arduous journey over many years from total denial to acknowledging to myself what happened, then entrusting this knowledge and my feelings to a few trusted souls. How much do I tell of how he molested me? Whatever feels right to me. I can't keep a secret because someone wants me to, and I can't share things because someone wants me to.

My love for my mother also impacts what I've included. We are continually rebuilding and renegotiating our relationship. Much in my life was motivated by my concern for her—feeling responsible to take care of her. As a child my mother often said, "I can always count on you." I believe I latched onto that role as a lifeline. If I took care of her, I might survive. There are many examples that demonstrate my placing her needs ahead of mine—as far back as I can remember. My mother tells the story of when I stopped breathing at the age of three and was rushed by ambulance to the hospital. En route I threw up, turned to my mother, and said, "I'm sorry, Mommy."

I agonized for years before telling her I'd been molested. There always seemed to be a reason not to tell her. I didn't tell her before she was going to France because I didn't think that was fair. Nor did it seem fair to tell her as she was leaving for Florida for the winter. I didn't tell her of the agony I was going through in deciding whether to attend a ceremony in my dad's honor. My father, by then deceased, the man who molested me, was being honored by his community. How could I go? How could I not? I decided to go out of love for my mother. It was crazy-making to know what he'd done, to be in such pain and still be protecting her, his name, and somehow myself by keeping the secret. He did so many good things. Molesting me was not one of them.

I never confronted my father—as a child or adult. By the time I would have been ready to confront him in my late thirties, he was pretty frail. I was afraid talking to him about what he had done would either kill him or cause a major rift in my family, or both. Much smaller confrontations had had serious ramifications. When I was thirty and didn't include my sister in plans to go out with a friend, he put his hand to his chest (where he'd had open heart surgery) and said how it made him sick when his children weren't getting along. He stopped talking to me for months and made life miserable for my mother, who then blamed me. I couldn't handle any of that. Instead I pulled away from both my parents as I battled the depression of remembering, put my knives in the trunk of my car, and kept myself alive.

I vowed not to perpetuate the pain he caused. I convinced myself that not telling my mother was stopping the transmission of pain he'd created. A few years after he died, that stopped working. To keep the truth of his violations from her, I had to keep away from her. She was always talking about him, about "Your Father." If I was to be in relationship with her, I had to tell her that her husband, my father, molested me. As I work to heal myself, I try to balance my need to disclose and mourn the fact that my father molested me, with my mother's need not to know and her desire that I tell no one.

I finally told my mother on a gray Sunday in October 1995. I had spent several hours with her, waiting for the right moment. I couldn't believe she couldn't tell I was going nuts inside. My heart was racing faster and faster with every hour we were together and I said nothing. I sat next to her on the couch in the den. I could give up and go home, but that felt too depressing. I suggested we go out to dinner. We went to a place she likes— a place I've known since I was in high school. I sat across the table from her. She was once again talking about how "our" father adored "us" kids. She always spoke of it with a tone of bitterness, of resignation. It felt as if she was mad at my sister and me because dad put us first. I was always angry when she said it. I didn't want the kind of adoration he offered. Finally, on this fall day, I said, "I wish he'd adored us less and adored you more." Our conversation meandered around some more. I kept hedging and praying for the courage to just say something. I said something I can't quite remember, and she said, "Did someone abuse you?" I said, "Yes." She said, "Your father?" I said, "Yes." She sat back and got a thoughtful look on her face. I don't know what I expected, but that wasn't it. She started to talk about how this made sense. She spoke of a night a few years back, during a time I'd pulled away from both of them. She and my father were sitting together in the family room. My mom asked my father, "What did we ever do that she would pull away like this?" My father said nothing. On the night I told, my mother was furious with him. A part of me had always wanted to believe she would have saved me if she knew. I was thrilled when, her voice full of outrage, she said, "If I'd known, I would have killed him."

"*What* did he do to you?" she asked, her voice rising almost hysterically. I told her one small piece. She physically recoiled, hand flying to her mouth. I stopped giving details. Some weeks later she told me of being haunted, by visual images of my father with me.

I got what I needed from her that night. She believed me. However, since then she has many times asked me if I was sure, who else knew, and if I needed to tell anyone else. "What's the point?" she would ask. "What good does it do to smear his name?"

It was painful to watch her fall into an isolated depression in the year after I told her. Because of her need to keep "the secret," she had only me with whom to talk.

I hope she never reads this book. I'm telling because I have to, for myself.

Yes, there was a secret. My father, who was president of his synagogue's men's club and a B'nai Brith man of the year, molested me. He entered my body with his in ways no child should ever know. I felt tortured, isolated, lonely, dirty. He manipulated me emotionally as well. I adored him. He molested me. He loved me. He threatened me. I lived in a nightmare of trauma, conflicted feelings and loyalties. I was not safe.

The background is red. The robe is his. My feeling is no. Its expression silent. This doll is playing my part. She was the only witness aside from dad and me.

My dance with a tornado began in the 1950s. I survived by the grace of God. I developed myriad coping mechanisms to keep myself going—to keep the secret—and to keep me from feeling. These were not conscious plans. They were just what I did. If I felt what he did to me and couldn't tell, I would have to explode, die, or go crazy. I had to run faster than my experiences while appearing to be a normal, happy little girl. To do this required that I keep silent and isolated.

I escaped into books. I read a lot. Books whose names I can't remember and others I can. Grimm's and Andersen's fairytales, *Double Date* and *Double Wedding* by Rosalind du Jardin, Robert Louis Stevenson's *A Child's Garden of Verses*, Betty Smith's *A Tree Grows in Brooklyn*, Lewis Carroll's *Alice in Wonderland*, and many more. Comic books and magazines offered escape into worlds unlike my own. I loved Superman and Casper the Friendly Ghost. Trips to the school library and the public library down the cobblestone street were a treat. I loved our local library with its warm, soft golden lights and row after row of books ready to transport me away. I read a lot.

I expressed my anger about things that were unimportant. I slammed doors. I took out my anger on my dolls and the cookie jar. Barbie was raped on a regular basis. How did I know what rape was?

One day I was filled with rage. I sat in the bathroom and shook one of my favorite dolls really hard. The rubber band inside her snapped. Her head and arms and legs fell off. I was terrified—at the damage I had done, at my violence, and I was afraid my mother would be mad. She wouldn't understand, because I couldn't tell her, that there was a very good reason I was so mad. Somehow I attached a new rubber band, but the doll was never the same.

I had nightmares. My dad said drinking a glass of water before I went to bed would help. I drank eight. Every night I'd stand at the bathroom sink and drink eight glasses of water. The nightmares didn't go away.

I managed overwhelming physical and emotional feelings and sensations by eating, eating, and more eating. I weighed 134 pounds at the age of ten and a height of 4'11". A diet doctor introduced me to amphetamines.[2]

I expressed my rage via the cookie jar filled with Oreo cookies. I'd take a cookie, slip off one side, and eat the one with the cream filling. Then I'd lick the noncream side and put it back in the cookie jar. My act of rage was never discovered. Why didn't anyone say anything to me about the pile of dark halves in the cookie jar?

I counted everything—steps, breaths, seconds. Counting occupied my mind, keeping me from thinking. I still find myself counting sometimes when I'm scared.

My body tried to help through somatizing. When I couldn't take any more, I'd get sick. It's not that I consciously said, "OK, let's get sick." It's what happened. When he hurt me, I often couldn't breathe. A hand over the mouth or the weight of an adult man on a child can do that. I also couldn't dare make a noise, so I'd manage to suppress tears, squeals, screams, and words, and eventually, within myself, even the awareness of all that was happening outside and inside. Then it would be over.

As I came back into my "self," my body would carry and express the pain that went far beyond the physical. I would gasp. They said I had asthma. I had many sore throats and upper respiratory ailments. By the time I was four and hospitalized with pneumonia, my mother said I was "such a good patient" that I "never complained."

I missed a lot of school. Nobody ever explored beyond the notion that I was a sickly child. The somatizing got me rest and, often, safe nurturing attention.

Actually, as I got older (seven, eight, nine), I remember sometimes I did choose to be, or rather "act," sick. I'd wake up and lie under the covers and pant to make myself "feel" sick to my mother's cool hand on my forehead.

She'd come in. I'd say with a small, weary voice, "I don't feel good." She'd touch my forehead and say, "You do feel warm. Let me get the thermometer." And back under the covers I'd dive for some more panting. It always worked.

I'd be both relieved and deeply saddened. I wanted so for her to catch me in this lie and ask what was really wrong. She never did. Not about this or the cookies or the messages I tried to send through my eyes to say, "See me. Help me. Now." Over and over I concluded she didn't love me and that I was alone. I know now she has always loved me and because of who she was couldn't or didn't notice. I needed her to notice. I needed somebody to notice.

Somewhere, sometime, I started to pick the skin from between my toes. I picked until it bled, until it hurt. Horrified at the damage I did, I still couldn't stop myself from doing it again. Sometimes it hurt to walk for a few days after I'd really done a number on myself. Scabs formed. Skin thickened. I don't know exactly why I did it. Sometimes I think it broke through the numbness I felt, to prove that I was real. It is yet another way I soothed myself or reduced my tension.[3] It is another way I hurt myself. These things didn't stop the molestation, but they did keep me going. They gave me ways to soothe myself, to discharge some of the frenetic energy inside myself. It would have been better if he just never molested me—if she noticed that there was something terribly wrong and interceded—if my ear, nose, and throat doctor or pediatrician noticed. But "they" say people didn't think about these things in the 1950s.

Those were the years of *Father Knows Best,* Wonder Bread, and *Ozzie and Harriet.* There were no talk shows or made for TV movies about incest in the family. Dinah Shore and Gary Moore didn't talk about it. It wasn't on the nightly news. Incest wasn't taboo, just talking about it was. I wonder how truly different it is today. After all, we know it happens to "them," not to "us."

Ironically, my story was mirrored in the life of Lauren Chapin, who played the youngest daughter on TV's *Father Knows Best.* While playing the role of a daughter in an ideal family, "Kathy 'Kitten' Anderson" was being sexually molested by her father and keeping the secret because Daddy said, "Shhhh." The girl we all thought had it made reports trying to hang herself in her closet as a child.[4]

How different my experiences might have been had I known I wasn't alone. But I didn't. So I coped mostly by forgetting and by talking myself into an illusion about who I was, who my parents were, who my family was. I idealized everything and pushed the pain of being molested and the awareness of it deeper and deeper inside until nothing was real. I was not present when being molested. I was not present when I wasn't. I acted as if all was well, and I got sick a lot until that day in 1986 when I decided to live—to choose myself over the family image—and thereby to remember and tell.

When I was little, after he was through, I would sit on my pillow, scrunched against the wall, stare at the windows and wait, praying for the light to come—knowing that when it came I'd be safe.

Drawing by Hadass G.

I'd like the light to come and to stay. The only way I can keep it light for myself is to pull up the shades and let in the light. Pull up the shades on the secrets in my soul.

Others are choosing to pull up the shades on their secrets—shining the light, remembering, and telling.[5]

Remembering and Telling: Other People's Stories
ᴖ

Hillary, now forty-six, a wife, mother, and Jewish educator, remembers:

Oral sex and intercourse began around the age of 7 and was most intense for the 1½ years I lived in my grandfather's house (till I was 8¾), but it did not stop completely until I was 15. Some people are appalled that my grandfather attempted sodomy and intercourse with a young child—but for me, the physical pain was not the worst part of the experience. Much worse for me were the lewd remarks, the whispered questions, and the threatening leer across the family's holiday table, and the French kisses he stole in front of my cousins. I was terrified whenever I was around Grandpa, and I was sure I'd die of embarrassment if anyone accused me of what they must be seeing.

I had no place to run, no place to hide (except under the porch), no place to find someone I could count on—not my rabbi, not my religious school-teachers, not even my Jewish neighbors. I had no choice but to submit and muddle through. In fact, when I did take flight at the age of 9½, I ran to the home of a Methodist family, for I intuitively sensed that their home would be a safe haven. I never made it into their house. I sat on their lawn for a while to see if it was the right thing to do. My adopted father found my sister and me before they could let us in. It was only at a high school reunion many years later that I learned that this family took in lots of runaways. If only I had trusted my instincts as a girl.

The Summer I'll Never Forget
by Hillary

1960 was a summer I'll never forget.
I lived with my mother and sister
In the third floor apartment
of my grandparents' house.
These are some memories of the
"Life and Times of Grandpa's House."

Black and white—
the colors of my TV—
The Jetsons,
Get Smart
and Lawrence Welk.
Red and orange and blue and green—
the colors of my comic books—
Mickey Mouse,
Minnie Mouse,
Donald Duck

and Goofy;
Batman;
and Dick Tracy.

Black and white—
the colors of President Kennedy's family on the news reel,
Annette and Frankie at the movies,
the metal jacks we played with using a red rubber ball,
and the race riots in the streets of Baltimore.
Pink and white—
the colors of my new two-piece bathing suit,
the udders of the cows at Cloverland dairy,
and Grandpa's penis demanding my attention.

The Summer I'll Never Forget
Collage by Hillary

ᛒ

Elizabeth, now thirty-seven, was born in Kharkov, Ukraine. At the age of sixteen her family moved to the United States. Molested by her father, Elizabeth writes in her poem about the invisibility of incest and how we come to rely on our best friends—even when they are supposedly inanimate.

Ghost Story
by Elizabeth

The girl is asleep now
Hands like matchsticks
Wrapped around her teddy bear
With one eye missing
Its body bruised and battered
Like her own.

A man comes into the room
The bear stirs
Its eye—a hungry moon
Teeth glitter in the darkness
The bear growls—a sound
That promises an eternity of pain.

The man falls to the floor
His heart stops—
The coroner concluded
It was a heart attack
Nobody wanted to speak
Of giant bear tracks
They found by the girl's bed
It is better to let
The sleeping dogs lie
Let the shadows claim their own,
After all
The girl was sound asleep
When her father died.

ᴧ

"For Fondling Me" was written by sixty-year-old Jerome, a business-man and writer, who was molested by his mother from the time he was eight into his teens. In response to the question, "While the abuse was going on, did you tell anyone?" Jerome writes, "I didn't have to; the family witnessed it. I didn't or couldn't comprehend how such craziness could exist in such a religious home. I've never completely or partially healed. I've never married. I've ended up physically and emotionally isolated and estranged. I have crippling phobias. I wish anything else than this had happened to me." Jerome's poem reflects some of the anguish and ambivalence survivors feel when the perpetrator is a parent or other relative.

For Fondling Me
by Jerome

For fondling me furtively, mother dear;
    for fondling me in front of family
too menaced by your madness to interfere;
    for fondling me in spite of plea after plea
of mother, please, please don't, it makes me feel sick—
    for all those sins, mother, for all those crimes,
with clubs, brass knuckles, axes and arsenic
    I'd kill you in my mind a thousand times.
And yet, in later years, did I not try
    forgiving and forgetting what you had done;
and wasn't I, when came your time to die,
    at bedside weeping same as any son.
We reconciled before it was too late,
and oh, the love I felt, and still the hate.

ᴧ

Laurie Suzanne Reiche is a forty-something wife, mother, writer, and student of feminism. Her poem conveys the flattening of her spirit as a result of having been brutalized by her father.

After Her Father Sodomizes Her a Little Girl Speaks
by Laurie Suzanne Reiche

Even in the burned forest the bird
has come back to sing (from "What's Not in the Heart" by Abba Kovner)

No bird has yet returned but I am not hopeless.
The stillness of this settled ash cannot last forever;
they say a heart is a mendable thing
and spring comes full of rejuvenation.

Still, I wait in stillness in this felled
forest of my heart,
an echo of silence heavy as any holocaust
thrumming on the curve of my skull
while outside the border of this bloody organ
people pound their flapping tongues
on the roof of their mouths
demanding my immediate
attention.

But everything has been destroyed
and I sit in darkness all alone
waiting for a bird
to sing.

⸼

Carol Greenfield is a college educator and writer. Her story, "My Only Sunshine," is a vehicle for her to tell the story of what happened to her as a child. It also demonstrates the anguish of remembering and telling.

My Only Sunshine
by Carol Greenfield

This will be quick. Promise. Then we can do what you want to do. Just try to forget you hate my stories because this one is important. It could be the last one. Maybe not. Turn left here.

I want to drive by Sohier Road. I used to live down there 'til I was seven. I *am* getting to it. Just pointing out the house will be quick but the house is not the story. I know. Big deal. It's a street. It's a house. I *know* I told you about the lemonade stand and the tires painted white that my *Zede* used as planters out front.[6] I told you about the egg man delivering the chicken manure each spring, but I didn't tell you about the basement.

This *is* the way to the beach. I know how to get to the beach; I'm just taking you the back way. Pull over. Turn around. Drive by it again. I haven't been back here for years. Bear with me a minute, will you? Slow down. Pull over. This will be short. God. It looks the same. They never even changed the color.

See the driveway? All gravel? One time when I was six, just after I got my glasses, I tossed two fistfuls of stones straight up in the air and looked straight up at them flying, forgetting about gravity, and just stood there like a young stupid turkey as the rocks pelted me and broke my glasses. Cracked my vision. I couldn't see straight then with or without them. Almost like now. I didn't know what to do.

That's *not* a cute story. It's a stupid story. It's not the story at all. The story is in the cellar. Dark. Where you can't see things clearly. Nana's youngest son Arnie lived down there. He must have been twenty or twenty-two. Over in a corner was an apartment without walls—a bed and bureau and a desk with a typewriter. Nana Gertie and Zede David lived on the first floor and we lived on top. Arnie was going to move out in a few months because he was engaged to someone named Rochelle. A real cheerleader type.

Don't worry. It's not clouding over. The sun's burning my face up, there's plenty of time to get to the damn beach. Now, listen! See if it makes sense. Can't we put on the air conditioner? It's so hot.

It was so cool in the cellar. Most of the time Arnie was working at my other uncle's bicycle store and I'd go down to the basement to play Market. Zede David had this chicken wire storage space with boxes of canned goods from his grocery store that I loved to stack and restack and reprice up and down. I'd have phantom sales on beans a lot because I hated them. I was scared to eat them because Annie Kulik would always sing about beans, beans, the musical fruit, and I was afraid I'd embarrass myself in class. Sometimes I played with the typewriter. I was six. I could read. I could write. But it was messy and my papers looked like a little kid's. With a typewriter, my writing could look like a grown-up's. Arnie found me there one day and told me I couldn't play with it. I must have cried because my parents usually let me do what I wanted. I kept saying please. I'd say please, pretty please with brown sugar on top. Arnie said it was expensive. I would break it so I could only use it when he was around. OK. That was OK. I'd say, Arnie? When can I play typewriter?

He said he had to watch me to see that I used it right. Here. Get up on my lap, he said. He'd show me how. It was better that way. I could reach better. I was typing whole sentences and then I felt him touching me. He sang, "You Are My Sunshine, My Only Sunshine." Touching me in my privates. I told him that was private but he said I was silly—he was my uncle. Privates are for family. Privates are private to strangers. I wanted to type. I just wanted to type. It was cool down there and dark and so hot outside and no one was around. Annie was gone to her cousin's house and Sandy was mad at me and my mother was way upstairs and Nana Gertie was watching her *bubby mayses* on her twelve-inch Admiral and I wanted to write a grown-up story and Arnie kept saying it was all OK.[7]

See what I'm saying? Just that day, or maybe it was more, I don't know, but one other day he said if I wanted to use the typewriter we'd have to play a game first. What kind of game, I said. Dolls. I wanted to go get mine, but he said he had one. He had one with him all the time. He would show me a secret doll only he had, but I should never tell. I hated his doll. I hated him. I hated the typewriter glowing in the corner. He kept singing and playing with his doll . . . "You Are My Sunshine."

When my mother asked me where I disappeared to I didn't even know, but one night when she was warning me about taking money from strangers and how I had to give twenty-one cents back to Mr. Katz down at the cobblers because he bought me a balloon and some men were bad men but not Mr. Katz of course, but she was just making a point, she said. I told my mother her brother showed me his doll.

A few hours later there was a family meeting. Arnie, my father, my mother's parents, me and my mother. Like being in a recital. I stood in the center of the living room and told everyone about the typewriter and the rules of the game and The Doll.

Before I knew it the moving trucks had arrived. Annie Kulik stood on the corner and waved good-bye as we got in my father's '37 black Plymouth and moved into a two story a few towns over that my other grandparents owned. They told me never to tell. It was private. These things were meant to be private.

So. Now you know. That's the story: two or four short long separate hours in a very small place. The new town was some dying leather town and the schools were nowhere near as good. I guess I got punished. We weren't near the sea anymore and I missed that smell so much, that salty, low tide smell. The center of our new town smelled like the banana oil they used to tan hides. Oh, god. Mostly now I just tighten up whenever I hear that song. That damn song. What's all this crap about family all of a sudden? Like it's some holy obligation. I can't do it. I just can't.

I'm soaking. You still want to go to the beach? Can you ever look at me again? Huh? Can you? At least start the car. And don't look at me like that.

Notes from Carol

The details of the story of the basement are true. To this day, I cannot bear to listen to any version of "You Are My Sunshine" without getting tense or repulsed. That's difficult, since it seems part of the national archive of old favorites.

It's important to know that this piece is "fictionalized." It's not raw material, or notes from a case study, or a transcription of a therapy session, that a psychologist would mold into his/her own. In this particular case, it means that I was not in a car with anyone I was in a relationship with, driving by my old house, and in fear that the story within would ruin a marriage, engagement, or whatever. The car ride was the vehicle to tell the story.

It's very common for children to feel as though somehow they did wrong: to tell the secret, to cause trouble in the family, to feel punished (in this case, *we* were the ones who left town). I feel the perception of how long people can carry that burden around with them is important. I was under strict orders Never To Tell. Which meant it was *bad*. And people would see me differently.

I have at least three other pieces that refer to this experience in various ways. It's *my story*. No matter how I tell it, it's mine.

These, then, are some of the stories people have shared with me. What Alice Walker said when speaking about female genital mutilation applies as well to sexual abuse: "What is painful is that what I am writing someone right now is living."[8] In the next chapter we explore how something so violent is so hidden, including why children stay silent.

TWO ✌

If It's There, Why Don't We See It?

Denial, Silence, and Some of Their Costs

RACHEL LEV

> When we deny our experience, we always move
> from something real to something fabricated.
> To live by this web of legend will always harm
> us. The truth may be difficult to open to, but it
> will never hurt us. What a tremendous relief to
> have the actual truth openly spoken: "There is
> suffering in this world."
>
> Sharon Salzberg, *Lovingkindness:*
> *The Revolutionary Art of Happiness*

> We cover the sabbath challahs while blessing
> the wine so they should not be humiliated by
> the fact that we are preferring the wine over
> them. How is it possible that anyone who has
> such a concept can humiliate a human being?
>
> Rabbi Abraham Twerski,
> speech on domestic violence, 1996

"But, No, Really? It Happens? I Can't Imagine It!"
✌

I understand your difficulty. When I sit at their table amid laughing and joking and feelings of warmth and affection, it is hard to picture this father slipping under his child's bedclothes at night, silencing protests with a glance; this mother oblivious to what he's doing, and this sparkling, animated child frozen in fear and at risk as this father closes the door and starts to unbuckle his belt . . .

It *is* hard to imagine.

On some level we know children across all cultures, all classes, and all religions are abused. A conservative estimate of sexual abuse incidents involving physical contact is one girl in three and one boy in ten before they are eighteen years old.[1] Due to the reluctance and risk of telling, there is every reason to believe that these are gross underestimates of the rates of sexual abuse. Children are most at risk with those they know. The 1995 Child Maltreatment Report states that "over 80 percent of sexual abuse where physical contact is made is perpetrated by either family members or people in the community who are trusted by the family."[2] According to separate research by Finkelhor and Cupoli, 81 percent of child sexual abuse is experienced before puberty and 42 percent of abuse is experienced before the age of seven. The most common abuse is the unwanted fondling of genitals.[3]

There is no evidence to indicate that sexual abuse in the Jewish community is any less than or different from what occurs in the general population.[4] As Rabbi Julie Spitzer wrote, "The *mezzuzah* on the doorpost is no charm, warding off the ills of society at large."[5] From the Talmud[6] to the *New York Times*, there are stories of sexual abuse and incest in the Jewish community. They aren't new. They aren't caused by external factors. They don't just happen among those who are somehow "different." People molest because they are wounded and because we do not stop them.

A report by the Shalom Bayit Committee in California states, "It is believed that the rate of abuse in the Jewish community is severely underestimated because there are few who are ready to listen to it and a lack of unified reporting services. Jewish Family Service agencies in Cleveland, Detroit, and Toronto found that the number of reports of family violence among their clients increased dramatically once their staff members had been trained to identify it."[7]

Why don't we see it?

We don't see sexual abuse because of the dynamics of denial and because of the nature of these abuses. Sexual abuse doesn't announce itself. Like other forms of abuse, it is about power and control. The abuser systematically disempowers, humiliates, and isolates his/her victim(s). Abusers often threaten to harm the victim more if s/he tells, or to harm people the victim loves. Unlike some other forms of abuse, molestation generally happens in private, without witnesses. In addition, children are often too young to have the concepts or language to describe what has been done to them. Without those concepts and language, their attempts to tell are often misunderstood, minimized, ignored, or dismissed. Add the facts that the symptoms of incest are rarely identified as such, that we are a parent-centered culture with a tendency to blame the victim (children are precocious, provocative, liars), and it gets easier to understand why the violation of children is often unseen and why children keep silent.

It may be hard to accept that some Jews molest children in part because it is hard for most of us to accept that anyone molests children. Beyond that universal reluctance to see something so awful, our history as Jews, the dynamics of abuse, and the deceit of child molesters have fed our worldview and thereby our denial.

We each have our own worldview—our way of looking at things. The experiences of our lives shape our expectations and create a filter through which we view everything and everyone. We bring our particular worldview into every experience in our lives. We may call it our worldview, our mind-set, our frame of reference or context. Ultimately it is how we see things, how we feel about things, what we believe, what we value. Our frames of reference are formed by where we lived and grew up, where we went to school, who our parents and/or caretakers were, what happened in our communities and the world around us throughout our lives, plus other life experiences. How we view the world determines what we see and how we react.

My dad gave me a purple passion plant which sat on the windowsill of my first apartment. One day I noticed lovely delicate orange flowers blooming on the plant. I called my father to tell him about them. He said, "It can't be. Purple passion plants don't flower." I stopped short. Then I repeated myself. He said, "No. That's not possible." I got very frustrated. I had called to share my wonder at this miracle, and now he was telling me it couldn't be. I found myself being swayed by his absolute certainty that purple passion plants don't flower. Then I thought, "Wait a minute," and I reached out and touched the flower. I said, "So, this flower that I'm touching and seeing on this plant isn't really there." "That's right," he said. "It can't happen."

Based on his worldview, "purple passion plants don't flower," and so he could not believe me. If he didn't know it, had not experienced it and/or labeled it as I had, what I said I saw could not be. I was touching the flower. I knew it was there, but he was my father and so certain of his view I began to doubt the facts and my experience. Purple passion plants do flower sometimes. He just hadn't seen it.

Sometimes we struggle to believe accounts of incest in our homes because they don't fit our frame of reference. Most of us have concepts about sexual abuse—what it looks like, sounds like. We have concepts of Jewish families and relationships. Many of us have no frame of reference for putting the two together. Abuse in Jewish relationships? We can't imagine it. Even as our denial is confronted by more and more people speaking out about the abuses they've survived as adults or children, our need to deny that abuse happens in Jewish lives continues. Why is that?

Denial is a natural human defense. It happens automatically. We deny when we feel scared or threatened. At the movies, when the images on the screen get too grisly, we cover our eyes. If we can't "see" it, it's not happening. While denying things that we see as threatening is understandable, in the case of child sexual abuse, to deny its existence and impact is unconscionable and hurtful. There is a "perpetuation by all of us," said Rabbi Dr. J. of the myth "that abuse doesn't exist among us." Because we do not have words or pictures for abuse in our mind-sets, he continued, even those who work directly with the issue often mislabel abuse as something else.[8]

"When we think about who is abused or abusive we think 'somebody other than us,'" said Sherry Dimarsky, domestic violence expert and attorney. In a presentation in October 1994, she said:

> The Orthodox assume it happens amongst the Reform. The Reform assume it happens amongst the Orthodox. The Conservative look in both directions. The young blame the old saying, "This is the way they were raised. They don't know any better." The old say it happens amongst the young. Those who live in the city say it happens in the suburbs where people lead lives of quiet desperation and those living in the suburbs say it happens in the ugly city. Middle and upper income people say it happens amongst the poor. No one says it happens amongst the wealthy—but it does. Who better to have the power and privacy to abuse? The truth is that all of us who are pointing fingers at other groups are right—it does happen there. But, so are those pointing at us.

In a letter sent to me in 1997, incest survivor Penny Royal describes her background, saying,

> I come from an upper-middle-class family that has grown in wealth over the years. Both father and stepfather are successful entrepreneurs. I was materially and educationally quite privileged, with a prep school

and Ivy League college education. The primary sign of trouble beneath the seemingly idyllic surface was my compulsive overeating (considered normal in my family), which became bulimia, as I grew older. In my family, compulsive overeating, addictions to nicotine and Valium, workaholism, and obsessive compulsive disorder all masked the presence of incest.

So perpetrators don't look like monsters and molestation doesn't happen only to "them." Then what do we look for in order to identify problems of sexual abuse?

Family and Community Denial—Preconditions for Abuse
๛

It is Thursday morning. Last night Dora's father molested her again. He crept into her bed and touched her inside private places. His lips smiled at her as he raised his finger to the *shhhh* position. Her nice daddy disappeared as his *shhhh* finger moved down from his lips. At the breakfast table Dora's mother notices something is wrong and asks, "Are you okay, honey? Is something wrong?" Dora whispers, "I can't tell. You'll hate me." (That's what her father had told her.) Mom, taking the milk from the refrigerator and grabbing the cereal from the cupboard, says, "Don't be silly. Talk to me. Tell me what's the matter." Mom turns toward Dora, who looks down and away. Several seconds later (an eternity for Dora, who so longs to tell), Dora says, "Nothing, Mom." "Well, honey, eat your breakfast. You know you can always tell me anything." Mom leaves the room, a lingering worry accompanying her, but thinking, "Well, Dora has gotten pretty private recently. I guess I just need to respect that. She'll tell me if she needs to." And with that, mom lets it go. Dora is eight years old.

About the same time a teacher notices Dora looking very tired and inattentive one morning. That was not like Dora, a usually eager student and exuberant child, so the teacher asks, "Dora, are you okay?" Dora looks down at the floor and shakes her head slowly from side to side—just once—as silent tears start to fall down her cheeks. The teacher takes Dora to her desk and asks if she should call Dora's mom. "No," says Dora. "Can I help?" asks the teacher. Dora shakes her head. Just then another student comes asking for help with an assignment. When the teacher looks back to where Dora had been sitting, Dora is gone. The teacher never follows up, never calls home, never brings in a school counselor even when she continues to notice how tired and inattentive Dora is some days.

In high school Dora finally told someone. She spoke to her school counselor, who said, "Well, if you don't have bruises that will photograph well, there isn't much we can do." She ran away and went to the police, who were very sympathetic and promised to help. They asked her who her parents were. Once she told the police her parents' names, they said, "No. It can't be." Her parents were well-respected leaders in the community. The police went from believing her to thinking she was lying or confused. One police officer said, "What, did they set a new curfew you don't like?" They called her parents, who came and picked her up.

Twenty years later, Dora, now thirty-five, meets a neighbor on the street. Their exchange goes like this:

Neighbor	*How are you?*
Dora	*Fine.* (Last night I made myself stay in bed, knowing if I got out I'd kill myself.)
Neighbor	*What are you doing these days?*
Dora	*Not much.* (I go to therapy four hours a week. I'm too depressed to have energy for much else. I'm not sleeping very well. Sometimes I wake up because I hear someone screaming. It takes awhile before I realize it's me.)
Neighbor	*Well, nice to see you. You look great!*
Dora	*Thanks. Bye.* (I look great! Ha! I learned to mask my feelings long ago. If you really knew, now, today, what would you do?) *You look great too!*

Fear and denial have shown Dora there are few, if any, places she can speak about being incested. Her experience is common. This is how people listen—good people—*menschen.*[9] This is what they see—nothing. People don't see, can't see, unless they really look and are willing to hear and know.

Sandy was ten when she was molested while walking to Hebrew school. She went on to the school and told them what happened. What she remembers most was the rabbi's emphasis on the fact that her mother's working kept her from being able to walk Sandy to school. Sandy, now in her late thirties, said, "It was as if my mother was the guilty party, not the neighbor who molested me." Familial and community denial silence child victims and adult survivors—that and the manipulation and threats by perpetrators.

According to Dr. David Finkelhor, abuse occurs when (1) it is possible for a person to think of being abusive, (2) there are no internal or external inhibitors (the abusers don't stop themselves, and no one else does either), and (3) the child doesn't feel it's possible to resist.[10]

The situation with Sheila's cousin Sol demonstrates the preconditions Finkelhor identifies. It was the beginning of the 1970s. Not quite a teenager, Sheila stood around and watched her cousin Sol as he gave the girls and women bear hugs while trying to unhook their bras. She saw him do this whenever she saw him. He was usually successful. The girls, including Sheila, actively squirmed and made faces while trying to avoid him. The women were more often able to keep him away. Sheila remembers grabbing his hands at the wrists, trying to keep him away from her. He was so strong. His hands felt cold, like steel. He'd say, "What's the matter? Don't you want to say hello to your cousin?" He laughed a kind of "gotcha" laugh. What was worst was the look in his eyes—a cold, mean gleam that seemed to communicate his certainty that he'd win. She was terrified. No one said anything. People laughed uncomfortably. Sheila's cousin acted as if what he was doing was funny. The family acted as if they agreed. This is denial. This is collusion. Any of the adults could have said to Sol, "*Stop that!*" I believe he would have.

Using Finkelhor's guidelines, Sol was able to think of being abusive, nothing within him and no one outside him said, "*Stop,*" and, although Sheila fought him as best she could, he was physically too strong for her to stop. Besides, everyone else was laughing. There was no place to go. The next story, by Hillary, also demonstrates the lack of support for children to set boundaries with inappropriate adults.

"Grandpa Morrie was a creepy man," writes Hillary.

> He was always kissing us with wet open lips. He touched us in places I thought only married people touched each other. He even conducted an arm-biting ritual in which all the grandchildren would line up by age and have our forearms slathered with mustard and ketchup to season us up for Grandpa's teeth. We'd get a nickel for a soft bite, a dime for a hard bite that left indentations, or a quarter if we let him bite our tushy. He was so brazenly creepy that he performed this ritual in front of an audience that included my aunts, uncles, adult cousins, and even great-aunts and great-uncles. Eventually, he would just take me into his bedroom, close the door, and do what he wanted to do with me—no matter who or how many people were in the apartment.

By then, I was too embarrassed to ask for help. I'd hide naked in the closet when someone knocked on the door.

As families and communities deny, children have no choice but to deny.

From such experiences with Grandpa Morrie or Cousin Sol, children learn that the family will not protect them. It is the beginning of self-doubt and fear. It is the beginning of questioning what we literally see, hear, and feel. How can this be real if no one else sees it or says anything? This is denial. If our family and neighbors see this and don't say anything, it must not be a problem. This is collusion.

Abuse is fed by individual, family, and community secrecy, silence, shame, and inaction. A story in the Talmud teaches that the mouse who steals the cheese is not the only guilty party. Also guilty are those who don't close the hole through which the mouse gains access to the cheese. Perpetrators clearly are responsible for their actions and must be held accountable; however, we must also look at what we do that makes it possible for them to molest. When we minimize, discount, or stay silent about the things that we see, we send a message to child and perpetrator that what is happening is acceptable. Too often people say, "Child abuse is a terrible thing, but we have to be careful, to be sure; after all, a man's reputation is at stake." We give the mouse access to the cheese.

Victims Deny to Survive
✢

Child victims deny in order to survive emotionally and physically. To experience and know the horror of what is happening, to know there is no way out and to function is impossible, so we block it out as much as we can. Some incest survivors talk about a day child and a night child—separating out—splitting off the tolerable from the intolerable. I idealized my father and my family and buried myself and my pain deep within me. This, too, is denial.

In this way, victims of child sexual abuse and incest are similar to others who have experienced or witnessed evil in action. To protect ourselves from overpowering feelings, "we must at times, avoid knowledge. . . . Erecting barriers against knowing is often the first response to such trauma. Women in Nazi concentration camps dealt with difficult interrogation by the Gestapo by derealization, by asserting 'I did not go through it. Somebody else went through the experience.'"[11]

Is it possible to compare child abuse and Holocaust abuse? In *Facing the Abusing God*, Rabbi David Blumenthal writes:

> Child and holocaust abuse are similar in some ways. Both are rooted in real historical events, both really happened . . . both deal with moments of utter victimization, of dehumanization. Both contain trauma that is massive in scope, penetrating over a long period of time into the psyche of the victim. Both entail a deep sense of aban-donment by those who should have helped. Both evoke psychic numbing, depression, suspiciousness, rage, isolation, and a conspir-acy of silence.[12]

Blumenthal also points out that child and Holocaust abuse are also dissimilar in significant ways.[13] He continues, "To speak of 'child' or 'family abuse' and to write about 'holocaust abuse' as homogeneous constructs and to compare them" is misleading. Yet "grouping the more severe forms of abuse together has an advantage. It enables us to compare the experience and healing process of two forms of deeply traumatized human experience. This, in turn, enables us to gain insights from one area which may be useful in the other."[14]

Blumenthal's comments resonate with the experiences of many incest survivors who, when reading stories or viewing films of Holocaust survivors, feel less alone. For me, there is a feeling that someone really understands pain that is often too deep to feel, that is impossible to describe in words, and that few are able to tolerate hearing.

I learned long ago that people don't really want to know—not about this. That necessitated my growing stronger and wiser and deepening my faith in God. I've been forced to tussle with God about how to live—how to reclaim my self—my soul—how to jettison the bitterness—to channel my rage—and embrace life—because "you" cannot know, do not listen, and too often leave or blame me if I upset you with the story of what happened to me in my home as a child. I'm not alone in that.

Carla told me:

> I am a survivor of incest. Growing up, it was like Mengele lived in our house. I am also a rabbi. I know other colleagues who are "out" to me about their childhood traumas, as well as various congregants and friends who have shared their stories with me. . . . When I speak with rabbinic colleagues about sexual abuse of Jewish children, they recoil in horror. . . . My openness about my history has hurt me professionally, as

if I were not the innocent child. Some days, I am sure that my incest experience has shaped me more profoundly than my identity as a Jew.

And when the experience that "has most shaped your life" is said to be impossible? Then, as Marcia Cohn Spiegel wrote, "If we say that Jews do not commit incest, then the child victim doesn't exist as a person or as a Jew."[15]

Distinguishing Deception from Denial
ᴕ

Denial is an unconscious mechanism. Deception is not. It is important to recognize both. Perpetrators consciously work to deceive and distract individuals, families, and the community from looking closely and seriously at their abuses. "In 10 years of counseling abusive men," wrote Rabbi Bob Gluck while a student, "I learned that the single most powerful factor contributing to domestic violence is the ability to get away with it."[16]

As we shine the light on sexual abuse, perpetrators will do everything in their power to continue having the freedom to molest without consequence. While we must offer them an opportunity to receive help and to heal, we cannot permit them to alter our course—safety for children that includes zero tolerance of child sexual abuse and incest.

Who Denies?
ᴕ

Thus far, this chapter has explored how denial shows itself. At one time or another, everyone denies. It is a defense against pain. Victims deny. Survivors deny. Witnesses of abuse deny. Family members deny. Perpetrators deny. Helpers deny. Friends deny. And anybody I missed denies.

"When someone you trust does something untrustworthy, your first reaction is disbelief—a questioning your own read of the situation," said trauma expert Renee Fredrickson at a workshop on clinical work with incest survivors. Denial is "a mental defense that cancels or negates external reality," writes psychiatrist Lenore Terr.[17]

Emunah told her sister that their dad molested her. Her sister said, "When, where, what?" to which Emunah replied, "I don't have to answer these questions. I'm just telling you I'm an incest survivor by our father. I don't need to be grilled. I'm not going to give you any details." A few months later Emunah's sister called to say she had recently been sitting on the couch at home when their dad grabbed her breast and said, "What is this?" She was so shocked she didn't even say anything.

"It's so sickeningly confusing," Emunah said.

> You think you're nuts. This guy is grabbing your boob and asking what it is, but it's so frightening and so altered you almost don't realize it's happening. His tone and manner are so normal, it's as if he's saying, "What color is your shirt?" But he's not. You dissociate. It's very creepy. After this incident with Dad, my sister told me she remembered that when we were kids and Dad tucked her in, he'd say, "I do different things to Emunah at night." She felt sick when he said that.

Kevin M. is a therapist who has worked with Holocaust survivors and Jewish adult survivors of child abuse. Kevin compares today's denial of child abuse in the Jewish community with stories Holocaust survivors tell about the reactions they received immediately after World War II. In Israel and America when these Holocaust survivors started to talk about what had happened to them or what they had seen, people would say in one way or another, "Don't tell me." World War II veterans experienced the same reaction—a turning away from the horrors of their experiences of liberating the camps—a community that said, "Don't discuss this. It's over. You're alive. Be happy."[18]

Lilith Goldberg is an incest survivor and author who was molested by her father, a Holocaust survivor. She writes eloquently about the dance of denial in her life:

> Because of the traumatic events that both my father and I lived through, our psychological patterning is eerily similar. We forget; we deny; we remember; we relive, and then, we forget again. And of course, it was easy for me to "forget" on a daily basis, because no one at school, or at synagogue, not even social workers, really wanted to hear about incest. Though I desperately sent out distress signals, I was told, over and over, in ways both covert and overt: "This doesn't happen in Jewish families."
>
> There was no one who would listen to the secrets of my soul. On my own, with no sympathetic other, I could do no better than "forget." By the time I was an adult and had retrieved memories of the perversities I'd endured, I could not bring myself to describe these horrors to anyone. Even in an incest survivors' group, I deliberately withheld details of my childhood traumas. It was too painful to be the "worst case," to receive the pity of those only slightly less abused than myself.[19]

Breaking through denial makes healing possible. *Lilith* continues:

> Recently I joined a group of daughters of Holocaust survivors, and, to my surprise, I encountered a number of women who were raped by their fathers in contexts very similar to mine. Together we examine and re-examine; we journey towards our deeper selves in great trepidation. Because of the support I feel from these women, I am slowly discovering the power of speaking out, of writing about my experience. I still often feel awash in my own shame when I articulate my pain. I still feel guilt-ridden, immersed in the suffering of an earlier era, but—even as I write—I move towards recognizing that the agony that my parents endured does not negate my own agony. As a second generation survivor, I struggle daily to live beyond the horrors of other times, other places. Slowly I unearth the last remaining images of war.
>
> And weekly, I light the Sabbath candles and recite the ancient words, continuing to bless whatever that spirit is that keeps me moving, feeling, existing, alive.[20]

In the spring 1993 issue of the newsletter *For Crying Out Loud*, Joy Shinnick reminds us, "The bottom line is denial, in any form, is only a temporary fix. The only way out of this nightmare is straight back the way I came. God grant me the strength for the journey."

If we didn't deny incest in Jewish lives, I believe there'd be a massive movement, money pouring in, people asking, "How can I help?" and then helping. Rabbis and lay leaders would actively work toward zero tolerance for child and relationship abuses of all kinds while teaching about healthy relationships, about respect. Abusers would be held accountable for their actions rather than their victims being ostracized, blamed, or ignored. More help would be available for victims, survivors, perpetrators, and their families. Helpers throughout the community would be exploring the possibility of incest and sexual abuse as a matter of "fact" when working with their clients, patients, congregants, and students.

Denial shows itself whenever someone says, "It doesn't happen here," when its impact is minimized, or when responsibility for prevention and intervention is not taken. There are solutions. In this section we've identified some ways to recognize denial. We will now explore some of the reasons we deny incest with the hope of shining a light on the harm caused when we buy into these beliefs.

Why Do We Deny?
ళ

Denial may seem a necessity for those who believe that to acknowledge that some Jews sexually abuse children will put the Jewish people at risk.

I was working on this book while on a writer's retreat in a remote setting where I was often a Jewish minority of one. People would ask what I was writing. As I told them, I found myself feeling uncomfortable, wondering if I was making Jews more vulnerable, wondering what "outsiders'" reactions would be. I felt guilty and defensive. I thought of publishing this book privately and disseminating it just within the Jewish community. It won't work. Many people for many years have been trying to do just that—quietly—one by one by one. It's not enough. Fear and shame can't be in charge anymore. And yet, I understand these fears.

Anti-Semitism, the PLO, Louis Farrakhan, the reality and memories of the Holocaust, and centuries of being a minority culture in the world (often targeted for extinction)—all have historically caused many of us to focus on the danger from these external forces and to deny, ignore, or minimize problems within our own community and within our families.

Since we are put upon by the "outside," it seems unthinkable that we would do anything to hurt ourselves or undermine our families. This veil of disbelief keeps us from seeing incest. Perhaps to feel safer, we collude with the worldview that Jews are different, especially when that means "better than." Myths of perfection feed denial. Whether minority or majority group, it is scary to confront incest. And whether in the past or present, sometimes it is scary being a Jew. There *are* dangers in the world. The shared belief that to disclose abusive behavior happening within our small circle makes us more vulnerable as a "people" parallels a "debate amongst researchers who study Holocaust survivors and their descendants. If they study the impact of the traumas of the Holocaust, thereby labeling people as victims, there is a fear that such labeling could be used as an excuse to harm Jews just as the excuses used to exterminate millions of Jews in Europe."[21] The desire to survive as a people feeds denial of incest.

I want to *shout* that being silent about our problems does not stop anti-Semitism or preserve our community. What could be more anti-Semitic than letting Jewish children be destroyed by their families and communities? Survivors willing to speak about what happened and communities willing to listen and help people build healthier relationships will be better able to repel and survive assaults of all kinds.

We hurt individuals and our community when we trivialize suffering that is not at the level of the Holocaust. Stephanie, a forty-two-year-old homemaker, language tutor, and mother of a small child, was incested by her father and grandfather from before she was two years old until she was nearly twelve. She never told anyone as a child, saying, "My grandfather lost his family in the Holocaust, so who was I to 'quibble' about a little 'yucky' touching? I also got the message that 'we shouldn't expose our dirty laundry to the goyim.'"

Families and survivors may feel denying and/or keeping silent is a necessity because they believe acknowledging sexual abuse will shame them.

Sally Weber, of Los Angeles' Shalom Bayit Committee, spoke about Jewish abused women who were interviewed as part of a study by Dr. Richard Gelles. The women shared horrific details of abuse they'd experienced. At the end of the interview they said, "There's something else. I don't know. This is so embarrassing. I'm Jewish." These women were more embarrassed that they were Jewish and abused than anything else.[22]

Artist and survivor Sherrie S. wrote:

> I cannot talk about my traumatic experience openly. I never believe that I have permission—that it's okay to talk, to discuss my thoughts or feelings or memories. I experience myself as shameful whenever the "public" mask slips or comes off. It is not just the need to protect myself from shame—from the humiliation of someone "knowing." It is the necessity of protecting my parents from humiliation and shame, even though they are both dead.

Orthodox women in therapy with any of the dozen *frum* therapists and rabbis I interviewed from across the United States expressed fears of letting others know they'd been molested.[23] One rabbi psychologist who wished to remain anonymous said, "These women have never told anyone, even as adults. They don't want to wreck the family. They feel responsible to hold the family together. If they say something about being molested they feel they can 'kiss the family good-bye.' If she talks about the molestation she fears she is casting a pall—a condemnation against her family. She is afraid of not being believed—of recriminations." Even though she was the innocent party, others are likely to label her and her family as damaged goods.

This is significant for those who fear that telling of their abuse as children will affect their marriageability or that of their siblings. Emunah spoke of her experience within her Orthodox community.

> When parents are wondering about a marriage for their son or daughter, they want to know about the family. When people fix you up they ask, "What's the family like?" It's a common thing people ask. They want to hear, "They come from a good family." "They're good stock." "They're going to make a good future for the Jewish people."
>
> People have this idea that if you come from a good family, you will be a good wife and you will be a good future. If you don't come from a good family you are suspect. So, obviously if you expose "Hey, I am an incest survivor. My dad raped me," that's not a good family. Who wants to connect to that? But the reality is incest is there and doesn't make me a bad person. I shouldn't have to be ashamed because someone molested me.

While this example comes from the Orthodox community, the often legitimate fear of being labeled defective is common regardless of religious affiliation. Too often, victims and survivors of child abuse are made to feel responsible, at fault, for what was done to them. They see and hear and believe that if they tell, *they* will be the ones in trouble or seen as "causing" trouble. They will be the ones who are censured, cast out. They fear being labeled as defective, less than. Many battered wives whose batterers are respected members of their congregations can attest to this inequity. It often is their husbands who are invited to dinner, welcomed in the shul, given *aliyah*.[24] Individual incest survivors may keep silent out of fear and shame. As community members we may deny because we are ashamed that abuse happens. Our collective self-image feels damaged, vulnerable if it is known that incest and sexual abuse happen at all.

We may deny because it is painful to know that sexual abuse happens and, for some, to remember that this happened to them, too.

During the Anita Hill–Clarence Thomas debacle, I remember women striking up conversations on street corners and bus stops. In one such conversation, an elderly Jewish woman spoke of her first job in a shoe store. She was sixteen at the time her boss asked her to accompany him to the cellar to "find something." Her head lowered and face flushed as she spoke emotionally of his hands reaching for her, her repulsion, and her quitting the job. She said, "I never told anyone until today."

When I told people in the Jewish community I was writing about incest and sexual abuse in the Jewish community, I was often met by silence, a serious or sad look, and questions about how I could write about something so difficult. "How did I handle the pain?" they'd want to know. The truth is, sometimes I'd have to lie on the earth, or take a walk in nature, or scream, or talk to God. Alice Walker was right: "The pain of writing this is nothing compared to the pain of living it." The pain of writing this is nothing in comparison to the pain of keeping silent and thereby disconnected from myself and unknown by others. My shame and fear kept me from saying, "I handle my pain by writing about this. You see, I was molested as a child."

We may deny because it is easier than confronting the realities and complexities of child sexual abuse.

How do we prevent incest? How do we help children and adult survivors heal? These are daunting questions. Denial protects us from having to figure them out. After all, we don't have to solve a problem we don't know exists. It protects the community when it doesn't have a response or answer because "we didn't know."

Jewish day school teacher Rose Alexander spoke to children about domestic violence at her synagogue's Tzedakah Fair. *Tzedakah* means to do service on behalf of others. The children were learning about problems people face and the importance of helping others by listening to presentations from various individuals and agencies. Small groups of children ranging from kindergarten through sixth grade came for brief periods of time to learn about the needs in the community so each child could decide where to pledge his or her support, dollars, or both.

A group of second graders came through. Rose asked them to identify the ways in which people hurt each other. Taking the subject seriously, one boy said, "Christians hurt Jews." Another said, "In World War II." Rose asked, "And what about Jews hurting Jews?" There was silence, wide eyes, and puzzled looks.

A group of sixth graders came next. One child's father stood behind him, his hands resting on his son's shoulders. As Rose and the children talked about ways in which Jews can be hurtful to each other in our homes, the father said, "Ha ha—did my son tell you I knock him around?" Rose said, "I certainly hope that's not true, but," while looking at the son, "if he does, I hope you'll tell someone." Then the dad said, "Well, I don't really do that, but did he tell you I slap his mother around?" Looking at him and making sure to speak conversationally, yet directly, Rose said, "I certainly hope that's not true either. . . . This is an issue that the Jewish community really has a hard time dealing with. We have a hard time recognizing this really does happen. People get embarrassed and ashamed about it."

His "joking" stopped, and he asked, "Well, does it really happen that much?" Rose gave him some information on the numbers of families being served and ways we could work together to help. She wanted to say, "Abuse is never a joke."

Later that week Rose was told the donations by the children to stop domestic violence in the Jewish community were more than to any other cause presented that day. Children know.

Survivors may deny out of fear of being victimized any more, of losing any more.

There is much legitimate fear of the consequences for telling. Therapists and rabbis who are also incest survivors have been censured and criticized by some colleagues. It has affected their ability to find jobs. Other survivors have been emotionally attacked by family members unable to let go of an idealized view of their family, the abuser, or both. Some continue to be physically threatened, harassed, or both. For some, it is implied or stated that they will be ostracized by the family, lose financial support, or both. As a result, many survivors stay silent.

Some survivors were threatened so much as children, during and around the abuses, that they are afraid, even after the abuser is dead, to speak out. Many were told it was their fault and that they wouldn't be believed. To speak out is a brave and sometimes risky act.

I've never been able to predict how someone will react to the disclosure that I've been molested. Usually I don't say anything more than "I was sexually abused as a child." In telling two women friends, I couldn't have asked for a more loving and warm initial response. I told them at separate times. Within weeks of my telling them, each stopped being in my life. One had been a good and close friend of many years. Years later she apologized and told me I had stirred her own memories, that she could not handle them, and so she could not handle being around me. Just being around me was a reminder, even though we never spoke of the incest again. Our friendship has not continued.

Denial, silence, fear, and shame about incest means that every time a survivor considers "telling," she risks losing connection. In addition, when trauma survivors speak about their experiences, they risk being labeled "defective." This is true with sexual abuse survivors and Holocaust survivors. Those doing research on the impact of the Holocaust on survivors and their children run into a dilemma.

> To describe severe symptoms as a consequence of trauma exposure, on the one hand, serves to validate the experience of the victim by acknowledging that the traumatic events, rather than some personal flaw, was the cause of resulting symptoms. On the other hand, an acknowledgment of the profound effects of trauma may also serve to further victimize and stigmatize the survivor by implicitly suggesting permanent damage, which may be quite contradictory to the survivor's perception that s/he has overcome adversity. Such a view may also promote hopelessness and pessimism in survivors, who may already be prone to these experiences. This issue is further compounded by the catastrophic magnitude of the Holocaust itself.
>
> Thus, the dilemma that is invariably created is how one goes about documenting the horrors and the permanent scars created by the racial prejudice as a result of the Holocaust while at the same time demonstrating the dignity of the Jewish people and their capacity to survive. To describe Holocaust survivors and their children as vulnerable, particularly if this has biological dimensions is to document traits similar to the ones that were actually used to justify the extermination of the Jews. On the other hand, to mitigate the scars of the Holocaust is equally problematic, and serves as an obstacle to providing the needed resources to help survivors overcome their mental health symptoms.[25]

This dilemma occurs when discussing child and adult victims of intimate violence as well. We need to find a way to talk about the awful impact of violence while not sentencing forever those who have been victimized to a "loser's" circle. We were victims and the impact is there. The thing is, the impact varies, and while some of the outcomes are negative, some are positive—not because the situation was a good thing, but because of what we were able to transform it into.

Survivors may deny their experience, and/or keep silent out of love, a felt obligation, or "loyalty" to the family or its "image."

Trudy, a successful, professional thirty-two-year-old, came into my therapy practice originally because of dissatisfaction with her career. In the course of our working together, she spoke of having been molested by her stepfather, David—a fact she'd never discussed with anyone before. David died some years before.

At the age of thirty-four, Trudy came in for her session saying her family was coming to town. Laughing, she said she'd like me to meet them. Trudy was curious about what I could tell from the dynamics. She liked the idea of my seeing what happens when her family talks about David.

"When the family gets together, everyone talks fondly about him," Trudy said. "There's an assumption I feel the same way." I asked her how that makes her feel. She said, "A little uncomfortable, a little angry, a little superior because I know something they don't." I asked Trudy, "But that also means you're disconnected?" "Right," she said as tears welled up in her eyes.

"I'm surprised by my sadness at this," Trudy continued. "I realize that this sets me apart from all of them. It's hard to stay connected to how I'm feeling. Part of me is willing. Part says it takes too much energy. All I feel I can do is let the struggle (inside me) play itself out—and then I dissociate," she said as she smiled. "It's not a word I use in everyday conversation."

We then talked about how far she has come to be able to recognize what happens to her as she starts to feel the pain of the consequences of what David did to her and the price of keeping his secret. We discussed the impact of being part of a community that ignores that incest happens and her feelings about an upcoming conference on child neglect and abuse in the Jewish community. She said, "I think it helps. I never thought about it—what happened to me—in terms of the Jewish community."

I asked what it would mean to her if the Jewish community said, *Yes, this is a problem. We're going to do something about it.* Trudy said,

> I can't get my mind around it. I'm trying to imagine it. I can't imagine people coming forward and participating. [And if they did?] Then everybody would know. [What?] If Marcy Goldfine participates in this conference somebody in the Goldfine family must have done something. It's like airing your dirty laundry. There's so little anonymity in the Jewish community. [How does that affect you?] It drives it all underground—especially with the Jews. Every Jewish woman I meet knows members of my family. There's no anonymity. People would wonder. I would care less what people in this community would think, "She's a survivor of abuse," than somehow it would get to my family and I would have to deal with it with them.

When asked what would scare her about that, she replied, "I don't think they would not believe me. I worry more they might minimize it and most that I'd be causing them that kind of pain and distress.

"I understand now that part of that concern is that if I make people feel bad or angry or uncomfortable, I might lose them. So all I try to do is make people happy and comfortable—even the saleswoman who shows me an ugly dress to try on."

Our relationships to our families are complex. We may love them and they us, yet we are often hurt by keeping this secret. We keep silent in order to keep in contact with the only family we've ever known. We keep silent because we're supposed to. I understand the feelings expressed by Trudy and Sherrie and so many others. I would have done anything—and tried—to not know I was molested. I almost died in order to keep this secret, to be loyal to my family. God how I loved him . . . how I wanted to avoid hurting my mother and sister. Ultimately there was no choice. If I was to live, I had to tell.

The Costs of Denial and Silence
～

Denying incest is expensive. Forty-six-year-old Hillary is a Conservative Jew, married with two sons. She volunteers as a Jewish educator. She was sexually abused by her grandfather, who assured her silence by threatening to hurt her, her mother, and her sister if she told. Hillary writes:

> The price I've paid for what my grandfather did to me, is not cheap. And I don't mean only in the financial arena. My kids had to put up with my emotional mood swings, my physical health problems, and my psychological crises. My husband has seen the rules in our relationship change almost weekly as I worked through the effects that my childhood experiences had on my adult sexuality, my ability to trust, and my confidence in honesty. Almost all my family of origin has removed themselves from my life—all of the extended family of aunts, uncles, and cousins, and even some of my nuclear family. My adoptive father has told me to stay out of his life, my mother and I have relatively cool and infrequent contact, and only one of my four sisters remains close (despite the taunting she gets from the others about maintaining a relationship with me).

"The cost to the community is huge," says Emunah, a thirty-three-year-old who was molested by her father.

> If someone is not working on their issues, they are not a whole person.
> There are so many people with a lot of potential who cannot perform.
> I did great in college but quit after two years. I started to break down
> for "no apparent reason." I think it's like a holocaust within the
> community. Only a small portion of the talent we have is being used
> and blossoming because a person can't use her talent or is very limited.
> I think a lot of LD [learning disability] is caused by incest. A lot of
> physical ailments, too. We don't grow spiritually. One of the most free-
> ing lines I've heard is, "You're as sick as your secrets." I believe it's true
> for the individual and the community.

With nowhere to go, molested children turn inward, often upon themselves. Rabbi, author, and family therapist Yehudah Fine writes about
wounded teens, saying that "they hold fast to their wounds and keep them
as secrets." Fine continues, their "secrets are toxic time bombs that can
affect generations. Traumas that are buried have an uncanny way of surfac-
ing and detonating in succeeding generations."[26] Many survivors choose to
not have children because of their desire to stop the abuse cycle and/or
their fears of what they or a partner might do to any child they have. Of
those who do have children, most with whom I've communicated have
said nothing to their children about what happened to them. They don't
want to "burden" or "harm" their children or partners.

This is a dilemma. Survivors often pay heavy prices for telling. There
are no clear guidelines for what to tell, how to tell, or when to tell a child.
There is no guarantee about how others will react to knowing. Whether
or not we tell is each individual's choice. However, when we don't tell, as
child or adult, others may be more at risk of being molested. Most perpetrators molest more than one child. Survivors who are parents often
anguish over this. Sally, whose father had molested her, told me, "When
my daughter was eighteen, she went to dinner with her grandfather—my
father. Over dinner he started touching her inappropriately and proposi-
tioned her. She was horrified. She walked out. When she told me about it,
I told her what he'd done to me. She was furious that I had not told her.
She felt I had not protected her from him. She was right. When I think
about what might have happened to her or her brother as children . . ."

Susie's story offers another example of the dangers of silence. Susie, now
a successful thirty-nine-year-old businesswoman and activist for safety for
women and children, was eight years old when her piano teacher, Mr. S.,

started unzipping his pants and having her perform oral sex. He showed her "pictures" of other girl students posing. Her mom found her crying one day and asked what was wrong. Susie told. Her mom told her dad.

"I'm still recovering from what Mr. S. did to me," says Susie. "My parents believed me, but no one confronted Mr. S. He continued teaching individually and later in schools. After my father died, I discovered the reason they never confronted him was because Mr. S. was a friend of some man with whom my dad did business. Dad didn't want to jeopardize that relationship. Basically, my dad sold my soul."

The abuse took place in her parents' house when her mother was home.

After Susie told her mom what Mr. S. had done, her mother remembered there were times she had seen Mr. S. with his zipper down. She had assumed he'd gone to the bathroom and "just forgot."

Susie's mother writes:

> I found out about the molestation about six months after the piano lessons ended. I was sick and wanted to kill Mr. S. It has been years since this happened, but I am so frustrated that I couldn't help her, and she had to seek help professionally—numerous times.
>
> She got no help at first because I wanted to confront this man and my husband wouldn't let me. I would like the Jewish community to know that the perpetrator was a Jewish piano teacher and that children cannot trust anyone.

How different this story could have been if Susie had been taught as a small child that it was her right to say "No" if someone touched her or spoke to her in a way she didn't like (even her relatives) and if she had been encouraged to tell her parents, teachers, or rabbi if someone did. How many child molestations could have been prevented if Susie's parents had spoken up at the time Susie told her mother what Mr. S. had done?

Moving Beyond Denial and Silence
⌁

Denial doesn't mean we're bad, just human. The challenge is (1) to confront our individual and community denial and get beyond it, (2) to see that the harm done by sexual abuse and incest is *greater* than the harm of disclosure, discussion, and confronting the realities of these abuses within the Jewish community, (3) to realize that we will not fall apart or undermine our community if we speak about abuses within our community, but rather (4) that we undermine individuals and community when we don't speak out, reach out, and heal the wounds caused by these abuses.

On a beautiful spring day in Jerusalem in 1973, I entered a cobbler's shop to get my shoes repaired. An angular, round-shouldered, bespectacled man took my shoes, put them aside, and insisted I sit down. He pulled out a large, flat book, with worn edges, and said, "You must know this." He proceeded to open the book that showed photographs of him and his friends in a concentration camp, while repeating over and over, "See . . . you must remember . . . you must know this." And so I looked at cadaverous men with lifeless eyes who stared out at me from the pages of this book. I was twenty-one. I remember it vividly. I remember the moment his sleeve rode up and the tattooed numbers on his arm were exposed. He was right. We must know.

We don't expect ourselves to feel comfortable or good while hearing stories of the Holocaust, yet we know we must hear them. We talk about it, write about it, make films about it, teach our children about it, at least in part, because we believe it can happen again, and if people know about it, we will be safer.

Silence and denial do not make our world safer for children. What is the solution? Melanie Kaye/Kantrowitz writes:

> The community, not the individual, is the unit of solution. Judaism specifically incorporates time for each individual to make private prayer, allows for a huge range of debate and disagreement. But one is not truly Jewish alone: one is Jewish in community with others. Problems are conceived of in collective terms, and solutions likewise. What this means in the late twentieth century, when problems are global, is that solutions must also be global.[27]

We can break through denial by making sure (1) the topics of child sexual abuse and incest are addressed when training rabbis, cantors, educators, administrators, and staff of Jewish social service agencies including their responsibility to act on behalf of children and survivors, (2) that our synagogues and community agencies receive training in this area, (3) that all Jewish organizations and institutions have policies for addressing these problems when they arise, (4) that programs are developed and available to teach parents and community members (including physicians and other health care professionals) about prevention and intervention, and (5) that programs for children are integrated into school curricula from early childhood throughout their education on topics such as respect, good touch/bad touch, healthy relationships, and where to go for help for themselves or others.

Hope lies in talking about these issues, confronting the denial. As more people speak out, we create momentum and permission to talk about incest and sexual abuse. By raising the questions we start the search for the answers. We promote healing. There are survivors who feel better knowing someone is asking questions, saying, "Yes, this happens. How can I/we help? What is needed?"

We must look with kindness and compassion for all concerned—for victims, perpetrators, their families, and community. This is the only way to avoid or lessen the resistance and backlash to knowing something so sad, so painful, and so evil. And as we drop the water of knowledge and compassion on the rock of denial, we will see what must be seen, know what needs to be done, and do it. It is the water on the rock theory of evolution. Even the hardest rock will wear away over time.

THREE

Jewish Law and Tradition Regarding Sexual Abuse and Incest

RABBI ELLIOT N. DORFF

Introduction by Rachel Lev
☞

In a proposal to the Rabbinical Council of America, Rabbi Mark Dratch wrote that community denial about physical, sexual, and emotional abuse of children

> remains inexcusable because we thereby shirk our responsibility to our children, denying the victims of abuse the safe haven of a caring and nurturing home and school, and preventing them from growing up with the physical and psychological security they need and deserve. It is for this sin of omission that our entire community must give *din vi-heshbon*, a complete and unequivocal reckoning. And it is to protect the bodies and souls of our innocent children that we must speak out and act.[1]

Religion can be a source of empathy—how terrible abuse is. It can also be something scary if we feel it is telling us we need to put up with abuse or be silent about it. I have learned in discussions with rabbis that Jewish law talks of respecting one's parents, fearing and honoring them.[2] I have also learned that that doesn't mean fearing for your safety. It doesn't mean physical fear. It doesn't mean never telling anyone about having been molested. Judaism doesn't condone violence. It doesn't say it's good to suffer. Rabbi Dr. J. said, "The Torah teaches the importance of respecting people, maintaining a healthy relationship with God and one's fellow man. It isn't a means to exploit or put people in chains."

In Rabbi Dratch's proposal he raises questions such as, "What obligations does Jewish law impose upon us in order to protect our children from actual or potential abusers? May we inform civil authorities? Are there problems of *lashon hara* (evil speech) or *hillul HaShem* (desecration of God)?"

In this chapter Rabbi Dorff answers these and other questions in ways that are sadly very different from what many child victims and survivors have been told. Why is this?

Marcia Cohn Spiegel points out that ancient Jewish texts share with the texts of some other religions and cultures a valuing of men over women and an acceptance of the use and abuse of women and children. The Mishnah (Jewish oral Torah)[3] and commentaries, which became the Talmud (the record of the rabbis' discussion, application, and amplification of the Mishnah),[4] color people's thinking whether we believe what they say or not.

For example, in early Jewish sources, while sexual relations are not condoned within families—"None of you shall come near anyone of his own flesh to uncover her nakedness" (Lev. 18:1)—the subsequent list which details those forbidden relationships does not specifically name incest between a father and his daughter. We are taught (Deut. 22:13–29) that if a girl is married and proves not to be a virgin, she may be stoned to death for doing a shameful thing.

Possibly the most disturbing statement of all is found in Kethuboth 11b: "Raba said . . . when a grown-up man has intercourse with a little girl it is nothing, for when the girl is less than this (3), it is as if one puts the finger into her eye; but when a small boy has intercourse with a grown-up woman he makes her 'as a girl who is injured by a piece of wood.'" The sage Maimonides reiterates this discussion in *Sefer Nashim* 3:11, where he says, "A father may betroth his daughter without her consent as long as she is a minor, and she also remains under his authority as long as she is a maiden. . . . [I]f she is three years and one day old, she may be betrothed by an act of intercourse with the consent of her father."

While we do not have evidence that any of these opinions were acted upon, contemporary men and women who study these texts could misinterpret or misunderstand the intent of the discussions and become insensitive to the sexual feelings of girls, women, and young boys, assuming that it is nothing to be concerned with.[5] As long as we study these texts without commentary on the ways children and women are objectified and diminished, we feed the denial that allows perpetrators to abuse and women and children to have no recourse when they are violated. I think it is not asking too much that those men (and women) who teach the Talmud could use this as an opportunity for education and sensitization of their students to respect and honor the bodies and sexuality of others—men *and* women alike.

As Rabbi Dorff writes, "These more controversial verses indicate clearly that to accomplish our expectation to be taught by the tradition, we must be aware of the twin duties we have as its heirs: we must learn it and preserve it, and, at the same time, evaluate it and reinterpret it when necessary. Only then can it continue to speak to us with wisdom and power."

Jewish Law and Tradition *Do Not* Condone Abuse
✖

Sexual abuse and incest happen in Jewish families.[6] This has not been part of our self-image. Somehow we were supposed to be immune from such behavior. Jewish families, though, suffer from family violence of all sorts, including spousal abuse, parental abuse, verbal abuse, and sexual abuse and incest. Moreover, it happens among those affiliated with the more traditional forms of Judaism (Orthodox and Conservative) as well as those who take more liberal stances (Reform, Reconstructionist, Jewish Renewal, secular).

We Jews often look to Jewish tradition for guidance on how we should live our lives. Nothing, including a strong commitment to Judaism, can provide a guarantee that domestic violence will not happen, for, as Jewish liturgy, theology, and law themselves recognize, human beings routinely sin and must constantly strive to return to the behavior that God wants of us. Nevertheless, the Jewish tradition has strong faith that we can do better, that we have both the free choice and the ability to act morally and compassionately. This view of human action is the major theme of the High Holy Days, but it is also part of the prayers that traditional Jews recite three times each day when we ask God to forgive us for our sins. Judaism can play an important role in teaching us what proper behavior is, in motivating us to act accordingly, and in showing us how to return to the proper path when we stray.

Matters of Method:
How Shall We Gain Moral Guidance from the Tradition?
✖

What, then, does the Jewish tradition say about domestic violence? In some ways, it seems obvious that Judaism would not allow people to abuse others, especially a family member. After all, in its opening chapters, the Torah[7] tells us that we are all created in the image of God.[8] The classical rabbis of the Jewish tradition, those who wrote the Mishnah, the Talmud, and the Midrash,[9] certainly understood that, to prohibit abuse for rabbinic law assumes that we do not have the right to strike others and provides penalties for those who do.[10] Indeed, the rabbis interpreted the integrity of a person to say that even those who slander others are to be regarded as though they had denied the existence of God. Rabbi Eliezer said, "Let your fellow's honor be as dear to you as your own."[11]

Given these underlying principles, we would expect that family violence in the Jewish community would be based on misinformation about our tradition, neglect of it, or the foibles of individuals. Unfortunately, when we probe Jewish sources from the Bible to modern times, we find some that permit forms of family violence and actually encourage it. For example, the biblical Book of Proverbs affirms the maxim "Spare the rod and spoil the child,"[12] and some medieval rabbis extended this to beating wives, ruling that husbands may teach them proper behavior through force.[13]

This raises major concerns about methodology: If we cannot automatically equate what the tradition says with the good, how shall we gain moral guidance from the tradition?[14] The method that Conservative Jews use to interpret and apply the Jewish tradition requires us to see sources within their historical context and to make judgments appropriate to our own time. The Jewish tradition has spanned many centuries. During that time it has not remained the same. Sometimes its development has been an internal unfolding of its inherent commitments in thought and in practice, and sometimes the example of other peoples among whom Jews lived produced changes within Judaism. Not all of the tradition is of an everlasting and compelling quality, and so generations of Jews have reinterpreted some parts of the tradition, all but ignored some, added other elements, and even taken steps to make some parts of the tradition effectively inoperative. For example, while the Torah permits parents to stone their children for disobedience, the rabbis circumvented that law with so many evidentiary requirements that once they had completed that job, they concluded that "the stubborn and rebellious son" of the Torah "never was and never will be"![15]

Historical understanding of Judaism is critical for identifying its contemporary message on any subject, including the topic of sexual abuse. We look to the tradition for enlightenment and guidance, and we often find it in a simple, straightforward manner. For example, the Torah's demands that we seek justice, that we love our neighbors as ourselves, and that we use honest weights and measures are as compelling to us now as when they were written thousands of years ago.[16] Sometimes, however, traditional sources say things that we find obsolete or even offensive. For example, the Torah permits owning slaves.[17] When that occurs, we have not only the right, but the duty to exercise judgment. We must determine whether such a mode of thinking or acting recorded in the tradition is a historical remnant that must be altered because contemporary circumstances or moral sensitivities have changed, or whether the tradition as it stands is instead an indictment of our way of doing things now and a challenge for us to change. Which of those, for example, is the biblical law prohibiting male, homosexual sex? Or the verse prohibiting heterosexual intercourse during the woman's menstrual flow?[18] These more controversial verses indicate clearly that to accomplish our expectation to be taught by the tradition, we must learn it and preserve it, and, at the same time, evaluate it and reinterpret it when necessary. Only then can it continue to speak to us with wisdom and power.

Jews expect their tradition to give them guidance beyond the demands of civil law, for we aspire to holiness. We certainly cannot interpret Jewish law to allow us to be less moral than what civil law requires.[19] Since civil law in most areas of the Western world now prohibits sexual abuse and incest, Jews must eschew it for that reason in addition to the grounds afforded by the Jewish tradition.

The Status of Sexual Abuse in Jewish Law
ᴣ

Throughout history children have been seen as possessions. "'Portable property' was Emerson's term for children, and most people believe kids belong to their parents, body and soul. As a practical matter, the courts have tended to uphold that view."[20] Even so, parents may not have sex with their children. The Torah states unequivocally, "None of you shall come near anyone of his own flesh to uncover nakedness: I am the Lord." After a long list of such forbidden relationships, it then states that such were the abhorrent practices of the nations that occupied the Promised Land before the Israelites. The land thus became defiled and is spewing them out—almost as if the land had gotten an upset stomach from toxic food. The Israelites themselves may remain in the holy land only if they eschew such practices and act as a holy people. Furthermore, "All who do any of those abhorrent things shall be cut off from their people. You shall keep My charge not to engage in any of the abhorrent practices that were carried on before you, and you shall not defile yourselves through them: I the Lord am your God."[21]

Part of what it means to be a People chosen by God as a model for others is that Jews must not engage in incest or sexual abuse. To do so violates the standards by which a holy people covenanted to God should live and warrants excommunication from the People Israel. Jews are expected to behave better than that.

Why does the Torah speak of incest and sexual abuse as "defilement" and "abomination" in addition to its usual language of "transgression"? In part, it is because the Promised Land was itself seen as alive and violated by such conduct, but surely the words refer to the human beings involved, too. One's bodily integrity is compromised when one is sexually abused. That is experienced not only as an assault upon one's body, but also—and usually more devastatingly—as an onslaught upon one's person. One has lost one's integrity—not only in body, but in soul. One no longer feels safe in the world; at any moment, one can be invaded in the most intimate of ways. The abuse is thus indeed a defilement: what was sacred and whole before is now desecrated and broken.[22]

Sexual abuse is also a source of shame. The Torah makes this exceedingly clear: "If two men get into a fight with each other, and the wife of one comes up to save her husband from his antagonist and puts out her hand and seizes him by his genitals, you shall cut off her hand; show no pity."[23] Despite the special justification the woman had for shaming her husband's assailant, the Torah demands drastic steps in retribution for the degradation she caused—although the rabbis transformed this to a monetary payment that she must pay. (Note that as the Torah recognized, feelings of shame and embarrassment are experienced by men who are sexually abused just as much as they are by women.) The Talmud, when determining the payment to be exacted for the shame involved whenever one person assaults another, uses this case as the paradigm for what embarrassment means.[24] We are humiliated when we are sexually abused—even just touched in our private parts against our will—for we feel that our sense of self has been invaded, that our honor has been compromised in the most fundamental way possible.

When children are sexually abused, the damage is even worse. Children depend upon the adults in their lives to help them master the skills of living. Their psychological well-being depends upon their ability to trust such people to act for their welfare. That is the only way that children can learn to trust themselves and others. When an adult sexually abuses a child, the child feels not only physically violated, but *betrayed*. Those who experience such violation and betrayal often have difficulty in forming relationships with others. In some cases, being sexually abused as a child also undermines a person's ability to trust the world enough to go out into it for any productive activity.

This assault on the body and the psyche of the child is clearly prohibited by all the Jewish laws prohibiting assault, sexual contact with one's family members, sexual contact outside marriage, and embarrassment of others. The Jewish tradition understands the Torah to ban not only sexual penetration, but any form of illicit fondling or inappropriate behavior for the purpose of gratifying sexual desire.[25] Indeed, in light of the extensive damage it causes to the future ability of the child to cope with life, without too much exaggeration I would say that, in the case of children, sexual abuse is akin to murder.[26]

Making Abuse Public
๛

When sexually abused children survive into adulthood, their survival and healing often require talking with others about what happened to them. What does Jewish law and tradition say about such discussions and the disclosure that they include?

Two commands within Judaism are sometimes misinterpreted to prevent someone from either helping others to extricate themselves from abuse or making one's own way out of an abusive situation. One is the prohibition against "evil speech" (*lashon ha-ra*), and the other is the Jewish need to avoid shame (*boshet*).

Defamatory speech. The Jewish tradition forbids several kinds of speech that are related, but distinct. These include (1) lies (*sheker*); (2) truths that it is nobody's business to know (*rekhilut,* or gossip); and (3) truths that, for all their truth, are defamatory (*lashon ha-ra*). Some people invoke *lashon ha-ra* to claim that Judaism prohibits an abused wife or child from publicly declaring their abuse in an effort to get help. Since complaints about the abuse will inevitably defame the abuser, the argument goes, the victim may not describe what is going on to others.

While it is important to avoid defamatory speech as much as possible, there are some very clear exceptions to the prohibition. One exception occurs when failure to defame the person will result in harm to someone else. If you are asked to be a reference for someone applying for a job, for example, and if your report will be generally negative, you are duty-bound either to refuse to write a letter of reference in the first place or to tell the truth, however negative it may be. Similarly, when failure to disclose abuse to the proper authorities will result in continued abuse, the victim and anyone who notices the abuse are obliged to reveal the facts. Even though notifying the authorities will inevitably defame the abuser, that is not only permissible, but mandatory when it is done in an effort to prevent harm to another.[27] As Maimonides wrote:

> Anyone who can save (someone's life) and does not do so transgresses "You shall not stand idly by the blood of your neighbor" (Leviticus 19:16). Similarly, if one sees someone else drowning in the sea, accosted by robbers, or attacked by wild animals and he can save him personally or hire others to save him, but he does not save him, or he heard non-Jews or informers plotting evil or attempting to entrap another Jew and he does not inform him . . . transgresses "You shall not stand idly by the blood of your neighbor."[28]

Indeed, if one person (A) is attacking another (B), any third party (C) has not only the right, but the obligation to stop A—even at the cost of A's life. This is the law of the pursuer (*rodef*).[29] Unlike the law in many American states, Jewish law would thus justify C in even killing an abusive spouse or parent if that were the only way to stop constant assaults on B, but only when there is imminent danger of the death or rape of B. In other words, Jewish law allows a third party (C) to do what B could legally do according to both legal systems as an act of self-defense.[30]

The law of the pursuer is based on a broader principle in Jewish law, that of *pikkuah nefesh* (saving a life). Specifically, the Torah proclaims the command to follow God's commands to live by them (Lev. 18:5). The rabbis interpreted this to mean that we must live by them and not die by them. Toward that end, the rabbis determined that we not only may, but must, violate all but three of the commandments if necessary to save a life. The three exceptions that we may not violate even to save a life are murder, incest/adultery, and idolatry. The first of those exceptions, however, applies only when we would be murdering an innocent person to save our own or someone else's life; if, instead, the person in question is threatening me, I both may and must seek to kill him or her first, and if the person in question is pursuing another, I must intervene, even to the point of killing the pursuer, as the law of *rodef* demands.[31]

These are extreme cases. They demonstrate, however, exactly how far Jewish law was willing to go to stop assaults. Civil law is not as supportive of those who murder family members to stop assaults, and even Jewish law would permit homicide in such cases only when the pursuer's murder or rape of another is imminent and unavoidable by any other means. People clearly need to extricate themselves from such situations before they ever come to this. Nevertheless, since Jewish law justifies even homicide to prevent assault, it certainly expects third parties to intervene in less violent ways to free abused people from the situations of their abuse, such as reporting cases of abuse to legal authorities. "One may not stand idly by the blood of one's neighbor," the Torah enjoins.[32] One who has information to report and fails to do so is in violation of that commandment and of Leviticus 5:1, "If he does not come forth with his information, then he shall be subject to punishment."[33] While in monetary affairs the witness may wait until summoned, in other matters, such as abuse, the witness must come forward voluntarily to "destroy the evil from your midst."[34]

This is true whether the abuser is a parent, a teacher, or anyone else. Abusive teachers *must* be removed from classrooms. The leaders of schools, camps, and youth groups must investigate the claim before taking such action, and the usual presumption of innocence applies to all parties involved. If the charges against the adult prove true, however, Jewish institutions have a clear duty to protect their students from that person's verbal, physical, and sexual abuse.

This raises one complication that inheres in cases of child abuse. Typically, the teacher or friend who reports the abuse is doing so on the testimony of the child together with supportive evidence. Since the testimony of minors is usually inadmissible in Jewish courts,[35] this evidentiary rule would preclude many interventions to redeem a child from an abusive situation. Some Jewish authorities, however, accept the testimony of minors if supported by other evidence, and that is the stance adopted by the Conservative movement's Committee on Jewish Law and Standards and by rabbis in other movements as well. Children are not to be presumed untruthful, especially in matters as painful and personal as this. In any case, the report given to civil authorities generally remains confidential and goes only to the governmental agencies responsible for child welfare. They, in turn, must investigate further. Consequently, the general inadmissibility of a child's evidence in court should not prevent adults who hear of child abuse from children and/or see evidence thereof from taking steps to have the complaint examined, and, if it proves accurate, acted upon.

Furthermore, before Enlightenment philosophies led to the creation of governments in which Jews were treated as full citizens deserving of fair treatment in court, Jewish law forbade Jews from turning over fellow Jews for prosecution in non-Jewish courts (*mesirah*) lest justice not be done and the entire Jewish community suffer retaliation for even raising the dispute.[36] Even then, though, Jews were allowed to refer the matter to non-Jewish courts when the perpetrator constituted a major threat to the Jewish community *(meitzar ha-tzibbur)*. In our time, secular courts can be presumed to be fair to Jews, and, moreover, abuse of spouses, elderly parents, and children has reached the extent of a *meitzar ha-tzibbur*—a menace to the community as a whole—in three senses. First, those who abuse others constitute a physical threat not just to the ones they have already abused, but to all potential, future victims as well and therefore to the entire community. Second, abusers pose a threat to the sense of well-being of the community as a whole by making it an unsafe place to live. Third, abusers are a source of pain and suffering for the Jewish community because they defame us as a community and God whom we worship, desecrating the divine Name (*hillul ha-Shem*). Consequently, it is within both the spirit and the letter of Jewish legal precedents of both Sephardic[37] and Ashkenazic authorities to assert that victims of abuse and witnesses to abuse may, and indeed should, enlist the help of governmental agencies.

The Jewish community is not perfect. Jews cannot expect flawlessness of themselves, and non-Jews must be taught not to expect that either. We ultimately do more for our own reputation as a community and for the Name of God, our covenanted partner, if we own up to the problems in our community and try honestly to deal with them. *Hillul ha-Shem*, far from prompting us to try to hide the abuse that is going on among us, should motivate us instead to confront it and root it out.

In the case of the abused party, the duty to disclose is even stronger than it is for other people. "Avoiding danger is a stronger obligation than any prohibition," the Talmud says, and saving your own life takes precedence over saving the lives of others.[38] This applies even to cases where the victim's life is not at stake through physical or sexual abuse, but where the victim is constantly subject to verbal abuse.

These Jewish legal principles together mean that abused adults have a positive obligation to ignore the issues of defamation of the abuser since that is necessary to save their lives, and their duty to report an abuser in the context of saving their own lives is even greater than their responsibility to disclose abusers of others. Minor children cannot be made legally responsible for this or anything else, but when abused by family members, children certainly have the sanction of the tradition to reveal such abuse to those who can help them, despite the defamation of the family involved.

What about adult survivors who need to tell their story in order to heal? Clearly, if the person who abused them is still actively abusing others, then there is no question: Leviticus 19:16 demands that we not stand idly by the blood of others. But what if the perpetrator is no longer abusing others, but his/her past victims need to tell their stories and maybe even confront their abusers in order to heal themselves?

The Jewish tradition makes significant, concrete demands on those who wrong others in order for them to warrant reconciliation and reinstatement in the community and in the eyes of God. Among those demands is that the perpetrator publicly acknowledge her/his wrongdoing and apologize for it to the victim, making whatever restitution is appropriate. This process requires that the misdeed become public. Moreover, anyone who causes bodily harm to another must, according to Exodus 21:19, provide medical care for the victim, and the same holds true for psychological injuries like pain and suffering.[39] Thus victims have a right to reveal the abuse as part of their healing, and perpetrators have the duty to listen if that will help to bring healing. Whatever defamation is involved is overridden by the victim's right to seek healing and the perpetrator's duty to provide it.

Shame.   The other Jewish value that sometimes stymies abused people from seeking help is the need to maintain the family's honor and to avoid causing it shame. Since disclosure of an abusive spouse or parent is an embarrassment to all concerned, some abused people feel that it would be better to continue suffering the abuse than to endure the shame of publicly identifying the abusing family member. Sometimes victims mistakenly feel that the abuse is at least partly their fault, which adds to the reticence to "come out of the closet" as a victim of abuse.

Moreover, the abused person's concern is rarely created in a vacuum; those near and dear all too often reinforce victims' impression that they should say nothing. The abuser her/himself, family members, friends, neighbors, or clergy can, by the shake of a head, the telling of a story, the click of a tongue, or a host of other cues, clearly send this message: "Sha! Telling is wrong and will only bring you and your family shame."

Personal and family honor are indeed important commodities. Our self-esteem is an important reservoir of physical and psychic energy to overcome the problems of life and to contribute positively to the world at large. The concern for honor, though, cannot be allowed to get in the way of preserving one's very life and health. Thus those who witness the abuse of others must forgo their concern not to embarrass them if that is necessary to save their life and health, and the same priority of values applies even more to people who must extricate themselves from threatening situations. It may be painful to "air your dirty laundry in public," but when your life or health is at stake, you must endure the dishonor in order to rescue yourself. Both children and adults caught in this painful situation can take heart in the fact that ultimately such bravery will not only restore whatever dignity they lost in the process, but actually increase their self-respect and honor as they escape the cycle of abuse and the mistaken self-blame in which so many are unfortunately enmeshed.

The Status of Parents
☙

Parents hold a special place in the Jewish scheme of things. The Torah demands that we honor and respect our parents, and this applies to mothers as well as fathers, daughters as well as sons. The rabbis understood "respect" to require that children not harm their parents and "honor" to insist that they actively provide for them:

> What is "honor" (*kavod*) and what is "respect" (*mora*)? Respect means that he [the son] must neither stand in his [the father's] place nor sit in his place, nor contradict his words, nor tip the scales against him [in an argument with others]. Honor means that he must give him food and drink, clothe and cover him, and lead him in and out.[40]

The Talmud, on the one hand, sets limits to these obligations, so that one may provide for one's parents out of their assets rather than from one's own.[41] On the other hand, stories in the Talmud recount instances in which specific people went to extraordinary lengths to honor and respect their parents, and these are taken as models for us all.[42] With this as a background, one can understand that the tradition, which prized honor and respect of parents so much, would in no way countenance parental abuse. Indeed, the Torah specifically prohibits striking one's father or mother, and it prescribes the death penalty for one who does so.[43]

These laws stand on their own, independent of any assessment of the quality of parenting that one's own parents provided. There are at least two rationales in Jewish sources to justify a duty to honor even bad parents. One is that the parents, along with God, are the three partners in the creation of children. Children owe their very existence to their parents, and for that reason alone parents have a call on the children's time, effort, honor, and respect. Moreover, the divine partnership in the creation of a person along with the parents means, for the Talmud, that "if people honor their father and mother, God says, 'I reckon it to them as if I dwelled among them and as if they honored Me.'"[44]

Not all parents are model human beings or paradigm parents; some are nasty or even abusive. According to some Jewish sources, one is required to love them nevertheless, either as a corollary of honoring them or as an instantiation of the command, "Love your neighbor as yourself,"[45] Maimonides, however, does not require love of parents:

> Know that the Torah has placed us under a heavy obligation in regard to the proselyte. We were commanded to honor and revere our parents, and to obey the prophets. Now it is possible for a person to honor and revere and obey those whom s/he does not love. But with the proselyte there is a command to love him/her with a great, heartfelt love . . . much as we are commanded to love God Himself.[46]

Moreover, one may certainly disagree with one's parents—although not in a way that they are publicly shamed, as the rabbinic definition of "respect" cited above specifies.

When parents not only fail to carry out their duties to their children but actually abuse them, thus violating Jewish law, a number of Ashkenazic sources (Rashi, Tosafot, Rabbenu Tam, R. Moses Isserles) assert that the Torah's commands to honor and respect them no longer apply. That would mean that formerly abused children need not muster attitudes of respect for their parents nor even provide for them in the way that Jewish law normally demands. Some also maintain that abused children, like abandoned children, need not fulfill the duties of mourning for their parents, for those rules are intended not only to help the bereaved, but also to honor the dead.

Sephardic sources, however, generally assert that the commands to honor and respect parents continue even in the face of abuse or other illegality. This is true for R. Alfas, Maimonides, and R. Karo.[47] Even Sephardic authorities would permit changes in the way in which one carries out this obligation in order to minimize friction and possible further abuse or retribution between parents and children. That is, the issue is not only *whether* one must provide for formerly abusive parents, but if so, *how*.

Specifically, children ideally should tend to their parents' needs themselves, for, as the Talmud notes, part of the honor of parents comes from their child's personal care for them: "'You are My children, and I am your Father.' . . . It is an

honor for children to dwell with their father, and it is an honor for the father to
dwell with his children. . . . Make, therefore, a house for the Father in which He
can dwell with his children."[48] When the relationship between parents and children makes that emotionally impossible, however, children may use the services
of others to fulfill their filial obligations.[49] That is true even when such negative
feelings are not the result of parental abuse. For that matter, even when the relationships between parents and children are good, people may choose to use
nursing homes and similar facilities when that proves to be best for all
concerned, although then they should visit their parents as often as possible,
by telephone if not in person, for the need we all have for family ties only
increases in old age. When parents have been abusive, though, children need
not care for them personally or even contact them.

Rabbis, communal workers, and members of an abused person's extended
family should not push the victim to abide by what is normally expected of
children vis-à-vis their parents, for that only exacerbates the situation.
Rabbinic rulings recognize that some of the specific ways in which children
demonstrate their honor and respect for their parents must vary with the
particular circumstances of the relationship. If a parent abused a child, rabbis
and others should not "put a stumbling block before the blind" in urging the
child to remain in close contact with an aged parent, for that may actually
tempt the child to get even with the parent now that the power relationship
is reversed and retribution is possible. Instead, formerly abused children
must be allowed to care for their parents from afar, if they are required to do
that at all.

One may not love one's parents, either for cause or just as a function of the
personalities involved. Furthermore, if the cause for such ill feeling is severe
enough, children may even be released from the commands to honor and
respect their parents altogether (Ashkenazic authorities) or at least from the
stringencies of these commands (Sephardic authorities). At no time, though, do
children have the right to assault their parents. Conversely, adults who suffered
abuse by their parents as children should not be made to feel that they owe their
parents the same kind of honor and respect that most adult children do.

Wholeness and Holiness
ᴠ

The Jewish tradition seeks to show us how to achieve lives of wholeness
and even holiness. Our ancestors harbored no delusion, however, that people
could always abide by Jewish norms. Hence three times each day we ask God

for forgiveness, and we devote an entire season of the year to that task. Certainly sexual abuse is a particularly egregious sin, one that not only wrongs another person, but undermines his or her sense of wholeness. The Jewish tradition bids us to avoid such behavior in the first place. When it occurs, however, we must take steps to protect ourselves from future abuse—and help others do so likewise. In those ways we can fix this troublesome part of the world as part of our effort to be "a nation of priests and a holy people" (Exodus 19:6).

"Honey, I'm Cold.
Put on a Sweater."

Family Dynamics and Incest

RACHEL LEV

Introduction

⟨ﾟ

Family is the place we first learn about relationships, about love, and what to expect from those who take care of us. Family is where we should be safest. If we aren't safe there, if this is the "best" we can expect, we wonder what the rest of the world will offer.

My father used to say he was the best father I'd ever have. I didn't understand the ironic truth of that until I was an adult. He was the best father I'd ever have. He was also the only father I'd ever have. I grew up believing that mine was a "normal" family and even "better" than most. What happened there was love. In many ways that was true. I was lucky. My parents loved me. We were bright and cultured and always had a nice roof over our heads. We never went to bed hungry. That was a lot, but it wasn't enough. It was their responsibility to keep me safe while teaching me to be interdependent and self-reliant. That is the job of every parent and the community in which they live. While the focus of this chapter is the family, the dynamics apply to communities as well.

The values and mores of the familial and community systems surrounding a child make sexual abuse and its discovery more or less likely. This is true whether the molestation is by relatives (incest) or by nonrelatives (sexual abuse). Each child's ability to take a stand for her/himself, to distinguish appropriate from inappropriate touch, and to ask for help begins in what is learned at "home."

In a healthy family parents recognize their role in their children's lives. In *The Prophet* Kahlil Gibran described how the relationship between parents and children should be.[1]

Your children are not your children.
They are the sons and daughters of Life's longing for itself.
They come through you but not from you,
And though they are with you yet they belong not to you.
You may give them your love but not your thoughts,
For they have their own thoughts,
You may house their bodies but not their souls,
For their souls dwell in the house of tomorrow, which you cannot
  visit, not even in your dreams.
You may strive to be like them, but seek not to make them like you.
For life goes not backward nor tarries with yesterday.
You are the bows from which your children as living arrows are
  sent forth.
The archer sees the mark upon the path of the infinite, and He
  bends you with His might that His arrows may go swift and far.
Let your bending in the archer's hand be for gladness;
For even as He loves the arrow that flies, so He loves also the bow
  that is stable.

To achieve what Gibran describes, parents must honor their children as separate and unique people, not as "theirs," not as property. Parents must know when to hold tight and when to let go. In my family we related more like the lyrics of "I Am the Walrus" by the Beatles: "I am he as you are he as you are me and we are all together. . . . I am the eggman, they are the eggmen. I am the walrus; goo goo g'joob." This chapter explores some of the dynamics that make molestation more likely to happen and to remain hidden.

Family Dynamics, Fuzzy Boundaries, and Incest
ॐ

Incest doesn't happen in a vacuum. It happens in a family where roles and relationships are confused. It happens when someone has been so deeply wounded and feels so impotent that he or she molests a child.

Incest is a violation of boundaries—at an emotional or physical level (or both). It can be overt or covert. It "isn't limited to specific acts of fondling and penetration. It occurs across a continuum from invasion of sexual privacy, to comments about your body, to being kissed in a way that feels uncomfortable, being touched in sexual areas, or being encouraged to have sex you didn't want. . . . Emotional boundary violations are characterized by family dynamics in which enmeshment, boundary ambiguity and identity diffusion are prominent features."[2]

Enmeshment? Boundary ambiguity? Identity diffusion? Isn't that how a family is supposed to be? That mergy, mushy feeling that can be wonderful sometimes—of feeling one with each other—of feeling like we, of course, understand—we're family, we're Jews. In "The Issue Is Power: Some Notes on Jewish Women and Therapy," Melanie Kaye/Kantrowitz writes:

> [W]hile you could say that Jews—like many other ethnics—have fuzzy boundaries, the issue of boundaries or their lack seems particularly acute for Jews. Boundaries between the self, the family, and community. Between the generations. Between history and the present. Between national identity and identification across national lines with the Jewish people. Perhaps this is why much of Jewish religion, in fact, involves drawing boundaries—between secular and sacred; between acceptable and non-acceptable food. The anguish of Israel and Palestine can be seen partly as a question of boundaries, geographical and metaphysical. Even one's body is barely one's own. A friend says, *you return from the toilet, and everyone wants to know: did you go?* The nosiness characteristic of Jewish culture relates both to responsibility and danger; if you constantly monitor information, you may be able to ward off disaster.
>
> Fuzzy boundaries between the self, family and community can be a sign of Jewish health.[3]

So, what's the problem? As the Cartwrights of *Bonanza* might have said, "The family that prays together stays together." Right? No. Fuzzy is one thing—boundary violation another. The tendency to view fuzzy boundaries as healthy may contribute to the difficulty in labeling boundary violations when they happen. Where is the line anyway?

Families as Systems
ᴖ

In my first year of graduate school, my direct services professor spent six months teaching systems theory. We studied and analyzed and studied again the case of one family in order to learn how to apply systems theory to working with individuals and families. We learned about the multiple systems that we are and that make up our lives. I, as system, am made up of heart, mind, body, and spirit. So is everybody. We are each an accumulation, an amalgam of everything that we are and everything that has happened to us.

We learned about homeostasis—the balance that all systems seek to maintain—even when what they're maintaining is hurtful. We learned about the impact of external systems on individuals and families from the quality of the air and water to racism and sexism. This professor handed me many keys to helping others and to understanding myself. The one I'll never forget is undifferentiated ego mass. You know, "Honey, I'm cold. Put on a sweater."

To understand undifferentiated ego mass, we have to understand more about how systems operate. Healthy systems have clearly defined yet permeable boundaries that allow for exchange—the import and export of the essentials of life. Each person is a separate system interacting with the other individual systems in their family. Each individual and family interacts with other individual and organizational systems in the community. We go to school or to work. The crossing guard helps us get safely across the street. We buy food at the grocery store. We deposit money and get cash at a bank. We interact and exchange in order to survive. The ability to exchange is healthy. The merging that occurs in an undifferentiated ego mass is not.

What Is an Undifferentiated Ego Mass?
∽

In an undifferentiated ego mass, people are not differentiated. Difference is absorbed, ignored, dismissed, criticized. "What do you mean you're not cold? It's freezing in here." "You must be hungry. I am." "You don't like chopped liver?" said with a tone and look that conveys you are *meshuggah* (Yiddish for "crazy"). At the core of an undifferentiated ego mass is fear. To be safe we must be more than like each other, we must be the same—indistinguishable. The more a family is like this, the harder it is for a child to speak up and to be heard. The more merged parents expect their family members to be, the less likely they are to see boundary violations as violations.

Another element needs to be discussed before going further in this exploration. As a child I had to find a way to behave that would help me survive and get the most favorable attention I could. Becoming the good girl, subsuming my own needs, even losing touch with them was what I did—through unconscious decision-making processes. As an adult, even though I had choices, I couldn't see them.

I had the same choices at age twenty-one that I do today. Without knowing it, I kept waiting for my parents to free me, to let me go, to tell me it was OK to grow up and away. Until I could see that it was my job to let go and move on, with or without their permission, and that I could, I was entangled in a messy, blaming, infantilized place. Also, because I couldn't express my rage and pain directly about the molestation, some of that spilled over onto situations that were less important. Even with all of that, I believe my family's enmeshed relationships made many things harder for me—as a child and an adult. Hopefully, the examples here will give a feel for the pain caused by enmeshment, boundary ambiguity, and identity diffusion. Some of my feelings and reactions can only be understood by combining the information on family dynamics in this chapter with the long-term effects of incest discussed in the next chapter.

Where individuals are not seen as distinguishable from each other, where systems do not have clear boundaries, where people form an undifferentiated ego mass you see or hear things like the following. Sarah asked ten-year-old Julie how her day was, and Julie's mother said . . . Or Dad put his hand on his chest and said, "When my children are unhappy, I get sick."

Examples of an Undifferentiated Ego Mass in My Family
❧

My father hated green. I was expected to hate green. We were to love what he loved and hate what he hated. He expected my mother, sister, and me as well as everyone else with whom he came in contact to think as he thought and do as he wished. At times he was playful about it, grinning and shaking his head with a little sparkle in his eye as he tilted his head back a bit, looking toward heaven, and spoke of how amazing it was that people weren't doing things his way. I saw this over and over again—at home, in the community, with extended family members, in work situations. Usually, he was not playful about it. He was dead serious. Not only did he expect people to agree with him, take his advice, and respect him, so did my mother, sister, and I. We were white blood cells joining together to fight off any nasty bacteria—that is, anyone who contradicted him. To disagree was to contradict and to contradict was to disrespect. Those were the rules—never stated—but demonstrated daily.

An undifferentiated ego mass is like a blob—like Brer Rabbit and the

Tar Baby. One being gets stuck to another and is forced to move as one. Undifferentiated ego masses don't let go. This is different from having a shared history and values. This is different from a healthy commonality in what people may like or dislike or believe. If my opinion is different from yours, you have to think, pay attention differently. In healthy relationships our differences can be a source of interest, an opportunity to learn and to grow. In healthy relationships our differences can be frustrating and annoying, but we learn to accommodate each other, to negotiate. In an undifferentiated ego mass, being different is a threat. People just want you to get back in line, or rather, in mush.

When feeling differentiated, I can say, My *body is not your body. No one else can know what I feel except me.* When under the influence of my family's undifferentiated ego mass, it is as if "they" know better than I do what I feel or need. As a child I became scared that if I differentiated I'd die. That belief has been hard to change. Transforming that belief has required seeing what happens and then deciding to do something differently.

When I say I'm hurt by something that has happened, my sister says, "That's your perception." NO, that's my experience. It doesn't have to be hers. Oftentimes if I persist in expressing feelings that differ from hers or my mother's, I'm labeled "sensitive" or "emotional." As I come more into my self, I learn to be less sensitive to these labels. It's my job to become less reactive. The wounded child part of me doesn't want to do that. She wants them to see what they're doing *and* to say they're sorry.

My sister and I traveled and lived in Europe after I had just graduated from college. I'd wanted to do as most of my friends were doing—travel alone or with friends through Europe. My parents would not allow that. They would let me go only if I went with my sister. I agreed to these terms.

We lived in Paris during the summer. I loved it. I worked as a secretary, took the Metro to work, made friends, and greatly enjoyed the freedom of being out in the world. I remember standing in the middle of the Tuileries one sunny, summer afternoon, arms outstretched as I thrilled to the awareness that no one knew exactly where I was.

She and I each had our own rooms in a charming house we shared with friendly people from all over Europe. One sweet and handsome man had a crush on me. If only I had been able to understand what he said.

My tiny but wonderful room was under the eaves of the house. Sweet lace curtains fluttered across the windows. An eight-inch contraption served as oven, stove, toaster, and broiler. I could bake six small chocolate chip cookies at a time. Friends from the United States popped in on a regular basis, sometimes sleeping on my floor. I made friends with people at work and dated a man named Henri who wrote of strewing the rooftops of the city with roses in honor of me.

The undifferentiated ego mass stretched across continents and oceans. Mail came from my parents. My mother wrote. "Your father misses you. When are you coming home?" My father wrote. "Your mother won't tell you this but she really misses you. When are you coming home?" One day another letter came. On the envelope was a note: "Come home already. Your father is depressed. I'm worried about him." It was from our mailman.

And so, on my birthday, I flew home. I was really sad as we boarded the plane in Paris. By the time we got to our street in the States, I was excited about surprising my parents, about making them happy. My mother sat at the kitchen table, on the phone. She looked up as I stood in the doorway. She looked stunned. She finished her conversation and sat there. No joy showed on her face, no excitement. I knew she was glad, but it was so "little." As she looked at me, I felt a terrible sinking inside. What a mistake I'd just made. I had been happy in Paris. I was twenty-two years old and didn't have a clue what I wanted to do with my life but knew, right then, coming home was wrong for me. I had thought this would make my mother happy, and when it didn't I felt bereft. I had given up so much—for nothing.

When I recently discussed this incident with a friend (Ann), she said she understood. Ann, too, had decided as a child that it was in her best interests to make her mother happy. It never worked. She would do things, certain her mother would be thrilled and she never was. Nothing Ann did was ever enough. She remembered how often her mother spoke toward the end of her life of being lonely and alone. At her mother's funeral Ann was surprised at how many of her mother's friends came and spoke of their years of friendship with her mother.

Holding on to an Illusion
✧

I don't think I ever felt there was anything I could do as a child that would assure my survival with my father. With my mother, that seemed different. Since I felt totally powerless in relationship to my father, I turned to believing that my life depended on making my mother happy. I thought I could make her happy. I could figure her out. I was wrong.

Since my earliest memory, at the age of three, my concern was for her well-being. I now understand that was connected to my notions of what I needed to do to survive—to physically and emotionally live each day. A major part of my survival was maintaining the image of each of my parents and the image of our family.

As a child I created a fantasyland in my head that may have had nothing to do with reality. Actually, I think it had to do with selected parts of reality that I wove into a picture I could pretend was the truth. Even the slightest jarring of that image was frightening.

To survive, I highlighted the good and ignored or minimized the bad and the ugly. I held onto snapshots of the "good." The glories of the theater on Broadway and dinner at Sardi's in New York. Barbra Streisand singing "People" all alone on a stage. Zero Mostel being outrageous in *A Funny Thing Happened on the Way to the Forum*. I had birthday parties at home with great cake. I don't remember those parties. I don't remember who was there or what we did, but I kept hold of the images captured on the 16 mm movies of parties and blended them with my parents' commentaries. I buried the pictures of the "presents" my father gave me in private.

I sold myself on the mythology of who we were. I was aided in this by my mother, father, and sister, our extended family, and neighbors. There is always some kernel of truth in myths. There were good things that happened in our house. My parents did love me. But how to juxtapose the four of us on a road trip, loudly singing "Let Me Call You Sweetheart," with being molested? How to enjoy and be grateful for the things that were fed rather than prohibited or destroyed by one or the other of my parents, like love of theater and music and creative expression? How to accept that my mother, who noticed everything around her, who was hypersensitive to sounds, didn't notice that I was being molested?

I created a picture of our family in which everything was fine. I was special. They were special. We were bright. All I wanted was to grow up and be like my dad. My dad adored me. Etc. etc. etc. And I lost my "Self." I stopped knowing what I felt.

I carried a variety of frozen images of my parents, individually or as a couple. In one they are going out for the evening—he in a black tuxedo, crisp white shirt, black bow tie, and cummerbund; she in an aquamarine satiny dress. They are holding each other as if they are dancing, smiling broadly, posing for the camera. My father loved to dance. I loved to dance with my feet balanced on his. I don't know if my mother did. Isn't that strange? I know so much about what my father loved and hated. So little about my mother's passions. That's kind of how it was. Her passions, likes, dislikes were overpowered, submerged to his, just like mine.

Learning to Differentiate
↶

In a differentiated, healthy family, children learn who they are, what they like and don't like, and how to make decisions. Much of what I believed were my likes and dislikes and the basis on which I made decisions were really a blind adherence to what my parents thought or a reactive rejection of their beliefs. I remember thinking about this while listening to Bessel van der Kolk talk about the impact of trauma on children's development. Traumatized children don't have the peace and safety and time to get to know themselves.[4] So, as an adult it often took heavy-duty somatic symptoms to get my own attention—to start to hear my inner voice.

I got accepted to law school and got my first migraine. I lay in the dark in sharp and nauseating pain. It was the first time I faced knowing that I didn't want to be a lawyer. More important was that I couldn't honor my father's wishes when they so went against my own. Something inside me said, "No more. Going so against yourself hurts. It's time you felt this." I know now this was about much more than picking a career.

My father wanted me to be a lawyer—or a teacher—or whatever he thought was best. When I decided to go to social work graduate school, he shook his head sadly and said I was making a mistake—that I'd break my heart. He was wrong. Being a social worker couldn't break my heart. He'd already done that.

When an individual is differentiated and you say something that differs from what s/he sees, hears, or feels, s/he may say, "*Gee, I don't feel that way, hear it that way, see it that way.*" Or, "*Hmmm. How come?*" Or, "*Gee that would be wonderful, terrible, interesting*" or even "*How did you come to that?*" or "*What makes you feel, think, see, hear things that way?*" or, with a grin on his/her face, "*You're weird 'cause you don't see it the way I do!*" We must be differentiated ourselves to see others as separate and unique with their own likes, dislikes, temperaments, and ways of viewing and experiencing the world. Without differentiation I am I and I am you and you are me and it's a mess. Without differentiation when I said I felt differently I was told I was wrong. That has led to a lifetime of apologizing for saying what I think, for having feelings that might differ from yours. How invalidating. How ridiculous.

I was on the phone with my friend Jerry, asking if I had offended him in a conversation the day before. "No. You didn't." Then he laughed. "What are you laughing about?" I asked. He replied, "You always do that—call the day after we're together to make sure you didn't say or do something wrong." I always did it but didn't know. It's really hard to write about this both because it's painful and because I am so accustomed to operating from an undifferentiated perspective that I struggle to identify how it operates. The bottom line is, when living in an undifferentiated ego mass, I often end up invalidated, feeling I was wrong when I was simply expressing myself, my needs, my experiences.

When Parents' Needs Are Primary in an Undifferentiated Ego Mass
ᴧ

In an undifferentiated ego mass, generational lines are blurred and roles are often reversed. I took care of my parents. They expected me to. Something else went on in our house. It wasn't just the mushiness of our boundaries that was a problem. It was also that I was too often an object on whom my parents projected their needs and desires. I was there to make *them* happy. I was there to mirror their wonderfulness.[5] So, add to the undifferentiated ego mass the fact that my parents' needs were primary—not mine—not my sister's. Sometimes it was my mother's needs that were primary, sometimes, often, my father's. Hating green because my father did, honoring my mother's fears and protecting her, were all part of the confusion of living in my house. It has to be part of why, as a child, I couldn't tell anyone about being molested—and why, when I did try to complain about my father to my mother, she couldn't hear.

It has taken years to see the cumulative impact of this pattern of diminishing my needs. It has taken years to find myself in the undifferentiated mess in which my parents' needs were primary, my father's being primary over my mother's.

When I was in my thirties, my mom mentioned she wanted to repaper the kitchen. I offered to go looking at samples with her. I enjoyed supporting my mother's creative expression, kind of goosing her along to figure out what she liked, and then encouraging her to do it. To see that it isn't a sin or dangerous to somehow do what you want. I think perhaps I should have spent more time doing it for myself. Perhaps I wanted to free her as a way of freeing myself, or out of a desire to have a partner in breaking out.

So we went to the wallpaper store. Mom found something she really liked, took a sample, and we left. Later on I got a call. I heard a cold, angry tone. She said, "Your father's mad at me and it's your fault. I showed him that wallpaper you liked." She wasn't joking. Hold on a minute. It was the wallpaper *she* liked. I was just along for the ride. Somehow this was about how mergy she was with him and how dangerous it was for her to differentiate from and thereby antagonize him. For me, it meant, help her be herself and differentiated from him and he gets mad and she gets mad and scared and blames me. What a mess!

I'm working on how scared I can still get when I hear a worried or angry tone in my mother's voice. It's not that there was any physical punishment for making her unhappy. It was more the absolute sense that I became useless to her—that she stopped loving me. The chill factor let's call it. It was terrifying to me—on some level it still is. To lose my mother's love was terrifying. Without her who was I? Nothing. Less than nothing. So I had to take care of her. I had to. She expected me to—still does.

Even today, when she asks, "How are you?" I feel what she seeks is reassurance that I'm OK. If I'm not feeling great and tell her, she gets worried. Then come the phone calls. A small voice asks, "How are you? I'm worried about you." Yes, she probably is. She has said she feels helpless when her children are sick.

In 2001, I'm able to experience that tone and message differently. She loves me. She worries. I don't have to do anything in particular in response to her. This is a new experience for me—the freedom to be myself and connect with her. This is what it feels like to feel differentiated.

It is hard to write about her part in the pain of my life. She never molested or abused me. Yet, she was unable to protect me or rescue me. That's pretty big. Today, she cannot comfort me. She can barely tolerate knowing I was molested. She gets angry when I need to pull away to work through the incest wounds. She gets angry and upset if I mention that's why I'm pulling away. She doesn't understand why we can't just enjoy each other's company. Sometimes I wonder that myself. She regularly "forgets" that the incest is a part of my life experience. Her forgetting is not because of her age. It's amazing what she is able to remember. I love her. I'm working as fast as I can to stop needing anything from her, to stop being reactive to her, to accept her as she is so that we can have more of a relationship before she dies. I'm learning how to balance things better. I can no longer act like I have no needs. I can no longer put her needs, which I understand so well, always ahead of mine. I can no longer feel guilty that my taking care of myself sometimes feels bad to her.

At times I'm still mad at my dad for the impact his abuse of me has had on my relationship with my mother. And, at times, I'm mad at her that she isn't different. I'd like there to be a clear and uplifting conclusion to this part of my story. There isn't. I hope she can handle and love my differentiated self. I do, and life is so much more wonderful this way.

Enmeshment, boundary ambiguity, and identity diffusion can happen in a family without it meaning someone is being molested. Whether molestation happens or not, when individuals in a family are undifferentiated, when children are primarily valued for their positive reflection onto their parents, something is very wrong. For me and other incest survivors, it is the cumulative effect of the primacy of our parents' needs plus the lack of healthy boundaries, including the molestation, that has been so destructive.

Maintaining the idealized image of my family and myself cost me much of my life. It required the development of elaborate coping mechanisms and defensive structures. Now, in my fifties, I work to discern who I am, what I feel, what I need and want, what is real, what is true. I struggle with a compulsion to overeat. I work to discover and trust my instincts, my "Self." I struggle to trust even the most trustworthy of people. I'm working to overcome my fears of love and intimacy. Normal, healthy drives for companionship, comfort, and intimacy seem fraught with land mines because as a child, they were. As my therapist said, the road map for relationships I received from my parents was missing some key arterial streets. So now I'm in the process of tearing down the fantasies, putting food into its proper perspective, learning to find an inner voice I can trust and to redefine love because much of what happened in my family was not the "love" I want in my life today. Confusingly, some of it still is.

From the Frying Pan into the Fire
On Being an Adult Survivor

RACHEL LEV
WITH HADIYAH C.,
LAURIE SUZANNE
REICHE, AND
B. B. ADAMS

The impact of being molested does not stop when the molestation stops. The impact varies from person to person and from day to day. Triggered by internal and external sights, sounds, smells, feelings, and events, many survivors travel, in no particular order, from hope to despair, to rage, to remembering, to shame, to mastery, to gratitude, to self-love and love of others, and back again. This chapter presents a profile of many survivors including some of the legacies of trauma.

Survivor Profile
᧒

Nothing on the outside distinguishes us from anyone else. You can't tell a survivor of childhood sexual abuse or incest—not by just looking. She looks like you and me, our mothers, daughters, sisters, nieces, grandmothers, friends, neighbors, and colleagues, and our fathers, sons, brothers, nephews, and grandfathers, too. She is successful at work or unemployed or underemployed. She lives in a lovely home or one that is ramshackle or she is homeless. She is in a committed relationship or not, married or not, with a wonderful family or not. She is heterosexual, bisexual, or homosexual.

She is bright and warm, kind and generous, a valued member of the community, and she wants to kill herself to stop the pain. She is cold and short-tempered, manipulative and controlling. She is a wonderful mother, a terrible mother, or fears never becoming a mother or being a terrible one. She plays myriad roles perfectly but lives on the periphery of a real life, real emotions, true connection.

She is Sephardic, Ashkenazi, Mizrahi, Iranian, Hispanic, Lubavitch,

Hasidic, Orthodox, Conservative, Reform, Reconstructionist, Jewish Renewal, and "just" Jewish. She grew up in the city, the suburbs, the country, everywhere and anywhere. She is any age, from twenty to nearly one hundred years old, as in the poem "Bubba Esther" by Ruth Whitman.[1]

Bubba Esther
by Ruth Whitman

She was still upset,
she wanted to tell me,
she kept remembering
his terrible hands:
      how she came, a young girl
      of seventeen, a freckled
      fair skinned Jew from Kovno
      to Hamburg with her uncle
      and stayed in an old house
      and waited while he bought
      the steamship tickets
      so they could sail to America
      and how he came into her room
      sat down on the bed, touched
      her waist, took her by the
      breast, said for a kiss
      she could have her ticket,
      her skirts were rumpled, her
      petticoat torn, his teeth were
      broken, his breath full of
      onions, she was ashamed
still ashamed, lying
eighty years later
in the hospital bed,
trying to tell me,
trembling, weeping with anger

Survivors often feel deficient and blame themselves for most everything. They have chronic health problems, somatize their feelings (experiencing illness, bodily aches and pains because they are unaware or unable to express emotions directly), suffer from depression, and often feel responsible for the world. They worry about what will happen to them. The next story by Hadiyah C. demonstrates how, so often alone with this terrible secret, isolated and mislabeled by health care practitioners, family members, and rabbis, survivors have to fight for their lives as best they can.

Declared Sane
by Hadiyah C.

Mealtimes were particularly trying for me. I held the fork, but the food wouldn't reach my mouth. I couldn't connect with putting food on my fork and getting it into my mouth. I was twenty-four years old and four months pregnant. The dining room was in Damasch, the Oregon state mental hospital.

Everything was always spinning so fast. I couldn't focus long enough to see how to operate in the everyday world. I had just risen from the table and was standing by my chair. I stared into space trying to muster enough energy to figure out what I was supposed to do next.

Two policewomen entered the large dining room. The room, filled with babbling patients and staff, became quiet, real quiet. The policewomen started walking in my direction. I didn't move. I knew. Instinctively, I knew they were coming for me. One policewoman reached for my hands. I didn't resist. I was handcuffed. Something snapped in me. I knew that I had to get sane. This was my last mental hospital, my last chance. If I didn't figure out what these people wanted, my life would be over.

I was in the back seat of an official state vehicle. The two policewomen sat up front. I was not told where I was going. As I stared into space, a voice in my head kept repeating, hang on you'll be all right. Hang on. We drove and drove. It felt like for hours. We didn't stop, not even once, although I had to go to the bathroom. I dared not ask. It was the longest trip I could ever remember, although in actuality I found out later, it was only a forty-five-minute trip. You'll be okay. I kept saying to myself . . . But, where was I going? Where was I?

Taken away. A long ride. It all feels familiar. I am being punished because I am a bad girl. I am going to be put away. Bad girl. Hold on, you'll be okay. My daddy is mad, real mad. Oh, my stomach.

We whizzed through the Oregon countryside, the blooming leaves were rich with the northwest rainfalls. The beauty was on the outside; inside I was in numbed terror. What was going to happen to me?

No place to go. Oh, my baby, my baby.
O

I was taken to the chamber of a small courtroom. There was a judge in a black robe, no jury. To my surprise, the large, redheaded nurse who chased me around the hospital floors was there as well. She was always trying to give me a shot to calm me down. I had read in Adele Davis that medication was not good for the baby. I refused to take the shot, and the nurse would chase me until the aides captured me as I screamed, "Don't, don't . . . the baby, the baby."

"Sit down, Miss Wold," I heard the judge say. Where is the bench? How do I sit down? Oh, this is awful. I want to pee. "Sit down," I hear again. The policewoman points her finger to the bench behind me, and I connect with sitting on the bench.

I was told that this was a sanity hearing to have me committed. If I was legally committed I would be sent back to New Jersey, to Greystone, the New Jersey state mental hospital. My father had made the arrangements. The baby would be taken away for adoption. I would be put in Greystone, the snakepit, for life.

> *Face in the room. All a blur. Standing alone. Face blank. Where am*
> *I? Standing in a room. People all around. Four years old. My daddy*
> *shaking me. Bad girl. My daddy's hand holding tight. Can't breathe.*
> *My daddy's hand—big dirty hand.*

"Miss Wold," I heard, "we are going to ask you some questions. Please answer truthfully. You know you are under oath."

> *What is the truth? My truth; my daddy's truth? I know. I know I*
> *must answer from another part of me. I must answer what they*
> *want to hear, not the truth, truth.*

"We see that you were involved in the civil rights movement. Tell us what you did and what is your involvement now."

> *Freedom rides, sit-ins. I tell them. But the other part of me answers.*
> *Grown-up answer. That's behind me. I intend to lead a quiet life. I*
> *will not participate again.*

Next question. "What do you intend to do with your baby?"

Oh, the baby's father and I are planning to get married. Did I really say that? And I have a part-time job waiting for me when I get out (true). The bottom line: the state did not want to pay.

The judge asked me to wait outside. I had to go to the bathroom. The policewoman took me to the bathroom. Handcuffed. She lifted my dress.

Daddy lifts my dress. Room spinning. Daddy's hands are cold. Daddy's hands smell of ham.

I peed. I didn't cry. I went back. Standing alone, all alone. The man in the black robe says I answered the questions quite well. He declared me "Sane: capable of returning to normal society." He wished me well and said I was free to leave.

Free? Free from what? My demons? My father? Would the memories ever get erased? Would I ever be free? My daddy was mad. I should be put away. Little girls don't tell. Shhhh, don't tell. I told. No one would listen. No one would hear. And there was nowhere to go except to my inner world that knew.

The redheaded nurse was told to give me a ride back to the hospital. I was unhandcuffed and put in the car. We were silent on the ride back to Damasch, a silent ride through the Oregon countryside.

Psychological and Physical Health Legacies
ᴧ

As much of this chapter will demonstrate, being molested is crazy-making. The inner dialogue described in Hadiyah's story is common among victims and survivors. We constantly debate within ourselves about what is real, what is "true." In *Man's Search for Meaning: An Introduction to Logotherapy*, psychiatrist and Holocaust survivor Viktor Frankl observed that an abnormal reaction to an abnormal situation is normal. Yet abuse survivors are often judged harshly by those from whom they seek help and by friends and family. As trauma expert Dr. Richard Kluft noted, "In situations where it's a parent's word against an adult daughter's, it may be easier to believe the adult who appears to be a normal, upstanding citizen, compared with a distraught woman in therapy. Perpetrators almost always look better than victims because *they* are the ones dishing it out, not the ones who are taking it."[2]

Dr. Judith Lewis Herman discusses the general lack of understanding of the impact of "prolonged terror" and the use of "coercive methods of control" on abused children and adults, prisoners of war, hostages, and concentration camp survivors in her book, *Trauma and Recovery*. One result of this lack of understanding is that those who have been held captive are often judged harshly. As we listen to survivor stories, many of us like to think we would have acted differently. We would have outsmarted our captors. We would have fought harder. We would have kept our self-pride. We would have escaped. And so, we judge those who didn't. We further believe that nothing could make us do something we didn't want to do. And so we judge others who do. We judge others because we don't understand the impact of being held captive and out of our fear that in such circumstances, this could happen to us. To quiet our fears, we do as much as we can to distance ourselves from "them," including saying that what happened was somehow their fault.

For example, hostage Patricia Hearst was found guilty for crimes committed while under duress and received a longer prison sentence than her captors. Heiress to the Hearst fortune, she was kidnapped in 1974 by a radical terrorist group and brainwashed, including spending days of her fifty-seven-day captivity blindfolded in a closet with loud music blaring at her twenty-four hours a day. She served almost two years of a seven-year term, then was released with help from President Jimmy Carter. She was not pardoned for another twenty years.[3]

Prisoners of war who break under torture may be labeled as traitors. Abused women who don't get away are censured. Those who were molested are assumed to be irreparably flawed. After World War II a question was raised about "why Jews were so passive. Why didn't they do more?" As if hostages, prisoners of war, abused women and children, or victims of the Holocaust had a choice.[4]

This blaming extends into the mental health world, where therapists often speak pejoratively of "borderline personality disorder" patients. Yet, when understood within the context of complex post-traumatic stress disorder, a diagnostic category suggested by Dr. Judith Lewis Herman and others, the actions and reactions of the borderline patient make perfect sense. When trauma is prolonged and repeated, the symptom picture is more complex than when it is an "event."

Speaking at a conference on adult sexual abuse survivors, Dr. John Briere pointed out that in an attempt to manage the unmanageable,

survivors display significantly more insomnia, sexual dysfunction, dissociation, anger, suicidality, self-mutilation, drug addiction, and alcoholism than other patients.[5] Research by Dr. Briere and others finds that
"fifty–sixty percent of psychiatric inpatients and 40–60% of outpatients
report childhood histories of physical or sexual abuse or both.[6] In one
study of psychiatric emergency room patients, 70% had abuse histories."[7] Yet, recovery and healing are stymied by health care systems,
medical and mental health practitioners, rabbis, and educators who are
insensitive and/or ignorant to the prevalence of childhood trauma and
its often long-term physical and psychological effects.[8] Psychiatrist
Judith Lewis Herman reminds us, "The bad old days, when patients were
told that they secretly longed for incest, are not far behind us. Most
therapists, even if they now believe their patients' reports of childhood
abuse, still shy away from exploring the history."

When medical and mental health practitioners understand the potential physical and psychological implications of a history of childhood
trauma, they make their own jobs easier and the possibility of helping
those who come to them much greater. In decades of medical care, only
three times has any practitioner asked me about a history of trauma—a
medical doctor who practices only acupuncture and Chinese medicine,
another who is a homeopath, and a third who is a gynecologist. None of
my therapists did.

The Legacies of Terror, Hypervigilance, and a Hardwired Brain
❧

As children, survivors lived in a world where danger could come at any
time and any place. Survival required being hypervigilant—ever watchful.

Lilith Goldberg, author and incest survivor molested by her father, a
Holocaust survivor, describes how the hypervigilance and terror of childhood affect her as an adult.

> I often have flashbacks of specific childhood moments. When I'm
> having sex, I remember scenes from early rapes; I have many night-
> mares; as I simply go about life, reading, shopping, eating, I frequently
> have momentary auditory or visual memories. I cringe at the sight of
> uniforms, at the sound of police sirens. To this day I am always early
> for meetings, wanting to check things out, make sure that I will not be
> in danger once a large group of people gather.

I check obsessively behind the doors and in the cupboards in my apartment, expecting some evil person to jump at me out of the dark. My hands at my sides are generally shaped into fists, perhaps to protect, perhaps to continually drain off a bit of the intense fury I feel at perpetrators of abuse. I physically sense the barbed wire limits of my childhood. Trapped also by the unseen ghosts of an earlier generation, I actually inhabit, at times, the painful past that rightfully is my parents', not mine.[9]

Lilith's hypervigilance and terror demonstrate what researchers describe as a hardwiring of the trauma survivor's brain. Trauma biologically resets something.[10] Dennis Charney, a Yale psychiatrist and director of clinical neuroscience at the National Center for Post-Traumatic Stress Disorders, found that even one experience of overwhelming terror permanently alters the chemistry of the brain.[11] Since the work of American psychiatrist Abram Kardiner during the early 1940s[12] we have known that what we now call PTSD (post-traumatic stress disorder) is a disorder that affects both the soma and the psyche. "Noting that sufferers from PTSD continue to live in the emotional atmosphere of the traumatic event, he [Kardiner] ascribed to them an enduring vigilance for and sensitivity to environmental threat,"[13] wrote Dr. Bessel van der Kolk.

Dr. van der Kolk underscores the fact that "the essence of the trauma experience is that it leaves people in a state of 'unspeakable terror.'"[14] Until the last few years I had nightmares at least weekly since childhood. I can now sleep through the night and rarely have nightmares. I have been suicidal, still struggle with a compulsion to overeat, and I get angry though now it is in context and I have vehicles for expressing it. When I least expect it, a common word, or the way someone smells, can trigger shivers, fear, or a flash of a memory. If someone asks, "What's wrong?" I can't always tell them because I don't always know.

Once traumatized, normal ways of thinking about something, of categorizing information don't work. When overwhelmed in this way, we cannot accommodate or assimilate the experience. The traumatic experience can then only be organized, as van der Kolk describes, "as horrific images, visceral sensations, or as fight/flight/freeze reactions. . . . Children are particularly vulnerable to physiological disorganization in the face of stress."[15] When, as adults, we "remember" these terrifying events through images, sensations, or reactions, our memories often show themselves in our feelings and actions.[16]

Shelley, psychiatrist and incest survivor, demonstrates some of the impact of the hardwiring from her childhood trauma on her as an adult:

> I get up in the morning in terror about what particular clothes to wear. I hypothesized I was raped because I was wearing the wrong clothes. We had gone to my room to change clothes, therefore I always have to be careful that I'm wearing exactly the right clothes. If I have the slightest sense that I don't have the right clothes, I'll change clothes four and five times a day. I used to carry a change of clothes in the car. I'm always in terror, and that's just one small piece of my struggle to be comfortable in the world.

Changing the hardwiring isn't always possible. Even when it is, it takes a lot of work. Shelley reports, "After starting recovery I would boast, *I can go to Starbucks and actually feel safe and enjoy myself and it's not terrifying.* So, after a couple of years in recovery and very hard work, that's my milestone, that I can go to Starbucks and feel safe doing that."

The Legacy of Disconnection
~

The writings and research of Dr. Judith Lewis Herman, Dr. Bessel van der Kolk, and Dr. John Briere helped me understand my experience and that of other incest survivors. I learned that a child whose molestation is prolonged, repeated, and severe is likely to suffer comparably to those suffering traumas such as combat, rape, kidnapping, spouse abuse, natural disasters, accidents, concentration camp experiences, and other forms of child abuse. Drs. Herman and van der Kolk helped formulate the concept of complex post-traumatic stress disorder for people impacted by these traumas.[17] Members of any of these groups are often judged harshly by society— as passive, compliant, cooperative. Why didn't they fight back? Speak out? It is as if by surviving, you are guilty.[18] In addition to implicitly, if not explicitly, being blamed for what was done to them, Dr. Herman writes about how trauma survivors suffer "not only from a wide range of psychiatric symptoms but from a profound sense of damage to their sense of self and their capacity for relationships with others."[19] She writes, "Traumatized people feel utterly abandoned, utterly alone, cast out of the human and divine systems of care and protection that sustain life. Thereafter, a sense of alienation, of disconnection, pervades every relationship, from the most intimate familial bonds to the most abstract affiliations of community and religion."[20]

I certainly felt that when I wrote in my journal, December 13, 1995, at 5:00 P.M.

Watch Out

I just want to be safe with somebody and don't believe that can ever be. My life, my future, in terms of healing this gaping wound feels bleak and empty and ragged and sharp and painful—and hazardous. Someone could get hurt if I even try and that someone is likely to be me.

Ragged edges of pain. That's all I see ahead. Sharp, ragged edges touched with blood. Brilliant red, delicately, yet boldly, displays itself along the edges and that's where I live—along the delicate bold, brilliant, jagged edge. People see it and are drawn to me until they get close, too close and then they see the danger and then stop or flee from me—a siren on a jagged edge—a danger to all who come near.

I'm sorry. I don't mean to be hurtful or dangerous. I want to be a gentle creature, a kind soul, a gift. But his abuse left me believing I am evil and deeply flawed, empty and frightened. So I beseech you to be careful before you touch my jagged edges—before you reach out to hold me because if you take me on your lap I may cut you off at the knees before either one of us knows what has happened and then we will both be sorry.

So, what is the answer? Is there one? Or, is it, as always, for me to leave—to stop burdening you and me. To stop hoping that it will ever be different. Just leave—not with a bang or a clang or an apology but with silence and sorrow wrapped up in a package that is me. A package that stays silent till it decays with age. A package left unopened—to save the world and myself from destruction.

I am so sad I can't see or feel or breathe.

It's still hard for me to read this journal entry. Such despair. I fought feeling it for so very, very long. I was disconnected from myself. I couldn't trust my own instincts and feelings because after years of pretending that everything was all right and I was "fine," I no longer knew what was true. It took me many years to realize my code word for how I really felt was to answer the question "How are you?" by saying, "I'm tired." "Tired" was a cover. It let me keep the secret while appearing to be part of the world. What was done to me impacted my understanding of love, of connection, of what to expect. Molestation is never an act of love. What was love then? Was I capable of it? Was it safe?

Psychiatrist and survivor Shelley described incest's twisted legacy when she said that "love and terror, trust and betrayal, nurturing and manipulation were intertwined." One of the greatest losses for survivors is the loss of heart—the loss of believing in ourselves and positive possibilities. We could believe in our dreams only as long as we ignored what was done to us. If we lived in the clouds, all things were possible. Living on the ground, with the rest of the world, only despair was possible. As adults, we have to learn how to keep faith and heart while walking on the earth. It isn't easy.

Psychologist *Avrum* discussed the disconnection he sees in Orthodox women clients who were sexually abused.

> These women, who feel they were violated in front of God, have an overlay of guilt and shame that is multiplied tenfold. They are filled with distrust. They fear telling their secret. Disconnection becomes the answer. Each disconnects from herself, her family, her friends and her community.
>
> They are unable to experience things that those who have not been abused can. What do I mean? A sense of safety with joy, with sexual intimacy, spiritual safety. They often feel so marred by the experience that repentance doesn't happen enough for full understanding. They feel beyond the pale of forgiveness and cannot forgive themselves for what was done to them. When asked, "Do you believe there is forgiveness for this in spiritual life?" they will say "Yes." When it comes down to it they are shackled and shamed and closed. Dead.

Regardless of religious affiliation, incest survivors often keep silent for years—some, forever. This legacy of silence isolates us. We feel like outsiders, strangers, alone, even in a group. We long to tell someone of our pain, to be believed and comforted. At the same time, we fear that once people know our secret, we will be blamed, shamed, disbelieved, challenged, ostracized, or abandoned. This fear is often legitimate.

For a long time I didn't tell many people about being molested because sometimes when I did, they pulled away. I had a friend, who after hearing a tiny bit of my story, went home. That night, as he tucked his daughters into bed, he was overwhelmed with horror and nausea as he associated what had happened to me with his cherished children. This is hard to know. It's also hard to tell, knowing it will cause the listener pain. I still have to tell some of the time. When I can't talk about being incested, I conclude that there's something wrong with me, something to be ashamed of.

For years, as I worked with families where divorce had occurred, I taught that children were resilient. It was the theme of the times,[21] but I also needed to believe it. I needed to believe that kids can bounce back—that I could bounce back.

My beliefs today are more complicated. Kids who are molested can be resilient depending upon what happened to them, how old they were when the molestation began, how long it went on, how severe it was, and what else was going on in their lives before, during, and after the molestation. What was their view of themselves and their molester before the molestation? Did they feel safe and loved somewhere? Survivors who had a grandmother or teacher with whom they were safe and loved fared much better than those who had no place to go but to the chaos of fear called home. I am so very grateful for my teachers and for the healthy, vibrant, and nurturing aspects of my childhood family life. I am also glad to have been able to provide a place of safety and love for the high school students I counseled early in my career.

The Legacies of Remembering, Forgetting, and State-Dependent Learning
⟋

Most survivors have always remembered what happened to them. Judith Herman writes that many "can remember detailed images, feelings, sounds, smells and tastes as clearly as though the abuse were happening in the moment. In other ways, survivors' memories are often confusing and vague."[22] Kate sees recurring images of frogs on a pool in Texas. As a child her family would visit her grandparents in a place like that. When she sees this image, she feels nauseous and scared, then sees parts of her grandmother's body coming toward her. She then feels disgusted, repulsed, and even more afraid.

Dr. Herman continues:

> Important parts of the story may be missing, and survivors may have difficulty putting the pieces together to form a complete narrative with an accurate time sequence. Furthermore, although traumatic childhood memories are deeply engraved, they are not stored or retrieved in the same way as ordinary memories. Many survivors have a period of amnesia during which they have no recollection of having been abused. In a careful follow-up study of two hundred women with documented childhood histories of sexual abuse, one in three did not remember the abuse twenty years later.[23]

Some of these eventually remember.

State-dependent learning explains one component of memory. It refers to the ways our brains link together what we literally see, hear, feel, and smell at a given time. This is true whether or not we are trauma survivors. Our bodies hold memories. Simply stated, it means that if we study for an exam while drinking a lot of caffeine, our ability to remember best what we studied will require a similar "caffeine" state. State-dependent learning explains why realtors put cinnamon or vanilla on the lightbulbs in a house they want to sell. For most people, vanilla and cinnamon are scents that "trigger" pleasurable associations and memories.

Memories of child sexual abuse and incest often connect a state of terror with body arousal. That is why many survivors talk about flashbacks being triggered when they are having sex as adults. This sensory remembering is different from recalling something that happened. How? The narrative story of what happened when these sensory connections were established is generally missing. We can't tell ourselves what happened. We just feel things or see flashes of fragmented images. Trauma survivors often contend with sensations and feelings that don't seem to make sense "today" but that make a lot of sense when understood as associational pathways laid down during the molestations.

While state-dependent learning describes some of how we remember, traumatic amnesia explains how some forget. This type of "forgetting" is well documented in Holocaust survivors, combat veterans, and incest survivors. In *Hidden Children: Forgotten Survivors of the Holocaust*, child survivor Ervin Staub says:

> Over the years I have been trying to re-experience those feelings, but they kept eluding me. I was cut off from most of my memories, and from reliving the anxiety of that time. I remember nothing about the time I spent with those people. . . . Not a face, not a voice, not a piece of furniture. As if the time I spent there had been a time out of my life. . . . What is missing? Why can't I conjure up those memories? I am staring into the darkness with occasional flashes of light allowing me to unearth bits and pieces of life.[24]

Holocaust survivor Ava Landy describes her amnesia:

> So much of my childhood between the ages of 4 and 9 is blank. . . . It's almost as if my life was smashed into little pieces. . . . The trouble is, when I try to remember, I come up with so little. This ability to forget was probably my way of surviving emotionally as a child. Even now,

whenever anything unpleasant happens to me, I have a mental garbage can in which I can put all the bad stuff and forget it. . . . I'm still afraid of being hungry. I asked my sister and she said that we were hungry. So, I must have been! I just don't remember.[25]

Some incest survivors do not remember what happened until something triggers their awareness and/or makes them feel strong enough to "know." For some, they are confronted with the pain of their childhood after being in a secure, loving relationship for some years.

Many don't start to feel strong or free enough to deal with their traumatic histories until their thirties or forties or until something in their life stirs the abuse issues. For example, it is often when survivors end an addiction, recover from an eating disorder, marry, become pregnant, go someplace that reminds them of their experiences, have a child who reaches the age they were when the abuse was going on, and/or when their perpetrator(s) or a parent they're protecting dies. For many it is when we've felt strong, safe, and independent enough that we can allow ourselves to fall into the despair of remembering and honoring our truths and to *tell*. Laurie Suzanne Reiche's poem expresses the shock, the confusion, and the terror of remembering.

The Gag
by Laurie Suzanne Reiche

1.
There is silence now, silence.
I hear nothing in my still sleep.
Children doze in this deep hour their breath
making bubbles of luxury that float through our small house
like friendly ghosts drifting from one safe room
to another, nothing breaking those perfect
mother-of-pearl planets
that brush happily past my closed
and quivering eyes.

2.
There is silence now, silence.
I thought I could hear nothing in this stillness called sleep
but a fat demon has pressed some button

at the top of my spine making me bolt abruptly
off my pillow smacking directly
into the black wall of night.

3.
This all happens in a matter of seconds, in silence, as all death does.
I cannot breathe and am choking.
I am a child with a mouth full of something thick and vile.
I am a child though a pair of thirty-seven year old hands
are clenching my throat as the rest of the house
hums in calm sleep.
I am clenching my throat to halt the choking.
My mouth opens in a paroxysm of panic.
I heave and a heavy ghost,
fat and slimy, spews from my mouth.
I gag one more time
am stunned
and then breathe.

4.
There is silence now, silence.
I am a woman sitting upright in bed.
I look around my room hoping no one saw,
knowing there was nothing really to see except this woman sitting upright
in bed.
I watch the gentle globes of my children's dreams
fill the morning with light and lay back down
eyes wide open in disbelief.

5.
There is silence now, silence.
I hear nothing on the surface of this deep hour
but I feel the earth rolling over my bones
and I remember, I remember, I remember the eruption
in my throat and the crushing weight
of dad's bones laying down on my face as he kills me;
and now, thirty-some years later
I am shocked at this moment

and the gag
a relief
like a newborn's frantic first breath.

The following story, "Cherries in the Russian Tea Room" by B. B. Adams, demonstrates ways associational pathways in our minds link seemingly unrelated experiences to each other and trigger a "remembering." Her memories of dinner at the Russian Tea Room as an adult trigger memories of another time she was there. Her story, like so many survivors, demonstrates what researchers talk about as state-dependent learning.[26]

"Working backwards to discover the origins of a suicidal depression led me to seemingly digressive moments and memories," B. B. Adams explains. "Why did I like maraschino cherries? What could be more artificial than a sour cherry soaked in almond-flavored alcohol and sugar and colored unnaturally bright red like no actual cherry? Why is 'cherry' a symbol of a virgin? These questions led me to write the story."

Cherries in the Russian Tea Room
by B. B. Adams

The smell of fumes isn't too bad. The station wagon engine started right up, as always. Paul picked it out, our first middle-class car, a Toyota Camry. A big step up from the tiny Pinto (the one with the gas tank that would explode on impact). Until the kids left, we'd always had big Ford wagons, nine-passenger behemoths filled to the gills with kids, dogs, candy wrappers, sticky spots from spilled sodas, stale potato chips, blankets and pillows for drive-in movies and camping trips. This sleek Camry is always clean.

The pills take the edge off the nausea.

Oh, Paul, where are you?

Remember when we went to the Russian Tea Room? Our twenty-fifth anniversary. How proud you were of our family! All the kids came. Those shining samovars in pea-green niches, the waiters in red silk cossacks belted with black cords. They looked like the dress I wore when Daddy painted my portrait—it was robin's egg blue, trimmed with Russian embroidery. I found the portrait a year ago. It was covered with dirt, so I had it cleaned. It hangs in the living room, the face of a solemn six-year-old none of my friends recognizes.

This engine purrs so reliably. You'd get so mad, Paul, when the old Fords wouldn't start on cold winter mornings. Do you remember that one bitter morning when you threw a cement block at the car? It cracked the window on the passenger side where I was sitting, holding the baby. You'd been out of work since Christmas—they always lay off construction workers just before the holidays. Unemployment insurance got us through the winter, along with meals at my mother's. You and she never got along. The night we celebrated finishing our M.A.'s, Mom refused to babysit. We found a stupid neighbor girl and Peter broke his arm running after Jeannie, and the babysitter was too dumb to realize it. I called Mom to come and stay with the girls while we took him to the hospital, but she wouldn't come. It's too late, she said. We put pillows and blankets in back of the Ford wagon and drove Peter to the emergency room, with Jeannie and Anita curled up in the back.

Daddy—what more can I tell you about him that you don't already know, Paul? You know how hard I tried to get him to see his grandchildren. You insisted we take them, uninvited, to his summer cottage. Rachel wouldn't even let the kids swim in their new swimming pool. Daddy made us drinks and gave the kids Coke, pretending nothing was wrong. Every year, Rachel sent us an expensive Christmas present. Mom always mocked them, "Don't they know how poor you are? What can you do with a glass paperweight? You need a washing machine and a dishwasher." Mom always reminded me I should hate Daddy. You protected me Paul, except when you got drunk and said, "Why don't you go home to your rich Jewish Daddy?"

The first time I went to the Russian Tea Room it was with Daddy and my best friend Betty Jo. It was my twelfth birthday. Betty Jo gushed about the samovars and the red-coated waiters and fancy food. She didn't know what chicken Kiev was, or borscht, or blinis. She was so jealous of me—said my daddy was the handsomest man she ever saw. Once, we took Betty Jo to Fire Island when Daddy rented a house for Mommy and me. I wore my first bikini. A blond boy who said he was fifteen took me up into the sand dunes and laid on top of me, rubbing against me. I was wearing lipstick and a kerchief wrapped around my head, like grown-up women. The summer before, when Daddy came to stay with us, I sat on his lap and he let me sip his Manhattan. He always gave me the cherry. Afterwards, he tucked me into bed and lay down beside me, stroking my back.

Daddy taught me to paint like him, holding my left hand and guiding the paintbrush. In nursery school, the teacher tried to make me use my right hand to draw, but Daddy yelled at her when I told him. He framed my first oil painting—yellow forsythias in a blue vase—and hung it in his den.

The garage looks funny, as if the walls were bending inward. Maybe it's the gas fumes. Now that Paul's car is gone, the garage is always half empty. I gave Jeannie his little red Tercel. I kept the snowblower, though it's too heavy for me to handle. I kept the self-propelled lawn mower Paul loved, and the three-speed bike I bought but never rode. Anita may want it to ride in the park. She lives in a Russian neighborhood in Brooklyn. Her Russian neighbors would never go to the Russian Tea Room. It's for rich Americans and looks too much like a leftover from Czarist Russia, they told Anita. I'll give the snowblower to the Carters, my nice neighbors. He's an engineer and she's a nurse. They have two sweet kids. They wouldn't understand if I told them about the Russian Tea Room.

Daddy has no taste for food at all. He'd eat cornflakes and cookies, if he could, all the time. Mom used to cook roast lamb, roast pork, roast turkey, and roast beef. He liked to eat in restaurants, though, to schmooze while he drinks Manhattans. He says he likes Chinese food the best, and Russian second.

The "Emperor" Piano Concerto! Beethoven's best and last one. This car radio has excellent speakers, better than the stereo in the living room upstairs. Are you doing this to me on purpose, God? You know it's my favorite. It's number 6 on WQXR's New Year's countdown of audience favorites. Just five more selections to go—I wonder what's number one? I may be asleep by then. . . . I wish I could stop crying. How long is this going to take? The pills should have knocked me out by now. Paul's favorite was Beethoven's Sixth Symphony, the "Pastorale." He said it was "our song." We listened to it in college when we made love for the first time. I bought the 78 rpm disc of Rudolph Serkin playing the "Emperor" when I was twelve. Daddy gave me an allowance every week, and I saved until I had enough to buy an album. Daddy bought me the Shostakovich Piano and Trumpet Concerto. It was strange, but I loved it. That's when I knew I wanted to be a concert pianist. When he left Mom and me, he rented a good piano for me to practice on in that smelly, furnished apartment. There was no sunlight from the grimy, second-floor windows shadowed by the big, expensive apartment buildings across the street. Mommy wouldn't give me his address or phone. Daddy never came to see me. Once a month, he took me to a restaurant and movie. I miss him so much! I remember . . . cherries.

Is that the phone ringing? Who could be calling me at this time of night? The gas tank is down a half. I wonder if there's enough left. It's so cozy with the heater on. Mom used to say she wanted to be a truck driver and drive all across the country and never come home. I've traveled farther than she ever dreamed of. I love to drive, especially at night, alone, on a dark country road.

The air inside the garage looks blue and furry, like the fake smoke they use in

Broadway plays. I made fake smoke with my chemistry set. Daddy gave me the biggest one they made when I was nine, with a picture of a boy on the yellow metal case. I got 100 percent on the chemistry regents. Daddy taught me grammar. Daddy talked French to me at supper. Mommy stared angrily, like she hated it when Daddy talked French to me. She couldn't understand a word.

I had shashlik for our twenty-fifth anniversary at the Russian Tea Room. Blinchiki for dessert. I remember! I had them before. Every Friday, Daddy took Mommy and me to a different restaurant in Manhattan—Chinese, Hungarian, Italian, French, seafood, Russian! We waited for him in his office, while he finished drawing an ad for Coty perfume. How ya doing, Squirt? Daddy said, pulling one of my pigtails. Rachel worked down the hall, painting flowers. I watched the skaters forty floors down in Rockefeller Center.

Mommy wasn't with us when Daddy and Betty Jo and I went to the Russian Tea Room. When I had shashlik and blinchiki the first time. Daddy had a Manhattan and gave me the cherry. Afterwards, Betty Jo went home on the bus. Daddy and I went to a strange apartment, not the one Mommy and I lived in.

This ball of tissues. They've piled up big as a basketball on the passenger seat. If the box of tissues runs out, I'll have to go into the house and get another. Or stop crying.

There goes the damned phone again. Must be a wrong number.

Shashlik! That's what I had with Daddy! My favorite Russian dish. Lamb marinated in lemon juice and grilled on a skewer. They bring it in flames to your table. Mommy wasn't there that night.

I was wearing the new white coat Daddy bought me. Betty Jo was so jealous of it. It had real silver buttons and red and gold embroidered trim on the neck and pockets. Daddy took me shopping when Mommy told him I needed a new winter coat, I'd outgrown the old one. Let your father pick one out—you're *his* child too, she said. Daddy took me to a shop on Fifth Avenue, not Klein's or Macy's. The fluffy white coat was hanging between ordinary dark-colored ones—navy, brown, gray. The minute I saw it, I fell in love. The saleslady smiled and helped me put it on, and I twirled in the three-sided mirror. She said it was just made for a grown-up little girl like me. She smiled at Daddy. How much, he asked. He scowled, and I held my breath. He wrote the check.

Daddy put me in a taxi with the big coat box. When I got home to the smelly furnished apartment, Mommy got real mad. I hugged the white fur closer. What a waste of money. You'll get it filthy in no time. He spoils you. I kept the coat spotless.

I'm getting a little sleepy. I've had insomnia ever since I was a little girl. I woke up every night, choking, unable to breathe. I thought I was suffocating. I was eight. Or six. It must be a nightmare, Mommy said. But something was pressing me down. . . .

Every week I met Daddy and Rachel at his favorite bar. I didn't know where he lived. Rachel sat beside him on a bar stool, wearing a tight black dress, her long black hair in a greasy ponytail, her eyes black as marbles. She smiled and patted my head as if I were a little kid. I knew she only pretended to like me. Daddy drank three Manhattans and gave me the cherries. Then Rachel said, I'll see you tomorrow, Jack, and kissed me on the cheek, leaving a red streak of greasy lipstick. Daddy would hand me his clean white handkerchief to wipe it off. As soon as she was gone, he'd say, Well, what'll it be, Squirt? Chinese, lobster, French? He knew my favorites, and taking my arm, led me to whatever restaurant I wanted. You're my date, he'd say. He would help me in the cab, help me take off my coat and put it on, holding the armholes just so, so I could slip my arms in. He said I had lips like roses and cheeks like cherries, *Vous êtes très jolie, Mademoiselle*. I was Daddy's little Colleen. I got Mommy's green eyes and auburn hair. He said I was prettier than Mom. My face felt hot. I was glad.

My stomach feels queasy. I hope I don't throw up. I wish the phone would shut up! If I weren't so tired, I'd go inside and take it off the hook.

Then what happened? Betty Jo got on the bus. The taxi to the strange apartment. Dark. A studio couch. Maraschino cherries. Daddy let me eat the bottle of cherries in his small fridge—there wasn't any food in it, just whiskey and cherries. I ate so many cherries and drank the almond-flavored juice. I got sick to my stomach. Daddy took me into the bathroom, took off my vomit-streaked clothes, and put me in the shower. He took off his clothes and got in with me and rubbed soap all over me. Then he rubbed me dry with a fluffy towel, wrapped me in it, and carried me to the opened studio couch. The sheets were cold, then warm. It was my twelfth birthday. Daddy said this was an important day for a girl. I never wanted to eat cherries again.

Daddy put me in a cab. It was very late. He handed me a twenty-dollar bill and told me how much to tip the driver. Daddy raised his hand and waved good-bye. I felt weak in the knees, remembering his lips, his hands. My little Colleen, he said. I wasn't Jewish enough. Fair game.

The gas tank is down to a quarter. I'm so sleepy, finally. I haven't slept for two months. The pills Dr. R gave me stopped working after a week. I found the Valium after Paul died. He left a shelf-full of medicines. I threw out all the rest, and counted out ninety-seven Valiums left from the one hundred prescribed for him.

Paul, I've been calling you and calling you. You were always there when I needed you. You came to me after you died—as I was waiting for the light to change, sitting in the Camry you'd picked out. The sun was setting over our hill. It was ten degrees, the orange slice of sun warming me through the windshield. It's been such a cold, cold winter without you. And then, there you were! I saw you, in the sun, its rays streaking behind you. You were looking straight at me, your beloved uncle Allen beside you. You were smiling, looking happier than you had for years. I was so glad to see you! You heard me, read my thoughts! You and Allen had been fishing, the creeks full of fresh trout, holding your poles as you paused in the sunset. You came back to me! For an instant. And then the light changed. I need you so much, Paul. You took care of me for a long time, even though you wanted to go back to New Hampshire. I'm sorry I needed you so much. I was selfish—I wouldn't let you go.

I wanted to tell you before you drifted away forever that Daddy is nearly dead too. He's in a nursing home in Nebraska. Imagine Daddy anywhere but in Manhattan—he's worse than Woody Allen. Poetic justice, I guess, exiled from New York. He has no memory, doesn't know who or where he is. Julia, my half-sister, takes good care of him. She has power of attorney. Rachel is in the same nursing home, in the psychiatric ward. She tried to kill another resident who she thought was stealing her food.

You were the only one who knew how Daddy invaded my dreams, waking me every night. They took hours to dissipate. I could never tell anyone else. I wonder about Julia, my half-sister—she and I have become friends, of sorts. She's an oncologist, and you remember I consulted her when you became ill. I was desperate to save your life, or I never would have contacted her, or found out that Daddy had lost his memory. Her professional advice came too late. We've kept in touch since then, talking on the phone, and meeting for dinner when she's in New York for a conference. My father never told her anything about me, as if I did not exist any more.

I asked Julia if Daddy had ever taken her to the Russian Tea Room when she was growing up. Never—too expensive, he said. Daddy always complained about not having enough money. Once a year, the token expensive gift came: the glass paperweight. I'm sorry I threw it at you, Paul. You made me so mad when you started giving up on life! But you never really hurt me, like Daddy. You gave me love, children, a life.

I knew I couldn't go on living without you. The stroke came suddenly, like an executioner's blade, to finish you off after the cancer had eaten your lungs. I held your good left hand and tried to tell you how much I loved you. I was sorry for ever being mean to you. I was so glad when you opened your good right eye and saw me clearly. You squeezed my hand hard, three times, with your strong left hand. You couldn't speak, but I knew you forgave me. For the cut wrists and bottle of pills—you saved me that time. Because of the dreams of Daddy I couldn't get rid of. You knew it wasn't my fault.

Julia says Daddy has no memory of either of his families any more. The story of Daddy and me is left unfinished—like a mystery book, with the last chapter torn out. I'll never know how it ends. Daddy forgot me. He erased me from his mind a long time ago.

I can taste the fresh brook trout you caught and cooked for me, Paul. It washed away the sickening taste of maraschino cherries. You've come back, Paul! You're opening the garage door . . . I knew you wouldn't leave me alone . . . no matter what I've done. . . .

A Mother's Story

MASHA GLADYS

The trauma of being molested as children affects those who love us, too.

A Mother's Story
by Masha Gladys

I couldn't believe what she was telling me. Jenny had picked me up at the airport after my trip to Israel. I was exhausted from the long flight, the struggle to get through customs, and jet lag from the ten-hour time difference. She made herself comfortable on my bed, as she watched me unpack. Abruptly she sat up.

"I have to tell you something that I have been dealing with while you were gone." Her face was grim. "Mom, you have to know that daddy forced me to have sex with him from the time I was a little girl. He forced me to orally copulate him as long as I can remember. I didn't tell anyone, but I've been having terrible flashbacks and memories for the last few years. They began while he was ill, that summer before he died. That's why I had such a hard time coming over to be with you then.

"I really thought I was going crazy. Then Ruthie told me that she was having the same memories but she didn't tell anyone because she thought that maybe they were bad dreams not memories. She was sure no one would believe her. We never talked about it, but we both had the same memories. I have finally gone to a therapist, and I don't know if I can ever come into this house again. Just being here has brought back all the memories and feelings that I had when I was little. I can't stay here."

I was stunned beyond belief. The first words I was able to say came without thinking; they just came out unbidden. "That explains everything," I said.

"Explains what?"

"Your brother's catatonic breakdown after his bar mitzvah, and your sister Ruthie's eating problems. And that time when I went to my brother's wedding in Colorado when you were sixteen. Do you remember how you called me hysterically to come home and not leave you here alone with him when he was drunk?"

"I don't know what you're talking about," she shouted. "I just told you the worst thing that could happen to anybody and your first response is to think about Isaac and Ruthie. No wonder I'm so f——ed up. You never pay attention to what is happening to me. I'm not sure that I can see or talk to you until I get this sorted out. I know that I'm not coming here again." She stormed out, and I just sat on the edge of the bed, dazed and breathless. It was some time before the tears began.

I couldn't sleep. My mind was sorting through everything that happened over the years. Where were the clues? How could this have happened without my seeing anything? I know the experts said that if a child was sexually abused by her father, that her mother was at fault, and that the mother may have colluded with the perpetrator. In order for the abuse to happen, if there was not outright collusion between the parents, then there were clear and obvious signs that were ignored by the mother; somehow she enabled the behavior. What did I miss? How did I miss it?

Despite Joe's drinking he always seemed to be a kind, loving father. It is true that he was not supportive of me, dismissed my volunteer work as meaningless, concealed the truth about our finances, and even belittled me in front of our friends. But he doted on the kids. Jenny was his best beloved child and Isaac the fair-haired son. He was proud of Ruthie, even though he didn't express it.

I first realized that he had a drinking problem after the children were born. Until then we never had enough money to buy wine or liquor except for rare parties. But once his career took off, he began to drink more and more. He had a cocktail before dinner: an on-the-rocks glass of gin, sixteen ounces and an ice cube. He had a highball after dinner: sixteen ounces of scotch and three ice cubes. Then he went to bed early. Passed out and snoring. But he was never angry, didn't raise his voice, never hit me. If he was mad he would simply stop talking to me. I think our first fight lasted three months, only I never knew we were fighting. In my family, anger was expressed violently. You shouted, you screamed, you hit, and then you threw things. That is how to be angry. I knew what that was. I didn't understand silence.

When we moved into the new house, we threw a big open house to celebrate his new job. Some celebration. He passed out on the bathroom floor a few hours before the company arrived, and never moved until the next morning. I entertained one hundred strangers, making excuses for his absence. And as soon as the last guest left, I packed the three children into my car and drove to my folks.

"I can't stay there any longer. He's a drunk. I have to get out of this marriage. Now!"

"What are you talking about? It can't be that bad. Look at who he is. First of all Jews don't drink. So if he is drunk you are obviously doing something to make it happen. He's a good man. After all, he married you, didn't he? He's earning a good living. You have a nice home. You can't stay here. Go home and get a good rest and you'll feel better."

That was not the kind of support I expected from my parents. I had hoped for a welcome that would allow me to leave and make a life for the kids and me. But without their help, there was no way I could do it. I had no job skills, no savings, and knew no one who had been able to make it on her own. In 1958 women didn't walk away from their marriages easily. I was reminded of my own worthlessness and insignificance, and my good fortune that this handsome, successful man would deign to be in a relationship with me.

I returned home and went to my rabbi. "Dear Abby" and her sister, Ann Landers, always told you to talk to your rabbi. Like my parents, he assured me that whatever was happening at home was clearly caused by my behavior and if I could find out what I was doing wrong and change it, then everything would be fine again. So I went to a psychologist. Joe agreed to go with me to make me happy. After listening to the story, the psychologist reiterated my parents and the rabbi, reminding me that since Jews didn't drink, I had to be the cause of Joe's drinking. And besides he understood that all Joe drank was a cocktail before dinner and a highball after, certainly not excessive. If I would stop exaggerating that would help.

Feeling helpless, I went to therapy weekly. Guilt piled upon guilt. But nothing changed. He drank more; I felt alone, and recognized that with no financial help I was trapped in the marriage. So I did the best I could. Despite Joe's drinking, I tried to build a life for the children and me that would give us a sense of happiness and accomplishment. I thought I had succeeded. The children were active in the synagogue youth group, in scouts, in clubs at school. They played sports. They got good grades. On weekends when Joe passed out early, we used to play games together, do puzzles, and just hang out sharing our lives. They would talk openly about many topics, and there was a wonderful sense of intimacy and closeness. Where were the clues? What did I miss?

I remembered when Jenny was little and starting to toilet train. Sometimes I would hear her whimper in the night and find her curled up on the bathroom floor. I thought she had come in to use the toilet and fallen asleep. I'd pick her up and put her back to bed. Once I even found her asleep in the bathtub and wondered about it. But she didn't remember why she was there. Since I had been a sleepwalker as a child, I just assumed she had walked in her sleep. It is true that sometimes she called for me at night, but Joe was up, having a drink or a cigarette, and I didn't see why we both needed to be up. I was exhausted from caring for the house and the kids and the car pools and happy that he could share in some of the responsibility of fathering. His favorite time with them was in the evening when I was doing the dishes. He would take the small children in for their baths. He would sing to them, and I could hear the happy sounds in the kitchen and smile at their being together. Despite his drinking he was being a good dad, and I felt like I was doing the right thing in making this marriage work.

It is true that I was not the good mother I wanted to be. I tried, but I was always tired and out of sorts. I felt abandoned by my parents, angry with my husband, torn apart by the demands of my children, my home, my synagogue, and community. I was trying to be all things to all people. I maintained my own family's model of dining, that is everyone sitting down to eat dinner together. But mealtime was uncertain. It depended on when Joe would get home and have his first cocktail. My mother had taught me not to spoil my appetite by snacking before dinner, and I taught my children the same rule. So by the late afternoon they were noisy and rambunctious and I was out of control. I wanted to hold my temper, but the anger won out, and I would scream at them to stop. I would warn them to calm down. Sometimes I would hit them or shake them, or worse, I would throw things at them. I felt remorse afterwards and promised myself that I would never do it again, but the next day there would be a repeat of the battle.

Isaac had suffered silently. Enormous tensions built up between him and his father. He was angry about the drinking and shamed before his friends. When Joe quit drinking just before Isaac's bar mitzvah, we were all elated at the prospect of a normal life. But the elation was quickly muted when Isaac became ill with Legionnaires' disease, which necessitated a long hospitalization. Shortly after he came home, he fell into a deep depression and would not eat, nor stay awake for more than brief periods of time. Sadly we put him into a psychiatric hospital. Joe refused to visit or participate in treatment. But Isaac was resilient and did what he could to get better. It was clear that Joe was deeply troubled by the illness. And once Isaac returned home and resumed his normal life and school activities, his illness was not discussed directly.

However, Joe and I started therapy with a new psychiatrist. The doctor loved Joe. It was clear that he did not respect me. Again I was reminded that Jewish men don't drink, and whatever caused Joe's problems earlier was the result of my actions. The problems within the family caused by the drinking, the blackouts, and the tensions were not part of our therapeutic discussion. Joe was apparently perfect just the way he was. Only I had to change. Again.

The children grew up, went away to school, and started their own lives. Ruthie came home to live after graduating from college, while she explored her future. Isaac was finishing high school, and she was looking for a job. The two of them were always bickering. She was clearly feeling down on herself about each job rejection, her weight problems, and her lack of a social life. I encouraged her to go into therapy. She found a well-known psychiatrist and began weekly sessions with him.

One evening after a session, Ruthie asked me if I could remember some traumatic event in her childhood. Her doctor believed that she suffered from the results of some mysterious event that she was struggling to recall. Nothing that I could think of would fill that description, although I knew that it had to be some terrible thing I did to her as a mother. I remembered how she refused to take either the breast or a bottle when she was very small, only wanting a cup. I thought that was strange. At the time I felt certain I must be doing something awful to cause that response. I remembered when she was three years old and tried to run away from home with her doll buggy filled with clothes and food. By now I had accepted that everything that happened was my fault. I was willing to take the responsibility, but I couldn't figure out what it was I had done.

While Ruthie was struggling with her memories, Joe said that he had enough of an adult daughter living at home and wanted her to leave immediately. He decided to stop payments for her psychotherapy, telling her that she should just go to work and pay for her own therapy. I was able to negotiate a few weeks leeway before she had to move, and to taper off payments for her therapy without cutting it off abruptly. A short time later she found a job, an apartment, and before too long stopped therapy. The mysterious trauma remained undiscovered.

All of these memories poured back into my mind after Jenny left that night. I played and replayed them, looking for any clues that would have said "Incest." But there were none. I recalled the close personal conversations the children and I had together at late night talk fests, but there were no hints of anything other than the issues around his drinking. I had left the marriage early, sought help, turned to all the appropriate people, but the only message I was ever given was that I had to change. Joe was good; Joe was successful; there was nothing wrong with Joe. This message was repeated wherever I went for help. Jewish men don't drink was what I was told. I was exaggerating. I was lying. It was all my fault.

My fury when I heard Jenny's story knew no bounds. Anger at Joe for the terrible things he had done to my children. Anger at my parents for not believing me when I asked for help. Anger at the rabbis, doctors, psychiatrists, therapists, and social workers whom I had reached out to. And shame. I felt enormous shame in having been so wrapped up in my own problems that I couldn't be the mother whose children could trust her to share their deepest secrets; shame that when they needed my full attention and support, I wasn't able to give it to them. And I was overwhelmed with enormous sorrow for what had been done to three small children that would color their lives forever. They had a mother who was a witch and a father who was a monster.

It has taken many years of therapy, working together, developing a sense of honesty with each other and trust before we could make changes. Isaac has not yet had the kinds of flashbacks that his sisters have, and decided that he wasn't ready to go into therapy to look for the secrets. He has made a choice to wait. It was a struggle for him as a young man to make peace with his dying father, and he is not ready yet to go into the dark places. Ruthie is still sorting out memories, dreams, flashbacks, and sensory images. Our relationship is fragile as we begin to reach out to each other. She and Jenny sometimes talk about their memories and have spent several sessions together in therapy, confirming for each other that their memories are real, and that they aren't crazy. Since they live on opposite coasts, they don't have many opportunities to be together. But this distance, and the fact that they each work with their memories in therapy before sharing them with each other, confirms the truth of their experience.

And true to her word, Jenny didn't come home for many years. There was a long silence between us. She struggled to make sense of what had happened to her before she and I met along with our therapists to confront the truth. I learned the details of how her father, my husband, threatened her with bodily harm if she ever told me anything about what was happening; and how he tried to prevent her from dating during her teens or seeing other men as she became a woman. While it was painful for me to hear the description of the horrors that had been perpetrated on her, it was also cleansing. She would describe an event, and then I could tell the story from my point of view, and she could respond with her feelings about it. The fact that I had gone for help was something that none of them had known. Although I was not able to protect them, they were relieved to know that at least I had tried, and that allowed our healing to begin.

I had to learn new behaviors. I learned how to listen to their stories without being defensive, without responding with excuses, without denying their truth. It was hard to sit silently and not say, "But you didn't know what was happening to me then." It didn't matter what was happening to me. It mattered what happened to them. I had to listen to the small, frightened child, speaking through this adult, and know when it was the child and when it was the adult to whom I responded. I had to say, over and over, "I'm sorry. I'm so sorry."

Years earlier, once I accepted that Joe had a drinking problem, I found my way to Alanon (a program for families of alcoholics), and there I found the support that I had never received anywhere in the Jewish community. At an Episcopal church I found meaning in Judaism that would sustain me through this ordeal. In working the program of Alanon, I was forced to seek my Higher Power (even though my rabbi had assured me that Jews don't believe in a Higher Power), to take responsibility for what I had done in my life, to admit to those whom I had wronged what I had done and try to make amends. For several years after Jenny told me her story, I would spend time reflecting on their childhood, particularly during the month of Elul which precedes Rosh Hashonah. During Elul Jews prepare for the Days of Awe by examining their actions through the year and asking forgiveness from those whom they have wronged. It is a time when I would write a letter to each of the children admitting my errors, attempting to atone for both what I had done and what I failed to do. While I couldn't take back their pain, I could at least acknowledge the reality of it. During the High Holy Days the practice of introspection and atonement were a further opportunity for me to do *teshuvah*, to make amends to my children. I had to examine my role in their lives without blaming others for my actions; I had to face my own shame in not knowing what was happening or doing something to make their lives better. This was a hard step for me to take, but the rewards have been in a renewed relationship.

I'm not sure that this story has a happy ending. I have become closer to Jenny and Isaac; I am renewing my relationship with Ruthie. We are now able to come together in joy at family celebrations, and share our sorrow at deaths. Jenny and Isaac come home for a seder or birthday or other special event, but Jenny still can't spend a night in my home. They are all working hard to find their truths and heal them. As each of the girls searches her life, she uncovers a new memory, works to heal it, and is ready to move on; but just when she thinks she has finished, another memory arises and the process begins again. Their pain goes on. We all share a deep sense of betrayal. I have been able to find solace in a Jewish spirituality that was denied me by my rabbis, but my children do not yet have such spiritual solace in their lives. We are conscious that we must tell the truth, hear the truth, and be honest with each other. This can be hard, and is often painful. But we are moving forward, moving away from the horrors and into the light. There is no ending, but a constant beginning.

PART TWO

Hope for the Future:
The Healing Journey
For Individuals
and Communities

SEVEN

From Terror to Triumph

RACHEL LEV
WITH "LEGACY
OF THE FORGOTTEN"
BY BRIANA ROSE

In this book, we've spoken about our pain, but there is more to us than pain. This chapter attests to our triumphs, our healing, and some of who and what helped us along the way.

Legacy of the Forgotten
by Briana Rose

The Burial:
Earth swallows ancestral bones without a sound.
Unbowed, unadorned, unidentified.
Soil seeps into ears,
settles between vertebrae, fingers and toes,
Soft flesh and silenced souls
slip
away.
Below ground . . . peace
above . . . survivors'
chaos begins.

The Haunting:
Pop Pop from Poland
came to New York
tailored, gambled
but never spoke
of the family left
behind.
Beat raging grief

into the body
of his young son
daily for fifteen years.

Such a successful son!
So handsome! So smart!
Drank J & B Scotch
with a beautiful wife
Drove a baby blue Caddy
and became Daddy
to a blue-eyed baby girl.

One night, his seething soul
reached for the child.
Buried his body in her warm flesh
for the momentary breath held bliss
that drew cruel boyhood
into the void
of oblivion.

The Healing:
Such a successful daughter!
So lovely! So smart!
Addicted, lonely
terrified.
Until she began
to remember
to re-member herself
as she puts together
scattered pieces
blown apart
by pleasure/pain,
don't feel/don't tell
his vampire eyes
as he filled the legacy
of death
with her life.

She will not run or hide, numb or blame.
She will lie on Earth's belly for comfort.
Her own flesh and bones are water, soil, tears.
For her father, her grandfather,
her forgotten family,
she will remember . . .
she will grieve . . .
and she will heal for us all.

Rachel Lev

Adulthood has been really hard. All the therapies and therapists, all the physical illnesses and medical care. All the despair. All the lost time. All the journaling and creative expression of my pain. I was often angry about how hard it was to heal. At some point a shift started to happen, and the incest was "then" and there was a "now." That was "then" and this is "now." I went from living in a fog, looking to the world like a grown-up and even acting like one to feeling grown up, feeling competent, accepting and beginning to embrace my responsibility for building my life. I began to see that I had choices. I could not have gotten there without first being able to own, honor, accept what had happened to me—the good, the bad, *and* the ugly.

Nothing could ever give me what I didn't get as a child, but I learned I could build something wonderful anyway. I was molested. That's over. A lot of good things happened, too. Now, how to put things in context so I can be all I am? Not to forget what happened, but to incorporate it as a part of the tapestry I am.

My healing had to include remembering and embracing all the wounded parts of myself. It had to include seeing my father for all of who he was—his controlling, abusive side and his affectionate, passionate, loving side. Healing had to include pointing a finger and saying, "Dad, what you did was terribly, terribly wrong" even after he was dead. Healing had to include seeing my mother's faults and frailties and getting mad at her, too. Glossing over any aspect of the pain and fear I'd experienced wasn't going to allow me to heal. I know, I tried it.

So often when someone is hurting we say, "It's over. Let bygones be bygones. Live and let live. Put it in the past where it belongs. Forgive and

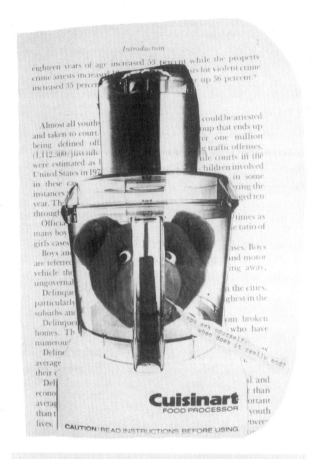

You ask yourself, "When does it really end?"
From Collage Book by Shauna Green

forget." Flashbacks and intrusive thoughts just won't let that happen, not unless you really want to go crazy.

Even when people are sympathetic, a lot of them reach a limit where they convey, "Hey, I know you went through something horrible, *but*. . . ." I now know this reaction is not personal. That person couldn't hear anymore. It didn't mean I had to completely silence myself. I wish I'd figured that one out sooner. So triumph means feeling through things anyway and getting lots of support from safe people. In my case that meant I saw a therapist a lot, still do. I feel grateful to have had people who could hold me and my pain safely, who saw my strength and wholeness before I could.

A Healing Coincidence: 199___

✧

One day, in a Twelve Step meeting, a woman stood up and announced that there was going to be a writing group and anyone interested should call or just show up for the first session. I don't remember the details exactly. All I know is I showed up—nine of us did and began a miraculous, loving, healing encounter for most of us for over two years. We started our journey using the book *The 12 Steps—A Way Out.*[1]

In this group I experienced the healing of hearing others disclose, the healing of disclosing, of speaking out in spite of the fear. I experienced the wondrous healing that came from *telling*. For the first time in my life, *all* of me was present—not just with a therapist. I will never forget the feeling of one woman's hand tightly gripping mine, telling me without words that she was not going to let go, as I trembled, fighting to let the words come out, to make sound. In those moments many things fell into place. I looked around and knew that I was no longer alone with my nightmares. I saw the tears, the compassion, and sorrow for me and the pain I'd suffered in the faces of everyone there. I have goose bumps even now, so many years later, as I remember that moment. Over time I heard their anger at my father for what he'd done—and saw that they did not see me as damaged but as courageous and wonderful. They loved my humor, my creativity, my kindness, and my wisdom. They loved me. How healing. How wonderful. What a triumph! I had other individual friends who knew my story. This group thing was somehow different. I continue to be grateful for this experience, this group I found through coincidence. Someone once said coincidence is God's way of remaining anonymous.

Other Triumphs and Terror: October 1999

✧

Triumph continues to mean taking risks that people in the "now" will not recreate the horrors of my childhood and that even if they do, I am an adult and can handle things I could not have handled as a child. It is beginning to mean, love. The old code for survival was avoid risks, don't feel, don't see. The new code of living says, take risks, have hope, reach out, stay present to yourself and the world around you and b-r-e-a-t-h-e.

Triumph means that sometimes I feel really safe in the world. Sometimes I feel incredible joy and gratitude. Today I felt delight at seeing a really fat bunny rabbit scurry into the woods. I felt awe and excitement when I saw a bald eagle from only fifty feet away. I felt sensual pleasure swinging on a wooden two-seater, leaning back, feeling the luscious air, and gazing at the deep blue sky through the needles of the pine tree overhead. Triumph means that my body is more and more a pleasure center than an alarm station. That is triumph!

Triumph means being more and more "me" with less and less apology. It means being able to say "yes" and "no." It means dropping the need to be perfect and accepting my own frailties and bad habits. When I make a mistake it means saying "oops" or "I'm sorry" rather than fearing the worst. And sometimes triumph means being terrified or depressed or outraged, and then asking God and my other helpers for a hand. Triumph is doing those things because I'm learning that I'm worth the effort and it's my job to take good care of myself.

Triumph means I often remember the huge array of tools I have available to me and use them more and more often—writing, praying, meditating, singing, stretching, walking, calling someone. Triumph ultimately means seeing more "light" everywhere.

As I find my voice and put myself together I go from triumph to *meshuggah*[2] to wisdom and gentleness to triumph again. I start to feel really good. And then—BAM—I get scared again. I believe the research that has indicated that trauma impacts the hardwiring of the brain.[3] I have often wanted to call Dr. Bessel van der Kolk or one of the other people involved in brain chemistry and hardwiring research and say, "Can you study my brain and tell me what's going on in there?"

In the middle of an otherwise fine day, I can feel compelled to slash my forearms. I now know it isn't a desire to kill myself, but that there is some pain that needs to come out. Hopefully I'll take the time to do whatever it takes to let it out or to comfort and encourage myself. Sometimes the compulsion is an ancient fear that has been triggered.

Hardwire Effect or Intuitive Sense of Real Danger?
◇

Triggers—sometimes identifiable and sometimes not—take me back to a physiological experience of being terrified. I suddenly imagine, in graphic detail, some man I don't know, doing terrible things to me. I'm not convinced that's just the hardwiring of my trauma. Some of that is the fact of being a woman in a world where a woman is victimized every six minutes—where a woman is most likely to be hurt or killed by those who "love" her, and where television, video games, and movies sensationalize these gruesome acts. So, some of my fears, while they may go beyond other women's, are understandable.

As I'm traveling, I meet other women who, like me, love nature, being out of doors, and hiking. They talk about being afraid to be out in the middle of nowhere by themselves. This is a fear I don't hear from the men I meet. I wonder if the men just aren't saying anything. Then I remember a self-defense instructor who described going into a law school class and asking the men, "What do you do each day to keep yourself safe?" There was silence in the room. When she asked the women in the class, they created a long list of things they do daily to try to keep themselves safe. All the women had something to contribute to the list.

So, I deal with the realities of sexism and violence against women, still affected at times, though less and less, by what was done to me as a child. It is not possible to separate one from the other.

I am tired of having bad dreams, being afraid of shadows, being triggered by sounds that make me hyper alert, make my heart race as I become conscious of all the sounds around me—and then, have to reassure myself, calm myself, remind myself that the door is locked and the windows closed and that I'm OK.

As I was walking in the woods the other day, I got really scared. I heard a bunch of kids laughing and was startled by the sudden noise in the quiet woods. I thought, "Oh. It's just teenagers," and was reassured. But then I remembered nightmarish stories about terrible things teenagers had done, and I got scared again. As I was walking I started imagining those terrible things and thought about cutting my walk short. I had to go through a number of processes to figure out whether this was my intuition telling me that there was, in fact, danger that I needed to honor, or that this was old fear coming up. To find out I needed to assess whether there was in fact danger. If there was no danger, I'd have to work to let go of the fear and worry. So, I checked and my intuition said, "Nope, no danger. You're fine." So now I have to calm myself. One of the things someone taught me is to connect to the light within me, moving through me, surrounding and protecting me. Instead of counting, which I have so often done over the decades, I replace it with something else repetitive that calms, affirms, and heals me. As I walk I speak in an internal cadence, "I am safe. I am an adult. I am all right." It replaces the counting and carries me beyond numbing trance, into an affirming sense of well-being.

This sequence happens in lightning speed. I am taking much longer to describe it than the speed with which it happens. It happens in seconds—the trigger, the fear, anxiety, the analysis, and decision making. It's emotionally and physically exhausting.

One of the things that came to mind on this walk was a self-defense class I took.[4] What a powerful experience it was. I believe it worked to replace the state-dependent learning of childhood molestation—to be silent, frozen, passive when in danger, with being able to act. While walking, I remembered things I can do. I can shout *No. Go away.* If someone doesn't honor those, I drop to the ground in a particular posture where I have all the strength of my body available to me, and if the person gets too close, I kick. Reminding myself that I have things I can do makes me feel better.

I didn't have that when I was a kid. As a child I didn't have the cognitive skills, physical strength, or the real-life options I now have. No kid should need to have such a repertoire of things to remind themselves that they can take care of themselves. That isn't what childhood should be about.

So triumph isn't perfect and it isn't seamless. I have not had the experience of those who can live at a level of naïveté that allows them to have a lot more energy available just for living. It allows them to have a far different attitude and hopefulness about almost anything. But this is living for me, and this is a thousand, gazillion, million times better than it has ever been. There were periods when my life was totally absorbed in healing these tragic things that happened to me and the consequences they left. It's not what my life is about now, at least not all the time.

I have the energy and ability to think about my relationships with people—attending to their needs from a very different place. I am able to laugh and play with friends of all ages which I've always had—but there is a difference—more and more I am p-r-e-s-e-n-t. And that's *much* better.

Some of what helps is my growing commitment to daily practices that keep me in touch with God, myself, and what is *not* wrong. I meditate, pray, practice acceptance and gratitude. I write frequently in a journal. I notice the natural world, and no matter where I am, I look for what beauty there is for me to see—right then. I also have a network of people who support me. I laugh, every opportunity I get—even when, or especially when, *nothing* is funny. I attend classes that expand my consciousness and support groups that connect me with people on similar paths.

Bad times happen. Right now I've got spasmed muscles in my neck and TMJ. I'm at odds with my mother and feeling horrible about it. As I finish writing this book, I feel overwhelmed with diametrically opposing feelings. These concerns are very different from being blindsided by pain, of feeling like dying and not knowing why, but both are helped by using whatever tools I can. A major one is: *accept.*

Accept.

It's a word I used to hate. It meant resignation, giving up, tolerating the intolerable. It's a word I've heard a lot in Twelve Step programs, and it's there that I began to understand what acceptance can mean.

"And acceptance is the answer to all my problems today. When I am disturbed, it is because I find some person, place, thing, or situation—some fact of my life—unacceptable to me, and I can find no serenity until I accept that person, place, thing, or situation as being exactly the way it is supposed to be at this moment."[5]

It is unacceptable that I was molested. It is reprehensible. Yet, it happened. I must "accept" that it happened and that there are consequences that impact me all the time—or almost. I must "accept" my feelings as they arise so that I can choose to deal with them rather than expend all my energy trying to make the facts be something other than they are. When I feel terrified, I feel terrified and I need comfort and protection, not an argument from myself. It has been really, really hard for me to "accept" this acceptance stuff. When I do, more often than not, I find greater peace, or at least some relief.

When I feel really scared, I find holding a pillow or a stuffed animal comforting. Sometimes I feel ashamed needing that. My job is to "accept" all of that and keep on moving. To accept is to surrender. As Sylvia Boorstein wrote, in her book *Funny, You Don't Look Buddhist: On Being a Faithful Jew and a Passionate Buddhist,* "Surrender means wisely accommodating ourselves to what is beyond our control."[6]

Accepting is one tool. Being grateful is another. The thought sometimes still makes me grit my teeth. Why should I be grateful? Wasn't I horribly victimized? Yes, I was. What I've found is when I realize there are things I am grateful for, I feel better. So being grateful is selfish—so why not? Part of my healing is separating my feelings out—being differentiated. I can be angry about one thing and grateful about something else.

Some nights, before I go to sleep, I review the day, noticing what I enjoyed or appreciated. Lately, that has included things that have pleasantly surprised me. Like one of my doctor's spontaneously commenting on how sweet I am, or my friend's three children running out to hug me when I came for a visit. Sometimes I have to really stretch. I don't know how it works, but it does. Maybe it's that I stop seeing things in absolutes. Maybe it's that my heart softens.[7] Maybe it's that just like "awfulizing" triggers a string of "ain't it awful" memories, remembering the things that please, sustain, nurture me, reminds me of those feelings and other memories.

I'm not saying "Fake it till you make it," to lie to yourself, but rather, to ask yourself, right now, is there anything you're grateful for? If all you connect to is rage, great. Express it. Write about it. Draw your rage. Paint your rage. Scream your rage. Just don't get in a car and drive your rage. And then, maybe, just maybe, sometime later you'll discover some gratitude that you could know you were outraged and could express it.

Life has to be about more than pain. Dr. Bessel van der Kolk establishes a contract with each patient involving a commitment to doing something he or she enjoys each week. When we're feeling horrible, we can lose sight of the good. I have found that any regular practice that keeps us in touch with what we appreciate, love, enjoy, helps us feel better, if not good. Any regular practice that keeps us connected to a Divine Source, Higher Power, God, reinforces that we are not alone. These help me find hope when I least expect it.

Years ago, when I was facilitating stress management workshops, I'd quote Epictetus, who said, "What matters in life is not what happens to us but how we perceive it." These days I think what happens to us does matter *and,* if we're lucky, we can work on our perspective to empower rather than entrap ourselves. My healing requires that I accept that there is both evil *and* good in the world and potentially in each of us. I need to choose which I'm going to draw into my life at this stage. Which path am I going to follow? There will always be evil to point at and say, "See, I told you. Ain't it awful?" And part of my life is about that. I feel like I'm a "pointer." That I need to help people see the evil abuse is so I can help myself and others heal and hopefully prevent future horrors for children.

Even though I believe that the hardwiring of my brain happened, I also believe I can heal and I am healing. Healing, for me, is a spiritual process. It is the Divine, God, Goddess, Love, whatever you want to call it, that ultimately brings healing. There is only so much medication, friendship, therapy, and positive thinking anyone can do. Incest attacks the spirit. I believe that the soul cannot be murdered, but the spirit can. Without spirit, you don't have access to your soul. I access my soul and inspire my spirit by looking for beauty, praying, meditating, and affirming the good (except when I am exceptionally crabby and then I *kvetch* [complain] and do some of these affirming practices anyway).

It's Not Black and White
ᴖ

My healing journey is not finished. I travel from terror to triumph to terror and back again. Healing is evident in the lessening frequency of terror or despair and in the quicker movement through each cycle. Healing is evident as I begin to have time to wonder about how I'd like my life to be. Where do I want to live? What work do I want to do?

Healing doesn't mean erasing my past. It happened. It hurt. It's over. I'm bigger than it now, and my life is better. It still impacts me, and I find it hard to believe that anyone who experiences multiple molestations at such a young age could just be done with it, over. I've noticed the women in my practice who heal faster than I have. I notice those whose lives are more constricted, with limited relationships, who are often frozen in worry and indecision. This latter group experienced multiple traumas and/or were under the age of three when the molestation began.

I can't write a happily-ever-after story because it isn't that way for many survivors and it's not fair to hold out that expectation, which can seem like a demand or judgment. *What's wrong with me/you that we aren't all healed yet?* The fact is, I'm lucky and grateful to have had the internal and external resources to deal as well as I have. There are many who didn't or don't.

Dr. Roderick T. Beaman, an osteopathic physician, worked for several years as a medical consultant at a state hospital. As a general physician for psychiatric patients, he treated Susan (not her real name) and became aware of her story. Dr. Roderick writes:

> *Susan* was known as a victim of incest. Her father had been in the army and retired as a non-commissioned officer. Once, she came back from a release time with him with some bruises. One of the nurses asked her what had happened. *Susan* said that she had gotten out of the car to get away from him and fell down. When asked why she had wanted to get away from her father, *Susan* replied that he had gotten mad because "she wouldn't fuck him."

I was shocked by this because I had always viewed the family as the cornerstone of Jewish culture. While I am not Jewish, I had always felt that it was impossible to understand Judaism without an understanding of the importance of the family in its tradition. Out of naïveté, it just seemed that Jewish incest was an oxymoron.

This patient will likely be institutionalized for the rest of her life. It is, of course, impossible to determine exactly how much the episodes of incest contributed to her destruction but there can be no doubt that they did. Other incest victims survive more intact.

I consider myself lucky that, for whatever reasons, I am alive and have many wonderful options in my life. I hold on to the hope and possibility of ever greater healing while trying to be gentle with myself about the ups and downs, ins and outs of my process. It isn't smooth. I am helped by others, like Rae. An artist, mother, interior designer, social activist, and thriver, she inspires me to live by the words of Rabbi Hillel: "I get up. I walk. I fall down. Meanwhile I keep dancing."

The ability to express ourselves creatively helps immeasurably. Chapter 8 presents "A Way Out: Healing through Creative Expression."

A Way Out
Healing through Creative Expression

RACHEL LEV,
SHOSHANA, RAE,
SHAUNA GREEN,
ASENATH BARZANI,
HADASS G.,
MARCIA COHN SPIEGEL,
AND ZENA DAVID

But let me impress just one thing upon you, sisters: Your imagination and your emotions are like a vast ocean from which you wrest small pieces of land that may well be flooded again. That ocean is wide and elemental, but what matters are the small pieces of land you reclaim from it.

Etty Hellesun,
An Interrupted Life, 1941–43

Rachel Lev
ᘒ

As a child I loved art and music in school. Family trips to New York introduced me to the wonders of theater and Broadway musicals. Lyrics of songs from *My Fair Lady, Funny Girl, A Funny Thing Happened on the Way to the Forum, How to Succeed in Business without Really Trying, Do I Hear a Waltz? Oklahoma, Fiddler on the Roof,* and more allowed me to communicate feelings that would otherwise have been silenced. Sometimes those lyrics were weapons.

My dad would ask me to bring him his cigars. I'd walk deliberately toward him, singing all the verses of "Just You Wait, Henry Higgins" from *My Fair Lady*, replacing Henry Higgins's name with his. At "as they raise their rifles higher, I'll shout *ready, aim, fire! Ah ha ha ___ ___,* oh ho ho ___ ___. *Just you* wait!" I would throw each Perfecto Garcia, missilelike, at his chest. He'd catch them and smile. How wonderful to have found a way to express anger and resentment even though indirect.

Throughout my life, the lyrics of songs first heard in childhood have come readily to mind and lip as I felt joy, sadness, or anger. "New York City Blues" sung by Bonnie Koloc captured my mood, "cause nobody knows how you feel." I came alive to the blues of Betty Carter, the jazz of Morgana King,

117

and the rock 'n' roll of Blood, Sweat & Tears. Throughout my life the sights and sounds of dance, theater, and music have gifted me. There has been an evolution from the unconscious expression and relief of sitting in an audience or singing and acting to expressing myself more consciously.

As an adult, the impact of writing, drawing, and working with clay as I exposed and healed the pain of my childhood feels as if it defies description. In the early years of healing, I didn't think about writing or drawing as "creative." I didn't *think* about it at all. I just did it. It was about survival. Get the stuff out. Put it on paper. Pour your rage and pain into something, onto something. Get it out. I wrote all the time. I loved writing *big* when my feelings were intense. I loved making large, sweeping swaths of red and black crayon across a page.

Art and creativity connect me to the life force—to what is good and powerful and potent even when what it is expressing is dark. I believe it helped me in ways I don't even know yet.

Art gives some of us a way out—a way through the pain—a way to speak our truths. Words on paper, paint, clay, crayons, photography, collage, and more offer safe vehicles for expression. Once expressed in visual form we see, in fact, that something can contain the pain. We can tear it up, smash it, throw it away. The pain gets smaller. Sometimes once we can "see" how we feel, we can cry, rage, vent. Sometimes when we share our creations with someone, they look at us, eyes moist and heart open, and we know we are not alone.

With each mark on the page, we reclaim ourselves. I am grateful for the support I received to freely express myself, without worrying about how it looked. One day, my feelings all bound up inside, my therapist handed me a fat red crayon, a fat black one, and a large sheet of paper. "Just move your hand across the page and see what happens," she said. What happened? Relief. Connection to my feelings. The ability to label, to name my experience. Joy. Rage. Sorrow. Healing.

The remainder of this chapter tells and shows the healing role of creativity—of writing, drawing, painting, and sculpting—in the lives of Shoshana, Rae, Shauna Green, Asenath Barzani, Hadass G., Marcia Cohn Spiegel, and Zena David.

Shoshana

When I open myself to creativity, I allow myself to reclaim my sense of identity, my sense of power, and my sense of connection to the universe.

Creativity unblocks the healing process. My daily life is a struggle against fragmented and racing thoughts, depression, anger, anxiety, and fear. When I
don't allow myself to channel this energy into something creative, the alternative is turning the anger inward. In this state I become self-destructive. I cut
myself, drive recklessly, overeat, overspend, etc. Creative expression has been
the only way I have found to distract myself during times of overwhelming
stress and channel this energy into something positive.

Rae

*The lady in red walks into the empty art studio. The smell of turpen-
tine lingers in the air. Over on the easel stands an unfinished portrait
of a woman and child. Over on the taboret is a tin can full of
brushes and pallet knives to sculpt a work of art. How was she to
know that she would be that work in progress, interrupted and
restrained for so many years and yet now awake—alive—a living
painting? In her head she still hears the strains of Brahms and
Mozart. She smells the Pinaud talc he used on his hands when he
was finished. Oh, her heart nearly stops as she sees the cut crystal
candy dishes, long since empty, and yet she still remembers every
treat, every whisper, every secret. The back rubs, the tickles, the
fingers gently touching her breasts, the warm endearments, the love,
the large hands and fingers reaching into her underpants, probing so
gently, and then his fingers finding that special spot. How wet she
was as he stroked her thighs. It felt so wonderful, so intoxicating.*
  "Oh Gramps, where did you put my new doll?"

I was born in 1950, eldest of two girls, to a nice Jewish couple. I grew up in
a residential area, not far from the city's center. My parents were upper middle
class. My father worked for the family business and owned two cars, a boat,
and belonged to a country club. To many it was an incredibly gifted and idyllic
existence. What they did not know was that underneath the normalcy was a
bizarre family secret that almost destroyed me.

Everyone told me how lucky I was to have both sets of grandparents until I
was ten. On my mother's side, Papa worked in the financial district. What I
remember most about him was his raspy voice and wild hair. He was a soft-
spoken man who could get me to come out of the bathroom when I locked
myself in. Nana was a *bubby*. She baked brownies, played on the floor with
us, and ran to get my gym shoes when I forgot them. Nana and Papa were

assimilated Jews who only went to services on the High Holidays. On my father's side, Gram came from an Orthodox background; however, she did not observe kashrut or Shabbat. She married Gramps, who didn't even attend his own bar mitzvah. My family may not have been religious, but they were culturally Jews. I grew up knowing I was Jewish.

The Family practiced *Tzedakah (with a capital "T")*. They believed in giving generously to Jewish causes in both time and money and had strong affiliations with the United Jewish Appeal, Devorah, Israeli Bonds, and Brandeis University. The Family name and reputation were sacred. We were always told, "Whatever is said here stays here." We were never to shame *The Family*. Like many Jewish families of the time, we did not acknowledge problems. When I thought about exposing the truth I thought to myself, "Who would believe the philanthropist or leader of the community was a child molester?" I did not want to hurt innocent family members. Furthermore, everyone would think I was crazy.

Gramps liked to play with us. I remember being eight or nine years old and going to his art studio to paint. Gramps was a dilettante. He played the violin and he painted. My sister and I both loved art, so we would spend Saturday afternoon at his studio. He would play classical music, set one of us up at the easel with a canvas and some oil paints, while the other one would sit on the couch for a back rub. It all started innocently enough. He would rub my back but then his fingers would inch around to my breasts or down into my underpants. I would wiggle and squirm but he continued. Sometimes he would rub himself on me or take out his penis for me to hold, lick, or suck. He never penetrated me, but he enjoyed himself. When he was finished, he would have my sister and me switch positions.

When I was painting I pretended not to see anything, but it was always there. This went on until I was thirteen. One day Gramps took a paintbrush and began to work on one of my canvases without asking me. I screamed at him to never touch my paintings again. He never touched me again.

This story is about abuse and the past, only to the extent that they challenged me to be the person I am today. This story is primarily about the path, the journey, of healing from sexual, mental, and emotional abuse—from survivor to thriver. It is my journey from an overly sensitive, intuitive, wounded child to a strong, courageous, and empowered woman.

In my youth I never told anyone about Gramps. After our sexual encounters he would offer me candy and say, "This is our secret. Don't tell anyone." I kept the secret. I did not tell anyone, but I acted out. I told my mother never to touch me again. I started to gain weight. In my family, no one discussed feelings. We were not allowed to be angry, slam a door, or shout "I hate you." Children were seen and not heard. No one ever asked me, "What's wrong?" After a time, I put it away. At times I even questioned my sanity. Did I make this up? I was lucky in that I received confirmation and validation from my sister. I was in my early twenties when I told my sister Gramps used to give me chest rubs. She said, "It happened to you, too?" When we told our parents, they laughed.

I believe my creativity, my rich imagination, and my artistic abilities truly saved my life. In my teens I was always dreaming about being in a tragic accident or having a fatal illness. I pictured everyone huddled by my bedside telling me how sorry they were. I read historical romances and lost myself in the character of a young French girl, Angelique, who was caught in odious situations but was always able to emerge victorious. She was able to use her wits and beauty until the Prince rescued her. Every book gave me hope. I kept waiting for Prince Charming to rescue me from my evil family. No one came.

I was a talented artist. Art was the one thing at which I truly excelled and for which I received recognition. In high school I painted people with no faces. No one asked why. I realize today that my people had no faces because I believed if you really saw the pain in their eyes, you would know my secret. I was attracted to bizarre and surrealist painters. I gravitated to warlike images and the grotesque. No one asked why.

As a young adult I began to try to figure out why I never fit in. I practiced yoga. I meditated. I read inspirational literature. I painted. I did a portrait of a young woman in such pain that I stopped painting for twelve years. The pain was too close to the surface, and I could not handle the suffering. I felt if I let it out, I would die.

Throughout my life art has been an incredible source of insight, growth, and transformation. For many years I used my paintings and drawings to understand and let go of painful childhood memories. In the beginning, I expressed my pain through images and color. I could give voice to feelings that had no name. Later I was able to self-direct my healing while painting specific themes that explored different issues in my life. When I felt like I had multiple personalities and was going crazy, I painted people with three arms and two heads. Later I used my artwork to explore social conditions that touched my heart, such as the homeless or violence against women. My artwork told me before cognitive understanding, I was no longer a victim and a mere survivor, I was a thriver.

As the creative process is being accepted into the medical profession for physical healing, I believe it is a way to work with spiritual illness or emptiness.[1] It is a way to come back to source. We are all inherently creative/spiritual. We have just forgotten. We are blocked. Through the creative process we can find our "true north," our true spirit.

In my personal work today, I often use the sacred art form of the mandala. *Mandala* is the Sanskrit word for sacred circle. This sacred art form can be found in many traditions including the Native American medicine wheel, Buddhist Tantric art, or the Chinese yin yang symbol. Carl Jung, the noted psychiatrist, used the mandala as a way of accessing the unconscious as a source of wholeness.

I usually begin my work with setting up an altar wherever I am working. I place flowers, a candle, and incense. I pray and ask for guidance. I ask my Spirit to bless my materials and make me an instrument for healing and love. I turn on music or sit quietly and wait for the images to come to me. I have used the mandala to honor my Spirit, to heal relationships, as well as express my joy and gratitude for the muses that inspire me.

Most recently I was asked to participate in an art show. Each artist was given a pair of ceramic hands about eighteen inches high. We could do anything we wanted. My *Healing Hands* represent my belief that creativity is spirituality, just as creativity is healing. Figures on the hands represent a combination of Eastern and Western healing images—an African healer, a Native American shaman, Buddha, and a Hindu goddess.

I don't believe we need to be artists to be creative. We just need to allow ourselves to create without judgment, to immerse ourselves in the process, not the outcome. Expressive arts therapy or creative arts therapy is a new and exciting addition to the counseling field. Believing that art therapies work best in an inter-disciplinary framework, Shauan McNiff, a pioneer in the field, uses drumming, vocal work, and movement in addition to painting when working with clients.

For me, painting and drawing were my favorite methods, but I have used movement as well. I believe we need to explore many avenues. It could be dance, improvisation, poetry, or storytelling. It is up to the individual to experiment and discover her or his own creative path, and Spirit.

Shauna Green

Shauna Green is a forty-something artist, therapist, and survivor of ritual abuse, who over the years recovered from dissociative identity disorder. As a child, Shauna never had the vocabulary to put her thoughts and feelings into words. She relied on the creative process to communicate. In the beginning her drawings seemed cryptic. As she learned to verbalize her experiences, her art became clearer.

Shauna created several collage books to document her experiences. She photocopied childhood photos of herself, immediate family members, and her ancestors and mounted them in a book. Typing text on plain paper, she created balloon forms around them and placed them near the pictures of her family. In one example Shauna's mother looks lovingly at infant Shauna. The caption reads "Secret touching may happen with someone you love a lot!" In another image of children playing Pin the Tail on the Donkey at a birthday party, the words from the blindfolded child read "Can you tell which ones are being abused?" On several of the pages, some figures are shaded in yellow. The yellow denotes someone who was molested.

Images throughout her art—a clock with no hands, tears of blood, lifeless trees, frightening and haunted faces, and eyes, eyes everywhere—convey some of the terror and despair she experienced while being abused and as she went through her healing process.

Silenced by fear and family, many of her pictures show people without mouths. During a time when she believed the only way to end her suffering was to die, headstones and cemeteries appear again and again. A therapist told her, "Your trees look dead, you should put leaves on them to make them come alive." Wanting to comply, yet not feeling that leaves were the answer, Shauna's trees evolved and sprouted roots. They began to dance in the clouds, doing ballet and playing on mountaintops. Her "dancing tree people" became her new voice.

Writing, as demonstrated throughout this book, is another way we release our pain and empower ourselves. The following is an overview of *Passing Over,* a play written by rape and sexual abuse survivor Zena David.

Zena David

"There are no problems; there are only solutions," my "good" uncle, Uncle Mossie, my mother's brother, told me all my life. I have to say "good" before his name so as not to confuse you with my "no-good" Uncle Will who became Uncle Lester the Molester in my play *Passing Over.* This "absurdly Jewish play" for Passover is about a young woman's need to get rid of the *chametz* in her soul as well as the *chametz* in her kitchen on the night before Passover. As part of the preparation for Passover, we clean our homes, change our dishes, and rid our homes of anything that is *"chametz."* The young woman's name is Miriam. Her fears and lack of organization, and some family members, both living and dead, stand between her and liberation. These people occupy the oversize cabinets, closets, and sink in her

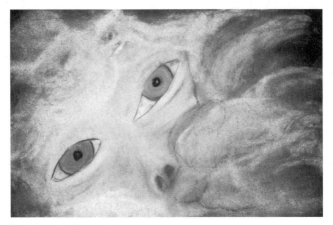

Pastel drawing by Shauna Green

"Frightening and haunted faces, and eyes, eyes every-where—convey some of the terror and despair I experienced while being abused and later, as I healed."
Shauna Green

Drawing by Shauna Green

"For a long time I believed the only way to end my suffering was to die. Headstones and cemeteries appear again and again in my art."
Shauna Green

Drawing by Shauna Green

Drawing by Shauna Green

"A therapist told me my trees looked dead and suggested I put leaves on them to make them come alive. I wanted to comply, but leaves didn't feel like the answer."
Shauna Green

Shauna's trees evolved and sprouted roots. They began to dance in the clouds, doing ballet and playing on mountaintops. Her "dancing tree people" became her new voice.

kitchen. Primary among the uninvited guests is the hand of Uncle Lester the Molester, Miriam's Pharaoh.

In the Passover story, G-d appointed Moses to deliver the Hebrew people out of slavery from the Egyptian pharoah.[2] In *Passing Over*, G-d appoints Lil, Miriam's former mentor and confidante. In the Passover story, Moses met G-d at the Burning Bush. In this play, Miriam, bemoaning the fact that she has no mother to help her organize her kitchen, meets Lilian as she opens her refrigerator.

Stepping out of the oversize refrigerator, Lil calmly hands Miriam some bread to throw away, casually commenting that Miriam always needed a mother. The sight of Lil almost shocks Miriam into a heart attack. Not only has Lil emerged from a refrigerator, she also has been dead for a couple of years.

Apparently, Lil has been assigned by G-d to perform a posthumous mitzvah (good deed). She must enable Miriam to "seize the day" and create a new personal Haggadah for herself, one that will end in her liberation. If Lil can provide skills for Miriam that will empower her in dealing with her family, Lil will be free to "visit" hers.

So what is this play? A farce. It is a farce and then you cry. Everyone needs to liberate some aspect of themselves. Often we need others to support us. Each one of us has a Haggadah that we write each year with archetypal core stories that define who we are. Each year more is revealed as we are able to face emerging truths, hard as they may be. Each year we discover the Moses and the Pharaoh in us. Two years ago, I discovered the Miriam(s) inside me. Ironically, I did not consciously intend to write such a play.

Two years before, I had attended a Jewish women's playwriting class taught by Susan Merson at the University of Judaism. Each week we had writing exercises followed by readings of works in process. I came each week empty-handed. Just before the first session ended, I was notified that my former mentor and confidante had died suddenly. I was shocked. I couldn't cry. Nor could I begin the grieving process. I was just numb. A few days after I returned from the funeral, I sat down at the computer intending to write my memories of Lil. Instead, this play tumbled out, outrageous, absurd, filled with corny jokes and silly songs. But it worked.

Time ignored its own limitations. Truths could be stretched (my mother isn't at all like the character Mother Mona) enabling deeper truths to emerge. A molester long dead could be raised up and "rekilled" in order to heal forty-five years of fragmentation and distrust in G-d. In the play, I get to "do it right" this time.

"*I experienced pain in silence. I did everything to keep the secret. I'd put my hand in my mouth, lock it in a safe. Therapy was the first place I told.*"

— Rae

Painting by Rae

There but for the Grace of God go I, *painting by Rae*

"*She's on the street soliciting. She's in bed nursing a broken arm and multiple contusions. She's in the hospital recovering from wounds she inflicted on herself. She's in the psychiatric ward for attempted suicide. She's in the corner, weeping, crying, shooting heroin. She's in the police car arrested for drunk driving. She's in the morgue. There but for the grace of God go I.*"

— Rae

"I felt great sadness, like I had a split personality. That's why my figures always had extra arms. I was controlled by my past and pain, thus the hand on the shoulder tying me to my past. But I always hoped I could give birth to myself."

— Rae

Woman in yellow dress, *painting by Rae*

"I was a great actress. I had a lot of masks and faces. I looked like a normal person, but when I looked in the mirror, I'd see my mother's face and blankness. The eyes are important. They tell it all. Two different colors. No consistency."

— Rae

Who am I? *painting by Rae*

"Tell them about how you're never really a whole person if you remain silent, because there's always that one little piece inside you that wants to be spoken out, and if you keep ignoring it, it gets madder and madder and hotter and hotter, and if you don't speak it out, one day it will just up an punch you in the mouth from the inside."

— Words spoken to Audre Lorde by her
daughter in The Cancer Journals
by Audre Lorde, Aunt Lute Books, 1980.

"I had such an ache in my chest. Drawing the physical sensations I was experiencing helped me identify, then express, emotions that had been bottled up."

— Rachel Lev

"This is a painting of me dancing around and around in a field. I painted it with the feeling that no matter how much I danced, no matter where I went, I could not escape the insanity of the world."

— Asenath Barzani

No Escape, *painting by Asenath Barzani*

"Whenever you write or paint or dance, you align with and open yourself to spiritual guidance. Like a flow of electricity, this spiritual connection is always there."

— Julia Cameron

Collage Book *by Shauna Green*

Suicide *by Shauna Green*

Endless Stairs *by Hadass G.*

Free Tree *by Hadass G.*

"Thirty-seven years old, I was born and spent most of my childhood in Israel. My pictures are a kind of mirror of my healing process from 'adult-victim' of severe childhood sexual abuse to a survivor. I always drew what I felt, the current mental situation I was in, and exactly dated my pictures. They became a pictorial diary of my healing process.

"Before I was aware of the abuse, I drew a lot of endless stairs.

"Creating these works helped not only as a vehicle for expressing pain, fears, and hopes, but also as I looked at the pictures. I hang each picture in different places at my home and office shortly after I paint them. This helps me go on and not fall back to well-known destructive patterns. It connects me to the present. Within a year of my current healing process, I see my great process and development through my pictures. It is a reminder to me that one can heal."

— Hadass G.

"I was raised in a nonobservant family who belonged to a Reform synagogue. For many years I never felt any connection to Judaism. I wanted nothing to do with God. I felt like an outcast, unable to share my past with anyone in the Jewish community due to the anger and denial I experienced from those in whom I confided.

"As I moved along in my healing journey, I began to realize that what I'd grown up with was not Judaism. I began to wonder what 'normal Judaism' was. Although fearful of past memories and having to work through horrendous flashbacks, last year I was able to go to a women's yeshiva in Israel to learn some of the basics. This opportunity came with a warning from the rabbi who told me not to discuss my past with anyone, since I would be seen as a 'kook' and, most likely, expelled."

— Shauna Green

"This is a slot canyon, a narrow canyon where the sun shines from late morning until midafternoon. If you enter the canyon early, it is dark, gloomy, mysterious. The path is obscured in shadows. When the sun emerges, brilliant, sparkling, and surprising colors, shapes, and forms appear. It seems to me that is a metaphor for our lives. We must remember in the dark that the sun will shine and beauty will once again appear."

— Marcia Cohn Spiegel,
activist for peace in Jewish lives

Antelope Canyon, Arizona,
photograph by M. C. Spiegel

Drawing by Rae

"GRATITUDE IS ONE OF THE SWEET SHORTCUTS TO FINDING PEACE OF MIND AND HAPPINESS INSIDE. NO MATTER WHAT'S GOING ON OUTSIDE OF US, THERE'S ALWAYS SOMETHING WE COULD BE GRATEFUL FOR."
BARRY NEIL KAUFMAN

"IF YOU WISH TO KNOW THE DIVINE, FEEL THE WIND ON YOUR FACE AND THE WARM SUN ON YOUR HAND."   THE BUDDHA

Drawing by Rae

"*Wherever I am working, I usually begin by setting up an altar. I place flowers, a candle, and incense. I pray and ask for guidance. I ask my Spirit to bless my materials and make me an instrument for healing and love. Then I turn on music or sit quietly and wait for the images to come to me. I have used the mandala to honor my Spirit, to heal relationships, as well as express my joy and gratitude for the muses that inspire me.*"

— *Rae*

Mandala *by Rae*

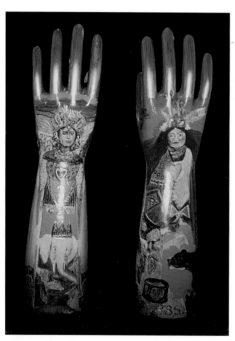 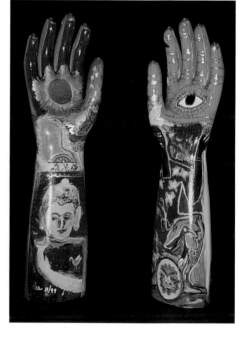

Healing Hands, *painted ceramic by Rae*

Several years ago, a rabbi prepared us for the internal Passover by suggesting that each of us make a list of the personal *chametz* that gets in the way of our own freedom. We were told to burn that list along with the food that is *chametz*. I had Miriam do that in the play, and each of the characters offered something to be burned. In Miriam's new personal Haggadah, her house is finally in order, and the exiled part of herself has been embraced and returned to her rightful home. So the problems found solutions.

I did not set out to write a play about a childhood molestation. My original motivation was to acquaint myself with the grief I felt over the death of someone who was instrumental in helping me navigate my preteen and adolescent years. The surprise and irony and awe occurred when other aspects of different parts of my life emerged, coming along for the ride. Rather than turn them away, I welcomed them and gave each of them a place and a voice. In giving them permission to be heard, I honored the relevancy of the words of a famous rebbe, Rebbe Menachem Mendel Schneerson. At the end of the play, Lil reminds Miriam to reflect on the wisdom of Rebbe Schneerson, "We are day workers. Our task is to shed light. We need not expend our energies in battling darkness. We need only create day, and night will fade away." Amen.

Expressing ourselves creatively helps many of us heal. But what of our identity as Jews? Chapter 9, by Sue William Silverman, "My Jewish Journey Home," explores the confusion of a little girl, then woman, whose understanding and feelings about being a Jew are complicated by many variables. Chapter 10, "Finding Something to Believe In: Religion, Spirituality, and Cultural Identity," describes some of the challenges Jewish sexual abuse survivors face, within ourselves and in interaction with the Jewish community as we search for if, where, and how we might want to belong.

NINE

My Jewish Journey Home

SUE WILLIAM SILVERMAN

I am an incest survivor. More specifically, I am a Jewish incest survivor. As a child, however, I didn't know the meaning of the word "incest." And I learned a confusing and contradictory definition of the word "Jewish." What did it mean to be a little Jewish girl in my family?

I am here, today, to tell you. I'd like to begin with a story told from this little girl's perspective, a girlhood of fear and magic.

I call this story "The Rosary."

Long after World War II ended, my mother remained terrified by the slaughter of Jews. Every night she told me scary stories about fates of Jewish children who'd lived in faraway countries, snatched from their beds, to perish at the hands of Nazis, hands that haunted my mother. "But you're a lucky little Jewish girl," she always whispered, carefully tucking in the sheet and kissing my auburn hair. "You're safe in America."

I didn't feel safe. For the war felt neither far away nor as if it were really over. Rather, *after* my mother turned off the light and said good-night, her insistent stories seemed to come to life. I gripped the edge of the sheet in my fists. I closed my eyes as tightly as possible. I knew that my father, an official in the Truman administration, and a man of peace by day, became one of those men of war by night, who searched for Jewish children in order to harm them. I knew how easily he always found me, so I felt as if a yellow Star of David were sewn to my chest.

As each year passed, I became more and more afraid of being Jewish. I began to wish I had straight blonde hair and a blunt pug nose. I wished my long last name could be short and Christian. I wished I could celebrate Christmas and Easter. I wanted to press the palms of my hands together and murmur Christian prayers or touch a holy Bible to my lips.

For the solution, I knew, was to mask my body in Christian camouflage, anoint it in Christian scents. I needed Christian amulets draped around the door to my bedroom to ward off all evil tyrants who tried to enter, tyrants who hated little Jewish children. *Pass by*, these magical charms would insist, at night, when the door to my room would open, when the shadow of my night-father would appear. *Pass by.* And then he would pass by—for it would be as if a crucifix were nailed across my bed.

But I owned no Christian talisman to guard me against the sultry midnight scent of my father, nothing to protect me from the wintry sound of his voice, insisting that I, his daughter, do whatever he demand. Nor did I know any prayer to silence the wartime stories my mother told me. The words "six million" gusted across the threshold of my bedroom. "Gas chamber" and "crematorium" seeped through the keyhole. I heard night trains roar past houses aglow with pale, delicate lampshades, houses where men wore starched uniforms—night trains roaring faster, blasting across oceans and fiery fields of war—until I heard black jackboots thudding up stairs, up the wooden stairs of my own house, down the hallway, toward the bedroom, a door cracking open, closer, nearing the bed . . . and all my mother's images fused into one phantom Nazi, my own stormtrooper father, who raped his daughter on her mattress stuffed with tuft after tuft of shorn auburn hair.

And each night ghosts of slaughtered Jewish children peered at us through my bedroom window. Their fingernails tapped the panes. Thousands of pale, bony fingers plucked at my skin. "Come with us," they whispered, with frigid breaths. "Come." Their souls floated across dark skies like patches of dull yellow stars, stars that could never light their way. "Come."

I refused to follow. Still, I waited to discover holy waters or Christian balms to save me.

Then, several weeks before Easter, I woke one Wednesday morning to a sound that seemed to reach me from a vast distance. It wasn't like harsh blasts of war. No. This was different. I opened my eyes and lay in bed listening to this soothing sound that rinsed the air in silvery light.

Bells. Church bells.

I believed they were an incantation or secret message meant just for me.

I slipped into a white dress and rushed outside. Now the bells seemed to sound more urgent. They chimed with more insistence. I hurried along deserted morning streets, my footsteps padding in time to peals reverberating through the soles of my feet.

There, towering before me, was a masonry structure laden with crosses and steeples. Stained-glass windows glinted. Spires pierced the sky. Now I clearly heard the secret message. Each ring pealed a syllable: "En/ter. En/ter. En/ter."

Pushing open a thick mahogany door, I was enveloped in cool, peaceful air. I heard the swish of silken robes. A priest sprinkling holy water chanted prayers. As I moved past the pews, I saw clean, well-fed children with bowed heads kneeling on velvet cushions. Wings of veined marble angels seemed to flutter. Faces of stone saints were raised toward the vaulted ceiling. For a moment I stood transfixed by the serene eyes of the Virgin Mother gazing at my own eyes as if in benediction. Then her gaze seemed to lower toward her outstretched hand. I, too, looked at the Virgin Mother's hand. Nestled in it was a rosary of ruby beads.

I knew the rosary was an offering for me. I reached for it my hand grazing her palm, and clasped it tight in my fist. I trailed the beads through the fingers of my own hands and felt, in the beads, the warmth of the Virgin Mother. Each bead seemed to glow like a miniature sun blessing my fingers, my hands, this warmth radiating up my arms, spreading through my body straight to my heart. I wanted never to relinquish the rosary or lose the sweet hushed breath of the chapel.

When I heard a shuffle of feet I looked up. The children were filing from pews to form a line down the aisle. I joined the solemn procession moving toward the altar and bent my head beneath an incandescent light. And on this most sacred and holy of Wednesdays, a priest decorated my forehead with a cross etched in charcoal. With this mark I felt anointed. With this mark I felt disguised. I knew the mark would remain on my forehead forever. I held the rosary to my peaceful eyes.

In bed that evening I trailed the rosary over my body. With this amulet, and with the cross of ashes on my forehead, no longer could I hear bedtime stories about fates of Jewish children. For now I was transfigured. Now, when my father opened my door, it was only the body of a lost Jewish girl who lay in my bed. While I, a radiant Christian virgin, wandered dark skies, far far away from nightraiders, my own rapturous soul transparent as flame.

After we left Washington, D.C., we moved to St. Thomas in the Virgin Islands. Still, my confusion as to what it meant to be a little Jewish girl continued. My desire to be a Christian girl also continued. Ironically, the first house in which we lived in St. Thomas was atop Synagogue Hill, beside the oldest synagogue in the Western Hemisphere. More ironic, perhaps, is that I attended an Anglican school for about six months.

Every afternoon I dreaded leaving the safety of the Anglican school grounds, located next to the Anglican church. I feared walking past the synagogue on my way home. Climbing Synagogue Hill, I gripped my rosary and rushed past the wrought-iron gate of the temple, my gaze averted, scared I would glimpse black jackboots just inside the door.

Did I ever enter the temple? A few times I did attend services with my family. I have vivid memories of playing in the sand that covered the synagogue floor. I remember staring out the arched doorway toward a sun-struck Caribbean sky. Yet I have vague memories of everything else, and can recall no rabbi, no prayer, no song, no spiritual light, no warmth, no guidance, no love. If I had a Jewish soul, I allowed nothing to touch it. Since my father still sexually molested me, I didn't know how to let anything touch it.

By the time we moved to Glen Rock, New Jersey, where I attended junior and senior high school, I'd lost the rosary. While my fear of Nazis had also faded over the years, I had not, however, outgrown or discarded my desire to be Christian.

Here in Glen Rock, where virtually all the students at my school were Christian, I wanted to look like them, dress like them, be like them, talk like them, eat like them. I wanted to learn, immediately, the secret language of Christian, New Jersey suburbs, learn the magic of Christian, New Jersey houses, towns, streets. In particular, I wanted Christopher, a blonde-haired, pug-nosed boy in my English class, to be my boyfriend. He, like the rosary before him, also became an amulet, as I substituted one Christian talisman for another. In the magical world in which I still lived, I believed that if he loved me, I would, almost by osmosis, be Christian.

The following is a short segment from my memoir, *Because I Remember Terror, Father, I Remember You,*[1] that reflects this time in New Jersey.

> Robin's Christmas party, which Christopher attends with me, smells of pine and cinnamon candles. An orange-blue fire in the fireplace warms the living room. On the mantel is a crèche. Carefully, I touch the miniature lambs, touch baby Jesus' head. I stand before the Christmas tree enchanted by bubbles of light. On top, a feathery angel, attached to a star, almost touches the ceiling.
>
> I believe, more than anything, this is what our family needs: a decorated pine tree placed before the window in our living room. If we had one, how would it be possible to rage at each other? The thin glass ornaments would shatter; no one would want to shatter them. If we had a crèche on our mantel, we would have to be careful not to wake the sleeping Jesus.
>
> But we will have no tree or crèche. Nor will we celebrate Chanuka. We have no Menorah or candles. Our family is without ceremony or myth to connect us to a life larger than our own existence. We are without comfort or means to ease the journey, deepen it past the parameters of our house.
>
> Christopher and I dance. All the couples dance, as the bubbles of light on the tree warm us. I inhale the scent of his wool sweater. . . . As each

record ends he releases my hand, but we stand together, waiting for the next record. Shyly we smile at each other. His front teeth slightly overlap. And while I know it's probably irrational, I decide I love this small flaw and hope he never fixes it.

"Does your house look like this?" I ask him. I nod toward the tree.

"Well at Easter we usually have baskets with stuffed bunnies and my sisters dye eggs."

I laugh—but imagine his sisters running downstairs on Christmas morning in slippers and robes to rip open their presents. "They still believe in Santa Claus?"

"The two youngest."

I realize I want to believe in Santa Claus and the Easter Bunny. I want to believe in Tinkerbell. But I also want to believe in Jesus, God, or Zeus. It doesn't matter.

"You go to church for Christmas?"

"Christmas Eve."

I imagine the flame of white tapered candles reflecting on stained-glass windows. I imagine voices singing Christmas hymns, imagine Christopher standing with his family, all in a row. When they return home after the service, his father will build a fire and his mother will fix hot chocolate. Christopher will plug in the tree, and his sisters will hold hands and whisper to each other what they hope Santa will bring them. And I want this as much as the church service, *this:* the fireplace, the hot chocolate, the lights on the tree. I imagine his sisters preparing for bed. I see them brushing their teeth and changing into pajamas. I see them pulling back sheets and nestling against pillows. But then, I don't know what else to see, what else I'm supposed to see. I want Christopher to tell me. Tell me: *How do your sisters sleep through night until morning? How much does your father love his daughters? What does he do to show it?*

It is only now, as an adult, that I understand I subverted my mother's stories and translated them incorrectly.

It is only now, as an adult, that I realize my equating Christianity with safety was illusion, as well as false, and that my desire to be Christian had nothing to do with religious philosophy any more than my flight from Judaism had to do with lack of belief in these principles and traditions.

As a child, I didn't even understand the profound meaning behind rosaries—or Stars of David, either, for that matter. My spirituality was founded and grounded in magic, in trinkets, in superficial icons, and in the unshakable, albeit magical, belief that a rosary of glass beads, a Christmas tree, a Christian boyfriend, could protect me because *they* were more powerful than my father—despite all tangible evidence to the contrary.

Why did I really need the rosary or Christian amulets? By sexually molesting me, my father stole my sense of self. He stole my little girl soul, and body, and spirit. I desperately needed something—anything—to substitute for this massive and comprehensive abandonment and betrayal. I tried to fill this enormous loss with a dimestore rosary.

In other words, as a victim of incest, I was so starved for spirituality, that anything, even false icons or superficial trinkets, were better than nothing. I certainly wasn't taught spirituality. In my incestuous family, I couldn't have been taught it. It didn't—doesn't—can't exist in an incestuous family. After all, can a family that hurts its most vulnerable member be a spiritual family? Can a child molester be a spiritual person? Can a child who has no sense of self, have a firm belief in anything? No.

What made me, finally, question what the rosary meant to me? In many ways, I began this journey by writing my memoir, *Because I Remember Terror, Father, I Remember You.*

Now, since finishing the book, what have I needed in order to help me claim my self? What I've wanted is for even one Jewish person to look at me, look at my book, even the book jacket cover, and say to me: "I am Jewish, and I want to hear your story."

This, I am gratified to say, has begun to happen. And so I have begun what I call "My Jewish Journey Home." And this is another story I'd like to tell you.

The first step on this journey was a chance encounter at the American Booksellers Association Trade Show, where I went to promote my book. The University of Georgia Press had a large poster of my book jacket hanging in their exhibit. At one point during the trade show, a woman approached the booth, looked at the poster, looked at me, understands that I am the author, and says she's from the Houston Jewish Community Center buying books for their bookfair, is interested in my book, and is pleased a Jewish woman was writing about incest.

Pleased? She's pleased because a Jewish woman wrote about incest? In one swift, stunning, overwhelming moment, all my childhood beliefs about my religion began to shatter.

For here was a Jewish woman and she wanted to hear my story.

The second step on my Jewish journey home occurred when I was giving a reading in Atlanta, and the Shalom Bayit coordinator of Jewish Family and Career Services came to hear me—not because I was an incest survivor, but because I was a Jewish incest survivor. And even though I had no idea what "Shalom Bayit" even meant at that time, I just kept nodding my head as she gave me pamphlets and brochures about her organization—an organization that helped Jewish women and children who were victims of domestic violence.

Jewish women? Domestic violence?

You mean I'm not the only one this has happened to, I thought? Ironically, even I, in some strange, convoluted way, somehow managed to believe that ancient myth that things like this simply didn't really happen in Jewish families, even though it had happened to me in my own.

And here was an organization dedicated to helping Jewish families in distress.

And their Shalom Bayit coordinator wanted to hear my story.

So, it is only now that I, as an adult, am able to discover a caring Jewish community that I never knew, as a child, existed—never even knew, as a child, that I needed. Please don't make today's Jewish children wait. Please don't make them flee past synagogues on their way home from school. Please don't make today's Jewish children seek safety and protection in the comfort of one thin rosary of cold glass beads.

Thank you for listening to my story.

TEN ॐ

Finding Something to Believe In
Religion, Spirituality, and Cultural Identity

RACHEL LEV,
JONATHAN,
ASENATH BARZANI,
RAE, SHOSHANA,
AND HILLARY

She called in tears and left a message: "I just wanted you to know, I'm almost sixty years old and I've done a lot of work healing the incest wounds. I saw your notice about your book. I didn't realize this piece needed healing. My Jewish identity. Thank you. It's the last piece."

Jonathan wrote via e-mail saying:

At the age of twenty-one a world famous rabbi tried to seduce me. It totally retraumatized me and left me not wanting to have anything to do with Judaism. I'd been raised secularly and came to this rabbi for help in learning about my heritage and religion. Instead, he used his position of power to try to use me. It was awful, and just like what had happened to me at home. A decade later, I was finally able to try again, and this time I found an incredible shul with a rabbi who is wise, and real and humble. She listened to my story and has been there to reassure me and root me on ever since I met her. Finally, just this year, for the first time in my life, I joined a congregation.

The human soul hungers for sustenance, nurturance, inspiration, for connection to something greater than itself. It glorifies the divine, the holy, and finds rapture in its presence. For some, this hunger is fed by the glories of nature. The sight of the sun setting, the sound of roaring ocean waves, the sweet seduction of a gentle breeze connects us to something grand and glorious. For some, this hunger is fed by the rituals and traditions of a religion or self-help network. For others it is fed by loving relationships. For some, it is not fed at all.

This chapter presents some of our souls' journeys. Where have we found

135

healing and inspiration? Where have we been fed? What draws us toward our Jewish roots? What repels us?

The Longing
☙

There is a joy and comfort, a coming home when I'm among other Jews. Sometimes. The rhythm of language, gestures, facial expressions, sights, sounds, and smells are so familiar, so like me. I went to my mom's condo the other day to drop off some groceries. As I entered her building, I grinned from ear to ear. The lobby smelled of potato pancakes, of *latkes*. On a cold and bitterly dry winter's day, the lobby was steamy and warm. I felt home all the way down to my cells. I long for more. I long to belong, to find a place I can call home. I long for a Jewish spiritual and cultural connection. It's not easy to find.

Identifying Some Stumbling Blocks
☙

For many trauma survivors, myself included, finding something to believe in and trust can be hard, regardless of our religious identity. "God" is often seen as just another perpetrator, someone who abandoned us, or as a concept created to control us. How can we believe in a benevolent Higher Power who allowed us to be so violated? Whether molested by a family member, rabbi, or teacher it seems impossible and unsafe to rely on "God" because as children it felt unsafe to rely on anyone or anything.

One of Judaism's teachings says, "Do not put a stumbling block before the blind" (Lev. 19:14). I am pretty blind when it comes to Judaism. I'd like to "see," to learn, but how? I have spent years attending different synagogues and "alternative" services. While I have occasionally found like-minded people, I have not found a "home." I continue to search. The entrance ways to Jewish learning aren't very clear to me, and there are so many stumbling blocks—even if I'd never been incested.

In "The Issue Is Power: Some Notes on Jewish Women and Therapy," author Melanie Kaye/Kantrowitz writes:

> Don't assume that reclaiming Jewish identity is simple. Jewishness is an intensely collective endeavor, to be pursued in a community of other Jews. Sometimes the work of re-approaching one's Jewishness involves exploration, the nature of which may well be mysterious even to the explorer. In this work we feel excruciating vulnerability.

We feel ashamed for not already knowing tradition, history, culture, language lost to us via assimilation. We feel exposed and foolish for wanting to encompass these things so little seen much less valued by the non-Jewish world.[1]

To this, we add the stumbling block of our individual histories of violation by a member (or members) of the community as well as people's resistance to facing incest and sexual abuse. We add the rabbis, therapists, family, and friends who said to us, "This could not happen." Rigid rules or ways of thinking, especially those that make us feel guilty or afraid of God's reactions to our talking about what happened to us, to expressing our anger at God about having been molested, create more stumbling blocks. If we live in the same community as those who molested us, or family members who don't want anyone to know, add several more stumbling blocks. Religious institutions can also create stumbling blocks, and not just for those who've been traumatized.[2]

In *The Masks Jews Wear: The Self Deception of American Jewry,* Eugene B. Borowitz talks about Jews who are seeking something, inquiring into their Jewish heritage. He says,

> What stands in the way of many of these Jewish searchers, I suggest, is less Jewish theology than the character of American Jewry's institutional religious life. Sensitive people are . . . turned off so regularly by our synagogues and our rabbinic style that they never find out what the Jewish heritage teaches about God and how that might relate to what they have sensed in themselves. . . . The synagogue instead of sensitizing persons, emphasizes decorum; instead of creating community, it builds an institution; instead of changing society, it serves itself.

An example of what Borowitz says occurred when I was introduced to a rabbi who was very enthusiastic about this book. He spoke of ways he might be able to help in getting it published and circulated. Then he asked, *Where do you belong?* I said, *I don't.* He said, *Well, when you're affiliated, let me know. Goodbye.* How can I affiliate without first knowing something about what I'm joining? The pressure to "join," to "be a member" starts immediately. I need a synagogue that will let me attend services and participate long enough for me to make that decision. I need more than that. I need to feel welcome before I pay any fees.

Kate found a synagogue she liked. She didn't feel comfortable continuing to go to services without joining. Membership for her and her husband for a year was five thousand dollars. They could not afford it, and she felt too new and uncomfortable to speak with them about the possibility of paying less. She stopped going. She is exploring other ways to have a spiritual connection. So is Chana, who says, "I feel awkward saying this, but I find greater welcoming and community in non-Jewish organizations. That is probably because of some combination of who they are and the expectations, fears, and hopes I bring. I have learned more about Judaism from a minister who is into the Old Testament than from Jewish sources. My hunger for a Jewish connection has grown, in part, through what I've learned listening to him."

The Need to Feel Welcome
ᴣ

Most people prefer to connect to places that make it easy to belong, where they feel safe. I have found these with groups of writers, groups of women, at personal growth workshops, Twelve Step meetings, and spiritual centers that value diversity as well as the divine feminine and masculine.

For anyone beginning to explore Judaism, or any religion, effort is required. Religious institutions can make it easier by thinking of ways to make newcomers welcome. Many years ago, I took a class on alcoholism. We were required to attend some open Alcoholics Anonymous (AA) meetings.[3] As I did, I discovered there were "beginner's meetings" for AA. In these four structured meetings I got an overview of the history and principles of the program as well as how it worked. It cost nothing and nothing was expected of me. I was given information that helped me see what I could get from these programs. Synagogues and boards of rabbis could do something like that, too.

I found a taste of a welcoming Jewish community in a Santa Fe synagogue during a visit to New Mexico in the mid-1990s. The rabbi spoke that Friday night in Santa Fe, about the upcoming holiday of Pesach— Passover. He painted a picture of the seder table in which we'd be surrounded by our families. He noted that we make room for the uncle or aunt who annoys everyone and that we need to make room for others. He encouraged people to include singles, the newly divorced or widowed, those new to the area, and the elderly—to make sure that everyone who wanted had a place at a seder table. He asked us to look around the synagogue and be sure to introduce ourselves to any newcomers. As he spoke about community as a place of caring and inclusion, he encouraged us to think about these things even when there were no holidays coming up. The rabbi's comments made it easier to stay around and mingle during the social time after services. His comments made it easier for congregants to talk to those of us who were not known to them.

The Fear of Connecting
✤

And, of course, there is always another "side." While we long to belong, we may also fear connection because we fear being known. One of the joys of being Jewish is that we often feel connected whether we know each other or not. A total stranger standing on a balcony at a Las Vegas hotel overheard my conversation and felt free to correct my Yiddish pronunciation of the word *ungapatshkied* (which I was using to describe the hotel's décor). As we laughed and began to talk, I was certain that, if we talked long enough, we would discover that someone I know knows someone she knows.

Within moments total strangers become kin, because we're Jewish. Because we, as Jews, are small in numbers and interconnected in so many ways, it is hard to remain anonymous. That is why many of those whose words and art are in this book use a pen name. Many survivors change their first and last names to distance themselves from their families of origin. Those women who marry are often glad to leave the family name behind, in part because they can avoid having to deal with the "Oh, are you related to . . . ?" or "I knew your father/mother/brother. What a great family!" If we are living in or near our abusers, it is almost impossible to avoid contact with them or people they know. This can cause another stumbling block, as is evident in Asenath Barzani's story.

Breaking the Chains that Bound Me
by Asenath Barzani

For years, I stayed away from my local Mizrahi synagogue. Not only did my father attend services there, but I had grown up there. Even after he moved to another town, I did not want to go and deal with a barrage of "Hi, Asenath, how's your father?"

I often feel stuck. On the one hand, I do not want to get into the details of my life with every person who asks me about my father. On the other hand, I do not want to play along with the "everything's fine" charade. I have found that if I try a third approach, such as, "I don't have a relationship with my father," or "I don't want to talk about my father," people suddenly decide that I am a stubborn, willful child; that I need to get over it and make peace with my poor, victimized father; and that they will be the ones to help me do that. Given the options, I have chosen to steer clear of any space where my father has left his shadow. As a result, I have spent a lot of time staying away from my community. The Mizrahi world is tight knit, and my father is prominent. For this reason, I have experienced a religious, spiritual, and cultural crisis in my life.

Not long ago I began tackling the dilemma head-on. At a meeting of Mizrahi women I spoke about being an incest survivor and how the experience was intertwined with my Mizrahi identity. It just kind of came out as part of the natural flow of conversation, and I didn't stop it. I felt very validated by the women's responses.

Some months later I read my story to an audience so quiet you could hear a pin drop. When I finished, the audience erupted into thunderous applause, and gave me a standing ovation. I leapt in the air in delight of my freedom, and when I turned around, there was a receiving line of all the Mizrahi women I had worked with, waiting to hug and congratulate me. I never felt so integrated in my life.

The following year, my tolerance for Ashkenazi racism and ignorance in America reached an all-time low. As I increasingly withdrew from "Jewish" circles, I found myself yearning to be observant yet completely cut off from Jewish life, on all fronts. I decided to take care of myself, so I wrote a letter to the rabbi of the local Mizrahi synagogue. He had been my teacher when I was a little girl, and I adored him. Why should I be cut off from someone who could provide me a spiritual home and religious guidance?

In my letter, I told the rabbi about my feeling of spiritual emptiness. I told him I desperately wanted to study with him and to continue on the traditional Mizrahi Jewish path. "But there is something I need you to know," I told him, "something that has been keeping me away." I enclosed the story I had read and asked him to read it.

I sent the letter from the airport on my way to Israel for two months. I was very scared of being rejected and didn't want to deal with it for a while. But when I came home, the first phone message to greet me was the rabbi's booming voice. "Asenath, I have one thing to say to you: You are always, always welcome at the synagogue. Call me, come and meet with me. We will talk, we will study." I cried with relief when I heard his message. Finally, I felt, I can be whole. I can go home. After a few rounds of phone tag, the rabbi suggested I come to the synagogue during services. He then wished me Shabbat Shalom "to you and everyone in your family. Everyone in your family," he said. I freaked out from his message. Did he not understand? Would I again risk the "willful child" reproach and resulting feelings of despair if I went to see him? He knew I had not spoken with my father for a decade, so why did he leave that message?

It took a year before I could bring myself to go to the synagogue. I finally went for Yom Kippur services and had a good experience. I wanted to start coming regularly for Shabbat services, but around that time I became observant again and did not want to drive. So I decided to check out the religious studies classes on Sundays. By that point, I had written most of my piece for this book.

I arrived late at my first class, apprehensive about what to expect. As I walked into the room, the rabbi was saying emphatically, "Tamar [who was raped] was ready to sacrifice her *life* rather than say who did it to her. It was better that she die than that she shame him. This is an extreme example that shows us how important it is in Judaism to *never* publicly embarrass someone." That week, I felt anguish about my decision to publish this piece. I went into deep meditation about why I write and why I publish. I reflected on the ethics of publishing my story. In doing so, I considered the fact that Judaism is in favor of publicly holding accountable people who steal or murder. Why is it opposed to publicly holding accountable people who rape women or sexually abuse their children? This issue is about power politics, not moral ethics.

I write and publish because I heal through speaking my truth to the Universe, telling my story, and releasing it to the winds. This dynamic process propels me forward in life, so that I always move through and beyond experiences, I always grow and blossom. Once I made a final decision to publish this piece, I found that freeing myself to speak the truth, to stand tall, to get rid of all the burdens of this secret . . . left me with a profound sense of peace, a feeling of *It's Over.* Opening my mouth and publicly speaking my story has broken whatever chains were still around me. Now I am free.

Asenath's experience mirrors that of many other survivors whose affiliation with Judaism or a specific Jewish community raises many challenges. Will we be accepted as we are? Will we be expected to stay silent about our life experiences, to act as if they either didn't happen or didn't matter?

While many survivors remain ambivalent about connecting to Judaism, some find themselves drawn toward that connection in ways that surprise them. Rae is one of the latter.

Judaism Full Circle
by Rae

It is hard to believe that today I am leading programs about Jewish meditation and how it can enrich your life. I spent most of my life searching for an
ideology or religion I could wrap myself around. I was angry at the God I grew
up with. It was not too long ago that I used to say Judaism only offered ritual,
no spiritual component. Now I find myself reaching toward spiritual renewal
through Judaism.

This part of my journey began in 1993 when I went to Ireland for a conference on the environment and spirituality. I took a workshop with Jack Korn-
feld, the author of *A Path with Heart* and one of the founders of Spirit Rock
Meditation Center. He was one of the most peaceful men I ever met. He was a
truly kind and serene soul. He practiced Buddhist *Vipassana* (insight meditation)[4] and combined it with some Jewish observances. I started exploring
meditation, which I had not really done in a consistent way for many years.
Most religious traditions have techniques to quiet the mind and discover the
divine within ourselves. Many practitioners believe that you must find one
form and stick to it. I found that I was not attracted to one form over another.
In fact, as I grew and changed, different forms served me better than others. I
used a mantra, a word or sound that was repeated. Sometimes I would use
movement or walking meditation or mudra, which is a hand gesture. Other
times, I would look into a flame or stare at a sacred symbol or a mandala.
Mandala is the Sanskrit word for sacred circle. I would draw my own
mandalas to release pain and sorrow as well as celebrate my healing and
wholeness (see *Mandala* in color illustration section).

In 1995, the book *The Jew in the Lotus: A Poet's Rediscovery of Jewish Identity in Buddhist India* by Roger Kamentz was published.[5] Listening to the
author speak, I became curious about Jewish practices. I went to hear some
Kabbalist lectures and heard one rabbi say, *If you can say om, why not
shalom?* A lightbulb went off in my head. Other practices I had been incorporating in my life were really no different from Jewish practices. Imagining
myself under a waterfall to wash away pain was no different from immersing
myself in a *mikveh* (ritual bath) for purification.

I bought some tapes and books on Jewish spiritual practices. To my surprise
I found there is a very ancient Jewish mystical tradition. According to Rabbi
David Cooper, the author of *A Heart of Stillness: A Complete Guide to Learning
the Art of Meditation,* Moses went on the first spiritual retreat when he went up

the mountain three or four times a day for forty days, without food or water, to gain a new level of intimacy with the Creator. Ancient Hasidim would go into caves or into the desert, withdrawing, praising God through the study of Torah and the psalms. It appears that throughout Jewish history, there have been Jewish mystics. Some emphasized the study of Torah, others prayer and service, and some combined them. It is only recently that people have been openly studying Jewish mysticism and the Kabbalah has become popular.

This year I had my own silent retreat and fast for twenty-four hours at Yom Kippur. I turned the phone, radio, and television off. I prayed formally from the prayer books, I spoke from the heart in a free-form prayer called *Hitbod-it*. I meditated, journaled, and read Jewish folktales for hours on end. I contemplated themes of forgiveness and love, and enjoyed visualizing a new way of living in joy with Shechinah, the female aspect of God, at my center. It was a beautiful and transforming experience. It has allowed me to appreciate my Jewishness and helped me to create my own meaningful rituals. Delving deep into my soul, I have created new artwork based upon inspirational quotes I have been collecting for a long time (see drawings in color illustration section). I believe it has been a long path home, but the more I have sought a spiritual life, the more I am drawn to my Jewish roots.

Judaism as a Constant
❧

As Rae has described, some survivors rediscover Judaism as a source of support and meaning. I heard from a few for whom Judaism has been a source of meaning, hope, and faith throughout their lives, including Shoshana, who writes the following.

Shoshana

In all the years that I was living through sexual abuse, the one part of me that remained clear and strong was my Jewish identity. My Jewish identity was a piece of me that no one could ever take away.

My volunteer work in my synagogue, helping to create women's liturgy for various events and women's retreats, has given me tremendous strength and empowerment on my journey to healing. I have also received support and love from several dear friends and a *chavurah*.[6] In this *chavurah* I put together and participated in a healing ceremony. What has been most helpful to me from this group is the unconditional love and support they have given me. When I first revealed my abuse, two other women in the group shared their stories as well. Out of twelve women in our group, three are survivors of childhood sexual abuse.

One of my therapists is a pastoral counselor, a wonderful rabbi who brings a spiritual dimension I have desperately been searching for. But this rabbi was not trained as a counselor for sexual abuse survivors, and it is only because of his generosity and willingness to read and learn that we are able to continue our work together. He has been able to help me through the use of prayers and *halacha* (Jewish law)[7] to stay connected to my Judaism and find strength and comfort as I heal. Bringing G-d and spirituality into healing work has been really important for me.

In an e-mail from Hillary, whose poem and collage are in chapter 1, she writes:

Despite the fact that the professional Jewish community played relatively no role in my healing, both the religious practices of Judaism and its spiritual underpinnings had a huge impact on my recovery. Practically, I found refuge in Jewish ritual—from Shabbat and holiday observance to synagogue attendance to immersing in a *mikveh* for purification and cleansing from my past. Spiritually, my struggle to rectify my God concept with my life experiences helped me find a new and stronger faith. God may not have immediately answered my childhood pleas to be rescued, but God gave me the strength to carry on between encounters with Grandpa. And God gave me the talents and skills I needed to find success in other arenas so that I could develop self-confidence and a strong sense of who I wanted to be at times when I hated who I was (a victim). Thus, while the Jewish community did nothing that directly aided me in dealing with the incest, Jewish synagogues, Jewish teachers, and Jewish leaders offered me a Jewish environment in which I found the meaning, hope, and faith to heal myself.

As Melanie Kaye/Kantrowitz writes, "claiming Jewish identity isn't easy." In 1963 I was the only Jewish student in my grammar school by the time I graduated from eighth grade. Our shul didn't educate girls, and my parents didn't involve me in other forms of Jewish education. I don't know the traditions or rituals very well. I'd like to. I find comfort in the sights and sounds of Judaism sometimes. Where to begin? I'm not sure. In 2000, I took a beginner's class on Kabbalah. I loved some of the teachings, but the autocratic style of the teacher and the sexist bias of the center made it the wrong place for me to affiliate. If I want more, I'll have to keep searching and be willing to be a beginner. I believe Jewish institutions and individuals could make this search easier. This will require their looking at things differently, perhaps broadening their mandate to include bringing in those who are disenfranchised whether by bad experiences or no experiences (with Judaism). Incest survivor Briana Rose says that in order to participate in any Jewish religious groups, holidays, or institutions, she would "have to find a group willing to talk about what really is going on in our families and how it has affected our trust—including our trust in God."

Whether certain or uncertain about what Judaism has to offer, the following chapter by Marcia Cohn Spiegel introduces some of the ways women have found to create rituals that heal, that integrate their Jewish selves. Spiegel's chapter also identifies some of the challenges that language, culture, and patriarchy present.

Survival and Recovery
Jewish Women Confront Abuse

MARCIA COHN SPIEGEL

> *In her heart she is a mourner for those who*
> *have not survived.*
> *In her soul she is a warrior for those who are*
> *now as she was then.*
> *In her life she is both celebrant and proof of*
> *woman's capacity and will to survive, to*
> *become, to act, to change self and society.*
> *And each year she is stronger, and there are*
> *more of her.*
>
> Andrea Dworkin,
> Letters from a War Zone:
> Writings 1976–1989

Introduction
೨

When I was a small child I never questioned my parents' right to hit me. It didn't occur to me then, nor even later when I was learning about violence in the Jewish family, that hitting a two-and-a-half-year-old with a belt buckle was more than inappropriate punishment. I knew that my folks were pillars of the Jewish community who could do nothing wrong, and I was constantly reminded that I was a very naughty girl. As an adult, married to an alcoholic, I sought help from my parents, my rabbi, and finally a psychotherapist. Each one assured me that it must be my fault that my husband drank, since Jews didn't do this. If only I would change, things would be better. To them I was still a very naughty girl. It took many years before my desperation led me to a Twelve Step recovery program for families of alcoholics.

As a Jew, I was nervous and uncomfortable attending meetings in a church and reciting the Lord's Prayer. I was filled with shame at what brought me to St. Peter's by the Sea Presbyterian Church. I felt that everything that happened to me was my fault. My Jewish roots were so strong that it was a struggle for me to embrace the program without abandoning the values and practices of my own religion. I learned to read the prayer book in a new way and to reexamine concepts that I had once accepted without a second thought. The love and support of others in the group nurtured me in my pain and taught me the importance of a higher power in my daily life. They helped me to find my own strength to survive. In that Christian setting I found a deeper appreciation of Judaism and my own ability to heal.[1]

At the same time, I was busy creating programs and religious services for my local synagogue, Temple Menorah. One of my projects was collecting prayers and poems by Jewish women for an anthology.[2] As I typed out the words of Jewish women through the ages, I experienced their feelings, their pain, their hopes, and their faith, and I took their words into my heart and soul. I identified so strongly with their experiences that I embarked on a journey to redeem their lives as well as my own.

I grew up in a world where it was widely accepted that Jews didn't drink, use illegal drugs, or commit acts of sexual or domestic violence. I assumed that I must have been the only Jewish woman in the world who had memories of beatings, or lived with an alcoholic. Recently these myths have been dispelled by newspaper headlines and magazine articles that describe how Craig Rabinowitz killed his sweet Jewish wife for her insurance money in order to support his stripper girlfriend;[3] how Shlomo Carlebach, beloved, saintly storyteller and singer, sexually abused girls as young as twelve;[4] how an Orthodox couple battle for custody of their teenaged daughter, who had been the victim of incest from a very early age;[5] and how two Chassidic rabbis fondled a young girl on a transcontinental flight.[6]

Even though these events were well documented, the community did not believe them and often tried to silence those who spoke out. Protestations of innocence were made to protect the perpetrators. The accusers were disbelieved or made to feel responsible. The Jewish community's first response was to protect its own image of abstinence and propriety. But the publication of these and other incidents of murder and abuse by Jews in major newspapers around the country have forced us to face unpleasant truths. Our secret is out. We can no longer pretend that violence and abuse do not take place in Jewish homes. We have to confront the unpleasant reality that has been concealed for ages behind the facade of *shalom bayit,* peace in the house.

The sages taught that God seeks peace in the heavens, between the nations on earth, and between husband and wife. They tell us that "the ultimate achievement of peace on earth depends upon its achievement in the smallest social unit—the family." For centuries, Jews created a protective barrier between themselves and the hostile world around them by portraying the Jewish family as a loving, supportive, protective unit. *Shalom bayit*, peace in the house, rather than the ideal toward which we strive, became the yardstick by which we measured ourselves.

This idealized image is inconsistent with both our tradition and our history. In the Bible we read about the murder of Abel by his brother Cain, the incest that occurred between Lot and his daughters, the violence of Joseph's brothers against him, the rape of Dinah and her brothers' murderous vengeance to clear her name, the rape of David's daughter, Tamar, by her half-brother, and the sacrifice of Jephthah's daughter to her father's pride and vanity. The Talmud (Sanh. 51a) debates whether stoning or burning is the appropriate punishment for perpetrators of incest. Ecclesiasticus informs us that "gold must be hammered and a child must be beaten." In turn-of-the-century Yiddish fiction, and in letters from the "Bintel Brief" (an advice column in the *Jewish Daily Forward*),[7] we learn about families in trouble, about rape and murder, and sexual abuse. Now, in addition to stories of battery and violence among heterosexual families, we are learning about the same behaviors in lesbian and gay couples. Community attitudes are slow to change despite the new information that contradicts our long-held beliefs.

For many centuries we women were silenced by our belief in the reality of *shalom bayit* and suffered indignities without protest to protect the reputation of our husbands or fathers, our mothers, wives, or children and to shield the Jewish community from shame. Nevertheless, with the close proximity of families in the shtetls (small Jewish villages in the Pale of Settlement) and in ghettoes such as the lower East Side of New York, the truth could not be hidden from neighbors. It was never, however, a subject for open conversation. Women remained mute, not revealing what happened behind closed doors.

As recently as twenty years ago, Jewish social service agencies rarely saw a client who revealed a history of sexual or domestic violence. When rabbis, psychologists, or marriage counselors heard a story of abuse, they were apt to say, "What are you doing to cause the problem? Jewish men don't beat their wives or children . . . or drink . . . or commit incest." The victim was blamed for the perpetrator's behavior. When a woman heard this response to her plea for help, as I did, it reinforced the idea that she was the only Jewish woman living in such a situation. Not only did she feel responsible for what was happening to her, she also felt tremendous shame for her own and her family's condition. She might never feel safe enough to risk telling her story to anyone else; she would continue to suffer silently and, possibly, even to die. Like me, she might find help outside the Jewish community, feeling guilty about sharing her secrets with non-Jews; or she might become involved in a cult where she found the spiritual comfort and support she craved. Some women left Judaism; some left home; others remained and continue to suffer.

In 1987 when Evelyn Torton Beck and I conducted a workshop on sexual abuse and domestic violence at a meeting attended by many Jewish women theologians, rabbis, philosophers, poets, and teachers, we were shocked that of the twenty-three women participating in our workshop, nineteen reported stories of physical or sexual abuse in their childhood. Since then, whenever I lecture or facilitate a workshop on addiction, spirituality, abuse, or creativity, women (many of whom are leaders in the Jewish feminist spirituality movement) tell me their stories of sexual abuse and violence. These stories still distress me, but I am no longer shocked. Although I do not believe that everyone who is struggling to change the patriarchy has been physically or sexually abused, I do believe that many women who have been abused are engaged in the struggle to reshape Judaism.

With the advent of the feminist movement we got a powerful new message that women are fully human and are entitled to be treated as such. In small groups the stories began to be told. Brave women spoke out to others who listened, who heard our voices, and who gave us the support we longed for.[8] We learned that we are not alone and that change is possible. Some of us went on to try to change Judaism to include our voices and our life experiences. We do the work of *tikkun olam,* repair of the world. We band together to create changes in existing religious institutions and community organizations; we create new organizations to reach out to others who have been abused; we create support networks; we tell our stories to force the world to hear our voices. Our own healing is strengthened and our lives made whole as we reach out to others.

In this chapter I will describe some of the methods that we are using to survive, to recover, to heal ourselves, and to find a place in Judaism that does not require us to separate into parts: woman, Jew, survivor. To survive, we are seeking the spiritual strength that allows us to go on, to learn to trust again, to believe in a God who will protect and nurture us. In my own recovery I had to reinvent God for myself so that I could awaken each day with a sense of purpose and joy. Healing does not occur in a moment. Healing is a process that begins with naming the pain and deciding to grapple with it. One prayer or ritual act, whether traditional or newly created, or one piece of creative liturgy will not heal the deep wounds. Rather, these are the first steps on a path of reentry into the Jewish community that many of us felt had abandoned us in our time of need. By framing these rituals, liturgies, and images within Jewish tradition, we create a comfortable setting to introduce a Jewish spiritual dimension to the process of recovery.

Speaking to God
∾

For me the hardest part of finding my "higher power" was defining my own belief in God. I could not accept an all-powerful male God who would allow the pain and suffering of His children or the bearded judge on the throne described in the prayer book. I learned that I was not alone; other women who have suffered abuse and betrayal by father, husband, rabbi, teacher, or another trusted man in our life struggle with our traditional invocation, "Lord our God, King of the Universe." We cannot find solace and comfort in an anthropomorphic God envisioned as father, king, or omnipotent judge; even shepherd no longer seems a benign image. We have difficulty praying to a God who acts in history. Where was He while we suffered? Why didn't He take care of us? Why did He abandon us?[9] We need a God of tenderness, nurturing, and caring; who protects us and is present in our daily lives, a God we can trust, who brings us peace.

Contemporary Jewish women who searched for these qualities in God found them in the ancient concept of Shechinah, the indwelling presence, who has become central in many women's prayers, rituals, and songs. She is a quality of God whom we can feel surrounding us as we go through the day. She is accessible to us, not removed by distance and power. We are recreating an ancient ideal, and redefining Her for our own needs. She is a source of nurturance and support. In my own search for a higher power, I recognized it in the words of Debbie Friedman's song "The Angels' Blessing" that reminds us that the spirit of Shechinah gives us strength, spiritual guidance, and healing and surrounds us with love.

When we first tried to replace masculine God language with feminine names, the result was often dissonant and jarring. All we had done was substitute a feminine hierarchical figure for a masculine one. Marcia Falk was one of the first Jewish women to explore traditional sources for nonanthropomorphic names and images of God that still retain the power and beauty of language and image in both Hebrew and English. Her *Book of Blessings* offers new ways to address God and prayers in which we become partners with God.[10] In one of her new blessing formulas, she has replaced "Lord, God, King of the Universe" with "N'varekh et ein ha-hayiym" (Let us bless the source of life); humans sharing the power of blessing with God. A few of the other descriptions of God that Falk introduces are: wellspring of life, source of life, source of faith, breath of all life.

One of the most important prayers in the High Holy Day liturgy is Avinu Malkenu, "Our Father, our King." The frequent repetition of the names and images of God as Father and King, in both Hebrew and English, can be profoundly disturbing not only to abused women but to other men and women as well. The solution of one women's prayer group, Shabbat Shenit, was to sing the traditional melody of the prayer while introducing a variety of new names and images of God, including the traditional "our Father, our King," but adding such alternatives as Mothering Spirit, Shechinah, Merciful Parent, Infinite Wisdom, Indwelling Presence, among others. Singing new words to the ancient melody was a profoundly important and moving experience for many of the men and women present. Retaining the familiar melody grounded the prayer in tradition while at the same time altering the discomfiting text.[11]

As we explore new language, metaphors, and images, we should be aware of problems that persist when we make these changes. If names and descriptions of God are related to parental or authority figures in our personal histories, no single alternative will work for everyone. Feminine God-language might be attractive to a woman who was abused by her father, but it may not meet the needs of someone who was abused by her mother. We must remember that sons as well as daughters are abused; men and women are abused; women as well as men are perpetrators. While we are still suffering, any gendered references to God may be difficult. References to power, might, and even protection and caring may trigger strong feelings of abandonment and may remind us of our betrayal at the hands of someone we trusted.

As we move into recovery, will we be able to accept a broader vision of the nurturing, healing qualities in masculine images and the powerful, protective vision in feminine images? Will we find comfort in nonanthropomorphic descriptions such as "the breath of all living things" and "the unseen sparks"? Do we need to picture God as a Being in order to feel a relationship with God? Will we find the courage to begin to express our rage at a God by whom we have felt betrayed and to rediscover our belief in a God who will not only protect us from harm but also empower us to protect ourselves?

Transforming Familiar Rituals
↜

Women have begun to invent new rituals to mark stages of their recovery from abuse. Many of these new rituals are based on familiar Jewish practices. Religious rituals, rites, ceremonies, and even folk traditions play a role in our lives, in family celebrations, life-cycle events, and death and mourning. We perform some in the synagogue, others at home. These ceremonies represent moments of transition in our life: joy and sorrow, life and death. Using elements of worship that are part of our tradition may give a new ritual the emotional resonance that makes it effective in healing and recovery. The rituals I will describe were created for women, but they can be adapted for men or boys.

One of the oldest religious rites is that of ritual immersion, *mikveh,* described in Leviticus 15. Ritual immersion was required to achieve a state of purity before entering the Temple in Jerusalem. It was also performed by both men and women to cleanse oneself after any bodily discharge. After the destruction of the Temple, the laws of *mikveh* applied only to women, regulating our ongoing cycle of menstruation, contamination, and purification, which were known as the laws of family purity. For traditionally observant Jews, the laws of family purity are considered of utmost importance in maintaining the sanctity of the Jewish home and the enhancement of the spiritual life of the Jewish woman. Many contemporary women, however, consider this control of conjugal relations and activities during menstruation, as well as the rigorous physical examination required prior to resuming marital sex after childbirth or menstruation, to be an onerous and humiliating experience. While many women have abandoned the practice, other women find that it enhances their relationship with their spouse, and even non-Orthodox women are incorporating this ritual into their lives. A transformed use of *mikveh* is becoming an important step in rituals for healing.

Women entering the *mikveh* immerse themselves totally, and allow the water to purify their body and their soul, and arise refreshed and spiritually reborn. While they are immersed, they can allow the painful memories of the past to be washed away as they envision a better life in the future. The ceremonies of healing in which I have participated took place not in ritual baths, but rather in rivers, streams, hot tubs, and swimming pools made holy by the spiritual act of the ceremony. Women recovering from incest, childhood abuse, or wife battering immersed themselves, surrounded by friends who floated them, supported them, and circled them with love, and they emerged feeling cleansed and healed.[12]

In biblical stories and legends, the prophet Miriam personifies the connection between healing and water. Miriam saved her brother Moses by putting him into a basket, which she carefully floated in the river. The Pharaoh's daughter rescued him from the river so that he could go on to become a great leader. The sages tell us that Miriam's presence was responsible for a miraculous well that provided water for the wanderers in the desert. The Well of Miriam disappeared when she died. Miriam's name is now being invoked in a blessing over water. For many women who have been abused and violated by a perpetrator who used alcohol, or whose own struggles with alcoholism and addiction resulted from her abuse, the traditional blessing of wine, recited every Sabbath and on all festivals and holy days, is not an acknowledgment of God's grace. The introduction by the feminist spirituality community of Kos Miryam, the cup of Miriam, which blesses water, or mayim khayyim, the water of life, provides a new opportunity for blessing, which includes the image of purity and sustenance. A ceremony developed by a women's group, Kol Isha, includes the following blessing: "Zot Kos Miryam. Kos Mayim Khayyim, Khazak Khazak V'Nitkhazeik. This is the Cup of Miriam, the Cup of Living Waters. Strength, Strength and may we be Strengthened. . . . N'varekh et Eyn ha-Khayyim she-natnah lanu Mayim Khayyim. Let us Bless the Source of Life that gives us living waters."[13]

The story of Miriam and Moses and the salvation of the Jews from slavery in Egypt is told as part of the traditional Passover seder. It is a time when families come together to retell the story of the Exodus and to dine on a sumptuous meal, but it is also a time when family relationships, tensions, and expectations are heightened. Many women feel excluded from the seder if the perpetrator of her abuse is present, and that abuse is still not acknowledged or atoned for.

Seders are held on the first two evenings of Passover by the traditionally observant, and only once by the Reform movement. We drink four cups of wine (or grape juice) during the ceremony. A special cup of wine is placed on the table for the prophet Elijah, who is expected to announce the coming of the Messiah. Many people are now adding a cup of water to honor Miriam; Kos Miryam symbolizes women's role in the redemption. In fact, artists are creating special cups to be used for this purpose. The name Egypt, Mitzrayim in Hebrew, is translated as "from the narrow place." The image of the struggle to come through the narrow place to a place of freedom is a metaphor for the birth canal, and the struggle of the newborn to come through the narrow passage. Jewish women all over the world have begun to celebrate a third, feminist seder that recounts the story of women's bravery, courage, and struggle.[14] Women in recovery at the Los Angeles Family Violence Project of Jewish Family Service created their own Haggadah to validate their journey to freedom and a new life.

Women have reclaimed Rosh Hodesh, the celebration of the new moon, another appropriate time for ceremonies of healing and recovery. All over the world, Jewish women, spanning the spectrum from secular to religious, gather on the eve of the new moon to perform rituals, to learn together, and to share their feelings and the stories of their lives.[15] In the Bible, the ceremony for Rosh Hodesh is described as a time for the blowing of trumpets and special sacrifices (Num. 10:10, 28:11). The Talmud says that women are not permitted to work on Rosh Hodesh. It was also said to be a time to wear new clothes, eat newly ripened fruit, and begin a new book. Tradition tells us that the celebration of Rosh Hodesh was given to women as a reward for saving their jewelry for the creation of the ark rather than for the casting of the golden calf. Because there are no descriptions of how women celebrated in the ancient past, we are free to create our own rituals. Many Rosh Hodesh groups read and discuss a text about women, relate it to their own experience, and give it a new interpretation. The groups are often small, and the intimate setting provides a safe environment where women who have been abused can feel safe to tell their stories and get the support and acknowledgment they need from other Jewish women. It has been my experience that when one woman tells her story, other women are given the courage to share theirs. Groups are often amazed to learn how many members have been abused. Together the work of healing can begin.

The final traditional ritual which I will describe is Havdalah, separation, that marks the close of the Sabbath. It is another ceremony that lends itself to healing and recovery. Havdalah is usually a short, simple ceremony that takes place on Saturday evening after the first three stars appear, marking the transition from the holiness of the Sabbath to the week that is starting. Blessings are recited over braided candles, wine or grape juice, and spices. Songs are sung to recall the peace of the Sabbath day and anticipate the arrival of the prophet Elijah (and in some groups to Miriam as well). The sensory richness of the candlelight, wine, spices, and music, and the clear demarcation between the holy and the profane allow multiple interpretations of the meaning of separation. We have begun to use this rite to separate from the pain of abuse and to mark a return to a state of wholeness and healing.

Creating New Rituals
ᴥ

In addition to creating ceremonies that reframe tradition, women are introducing new rituals that use familiar symbols, prayers, and music. Savina Teubal created such a new celebration for her sixtieth birthday, a Simchat Hochmah ritual, to mark her transition into aging and to acknowledge the accumulated wisdom of the elders.[16] Inspired by Savina, I celebrated my sixtieth birthday with a Simchat Hochmah Havdalah. I adapted the Havdalah service as an appropriate transition from the turmoil following the deaths of my husband and parents and to mark my own recovery as I entered a new stage of life. I accepted the inevitability of aging, assumed full responsibility for my life and its consequences, and let go of my anger and blame for past events. Preparing the service enabled me to focus on the lessons of my life, what I chose to hold on to and what I chose to let go, remembering that life is part of an eternal cycle.

I combined familiar elements with new prayers and music so that the service would seem familiar to the congregation despite innovations, such as a naming ceremony and sukkat shalom, a tent of peace. Friends who were in need of healing for physical and mental pain came forward to be wrapped in my grandfather's tallith (prayer shawl) while Debbie Friedman sang a prayer of healing, "Mi Shebeirach,"[17] whose words were based on the traditional prayer of blessing for renewal of body and renewal of spirit.

Savina and I both took on new Hebrew names at our ceremonies. Changing one's name or adding a new name is a way to mark a new stage of life. When Avram made a covenant with God, his name was changed to Abraham, and his wife, Sarai, became Sarah. A convert to Judaism takes on a Jewish name. According to folk custom, the name of a dying person might be changed to outwit the hovering angel of death. At her Simchat Hochmah service, Savina took on the name Sarah because of her identification with the biblical matriarch. Our parents gave us our names, usually honoring a deceased family member if we are Ashkenazi or a living relative if we are Sephardi. Names may be reminders of events and people with whom we want to disassociate ourselves. Our names define us; a new name can redefine us and help us see ourselves in a new light. The power of naming was given to Adam by God, and naming ourselves gives us the power to create ourselves anew.

At my Simchat Hochmah service, those in the congregation who wanted to rename themselves came forward to stand under my grandmother's hand-crocheted tablecloth. The cloth was held high by friends, like a huppah (a wedding canopy). Together we recited the blessing, which Marcia Falk had written for Savina:[18]

Let us sing the soul in every name,
and the names of every soul.

I chose to take the name Miriam because of my identification with the prophet's bravery and because of her survival in the face of adversity. I use my new name whenever I am honored by being called to the Torah. You can imagine my pride when, on the occasion of her adult bat mitzvah ceremony, my daughter Linda was called to read from the Torah as the daughter of Miriam, and later when I was called to read from the Torah at my granddaughter's bat mitzvah by that name.

Savina conceived the idea of changing from ordinary clothing into a kitel, a white garment normally given to men to wear at their wedding and then worn for Passover and Yom Kippur services and, finally, as their shroud. I recognized the inevitability of death as part of life's cycle as I changed out of the black dress of mourning into the white gown which for me symbolized both hope and death. Each time I put on this kitel, for Passover seder or Yom Kippur, I am reminded of my hopes for renewal and recovery. Savina and I also each planted a tree, recognizing that we sow now for others to reap. We each made promises for our lives, and for charity, our own covenant with God. My vow was to continue in the work of helping others move into recovery and heal their wounds.[19]

In addition to words of Torah and prayer, I told stories about my life. Storytelling has traditionally been a way for women to share the truth of our lives. In a story, we can use the life of another woman to represent our own experiences; we can portray evil at its worst and heroism at its finest; we can express our sorrow and our outrage; and we can experience redemption, even justice. This ancient part of our folk culture has become significant in the creation of new rituals for all women and is another powerful tool for women recovering from abuse.

For most of Jewish history, retelling and interpreting biblical stories, creating Midrash, was exclusively a male activity; now as women add their voices, new meanings are given to old stories, and new understanding from traditional texts. One exciting use of storytelling as ritual took place on the night of a midsummer full moon, Tu be-Av (the fifteenth day of the month of Av). A group of women gathered out-of-doors to exchange white garments and to retell the story of the sacrifice of Jephthah's daughter by her father to fulfill his rash pledge to God. We also told the horror story of the rape and murder of the unnamed concubine of Bethlehem. Under the bright light of the moon, we turned the stories around, changing the endings to add women's redemption and survival to these brutal tales of murder, rape, and abuse.[20]

I have described only a few of the ceremonies in which I have participated; many other new ceremonies are being developed throughout the Jewish community as women seek a path to healing that uses Jewish ritual, is grounded in our past, and allows us to move into the future. Each Jewish holiday, season, and celebration offers additional symbols and ceremonies to be adapted and used for transforming our lives and for healing from abuse. Incorporated into a new ritual, these symbols still resonate with tradition. Rites of joy and celebration may help us to move on, while other rites may allow us to act out our rage.

More than one ritual will probably be needed as a woman moves through the process of recovery. Different stages of recovery can be marked by different rituals. It is important to remember that what works for one woman may not be appropriate for another. A woman who has negative associations with *mikveh* may not want to use immersion as a rite of purification. A woman who is uncomfortable exposing her body to others will not find spiritual strength if she is forced to disrobe for the *mikveh*, even with her friends. A woman who has not been involved in Jewish ritual life may find meaning in ceremonies that will provoke quite a negative response from a woman who comes from a traditional background. Sensitivity to each individual must be the guide. The recovering woman should participate in the planning so that the ritual will meet her needs at that moment. As she moves forward in recovery, her needs will change and so must the rituals created for her.

Repentance and Reconciliation
 show

The High Holy Day season is a time of repentance and reconciliation. Elul, the month preceding the New Year, Rosh Hashanah, is supposed to be spent doing the work of atonement, making amends to those whom we have wronged and healing spiritual and emotional wounds. This solemn time culminates in the Day of Atonement, the Yom Kippur service. The Kol Nidrei prayer, recited on the eve of Yom Kippur, is one of the most solemn prayers in Hebrew liturgy. It is chanted three times as Jews ask forgiveness for their transgressions against God. (Transgressions against another person can only be forgiven by that person.) A contemporary interpretation of the Kol Nidrei prayer is to allow ourselves to forgive our shortcomings as we vow to behave differently in the year ahead; we can use this time of introspection to rewrite our life's script. It is a time of cleansing, purification, and renewal. For all Jews it is a time of healing.

These holy days are often a particularly stressful time for survivors of abuse because of the focus on forgiveness. How do survivors live with the painful memories of acts of cruelty perpetrated against them, acts that are truly unforgivable? Judaism does not teach us to automatically grant forgiveness to those who have wronged us. Rather, it is the wrongdoers who must come forward to ask forgiveness for their deeds. It is they who must do *teshuvah*. *Teshuvah* means to turn away from evil, to turn toward good, to return to God. In the twelfth century, Maimonides ("Hilkot Teshuvah," Sefer ha-Madda) described four steps of *teshuvah:* regret or remorse for one's actions, renunciation of the behavior, confession of the wrong and a plea for forgiveness, and finally a pledge to change one's life so as not to repeat the act. (The twelve steps of Alcoholics Anonymous are a parallel to those described by Maimonides.) The proof that one has done *teshuvah* is that when confronted with the same scenario, one behaves differently.

The dilemma for the victim of abuse is how to relate to a perpetrator who does not admit to the evil, who does not take responsibility for his or her deeds. How do you heal or feel complete when someone whom you loved and trusted betrayed that trust and does not make any effort to bind up the wounds? How do you interact with your family when the perpetrator is safe and secure while you are forced to flee? How do you respond to parents, grandparents, or other family members who act as if nothing has happened to you, who may even blame you for being a reminder of a part of themselves that they would like to forget? Why does a daughter or son refuse to celebrate a holiday with the family, come home for Passover, or attend a wedding or a bat or bar mitzvah? One friend of mine who could not attend the family seder reminded her mother that she had not yet come to terms with her father's acts of rape and incest; she was told by her mother, "But that was so long ago. You should forget about it. Let bygones be bygones." For someone who is still suffering from flashbacks and night terrors, who is struggling to recreate herself, "forgetting about it" is impossible. In addition to her pain, she suffers the denial and abandonment of her family, another betrayal.

If the perpetrator of the violence or abuse is dead, the problem may be complicated for the survivor. The yearly cycle of Jewish holidays contains many special moments to honor and remember the dead.[21] Yizkor, a memorial service, is part of the worship service on each of the four major holidays, Yom Kippur, Sukkoth, Passover, and Shavuot. During Yizkor we ask God to remember close family members who have died. Kaddish, the traditional prayer recited for the dead, is said by the mourners. Kaddish is thought by many people to be a prayer that praises the memory of the dead. Actually it is a prayer that praises God, and the power of God in the universe. The Kaddish prayer, said in community with a minyan (quorum of ten people), is recited daily for thirty days following a death in the family. When a parent dies, Kaddish is recited daily for a year. After the initial period of mourning, Kaddish is recited on the anniversary of the death as well as at the four Yizkor services.

How do victims of abuse memorialize a dead parent, spouse, or sibling who did not do the work of *teshuvah,* who never acknowledged his or her behavior or asked forgiveness? How is that person eulogized by the community if his or her acts were known? If they were secret? Do we who were victims say Kaddish? Do we attend Yizkor services? How can that time of memory be used to reconcile our feelings of loss, anger, and betrayal so that we can move beyond them? Those of us who have not shared our story of abuse will be reminded of the pain each time Kaddish is recited. If we continue to worship in our family's synagogue, we will hear the perpetrator's name read "in loving memory"; we will receive notices of the anniversary of the death every year, and we will sit in services where parents, spouses, children, and siblings are remembered for their loving, caring, nurturing presence on earth. The very act of putting up a headstone on the grave becomes a reminder of abuse. It may help a mourner to consider the recitation of Kaddish as a time to allow God's power to help move them forward in their healing, to become a partner with God in life. The following reading was prepared as a preparation for the recitation of Kaddish during memorial services:

> As we prepare for the Memorial Service, we must acknowledge that for some of us, this is a particularly difficult time. Many of us mourn for loved ones whose memories are a blessing; others of us have troublesome memories, unfinished business with those who died. Those of us who have not reconciled ourselves with family members cannot extol their lives, exalt their memories. But we cannot live forever with bitterness, anger, or rage in our lives.

While Judaism does not require that we forgive those who have perpetrated evil against us, in order to move toward *shlemut,* wholeness and personal integrity, in our lives, we can use this time of memory for our own personal healing and growth. Kaddish is not a prayer that praises the dead, it is a prayer that praises God, and the power of God in the world. As we recite Kaddish together with Jews all over the world, we remember that death is an inevitable part of life, we mourn those who died before their time, those who died in suffering and pain, those whose lives enriched the world, and we remember the living, asking healing for all who suffer so that they can move on.

For some of us victims of abuse, the first step toward healing may be an opportunity to express rage, anger, disappointment, loss, and betrayal. Most of us have been trained to keep these feelings to ourselves, and expressing them is frightening both to us and to those around us. There is fear that we will become uncontrollable. Society is quick to demand forgiveness for acts perpetrated against victims but does not allow us to express our feelings. Jewish ritual provides many opportunities for an individual to express remorse for the sins that he or she has committed and for which he or she must atone. No such prayer or ceremony exists, however, for expressing the feelings of a victim whose perpetrator does not acknowledge the wrong. It is possible that a ceremony, as part of a formal ritual, can provide us with an opportunity to express this anger in a safe, controlled setting. Keening and mourning rituals may be very useful; donning dark clothes, sitting on low stools, wailing and lamenting the lost inner child, releasing her spirit to allow it to grow and change might prove to be comforting. Other symbolic actions might involve breaking, tearing, crying, burning, casting out, and separation. By performing these ritual acts, we may be able to let go of the rage and move forward in recovery.

Conclusion
ﭏ

Following Maimonides' steps, the Jewish community can begin to do the work of *teshuvah* by speaking out and telling the truth. We can stop pretending that Jews are different from other people and accept the reality that physical and sexual abuse happens in "nice Jewish families." We can recognize that *shalom bayit,* peace in the house, is a goal toward which we strive, not a measure of who we are. Each family responds to the stresses of life in different ways, some functional, some dysfunctional. We do the best we can, and if we fall short of the sages' ideal, we recognize that we are human. It is not the community's shame when an individual fails. Rather, it is the responsibility of the community to recognize the problems, to reach out to the victims and encourage those who are suffering to seek help when they are in pain and in need of healing, and to provide the services and a safe environment for that healing to take place.

Other steps that the community can take to do *teshuvah* are vowing to change our ways and not continuing on the wrong path. We must begin this work of *tikkun olam* (changing and repairing the world) by reaching out to each other. We should advocate that synagogues and Jewish family agencies address the needs of those who are abused. We can work within our community and with other communities to make sure our voices are heard. We are beginning by doing healing in ceremonies, rituals, and new celebrations using stories and song, adapting old customs with new meanings, and banding together to force political and institutional changes. The work has only begun.

We seek *shlemut* (from the root of *shalom*), which means wholeness, harmony, completion. With *shlemut* we can achieve personal integrity, joining together the fragments of our souls, our bodies, and our psyches; we can reach out to family and community. In the *Guide for the Perplexed,* Maimonides sees this completion as the result of our unity with God, which manifests itself in our behavior. According to Rabbi Nachman of Bretslav, a human being reaches in three directions: inward to self, outward to other people, and upward to God. The secret, he adds, is that the three are one. When we are connected to self, we can reach out to others; when we reach out to others, we may come to know God.[22] Rabbi Tarfon tells us that "you are not expected to finish the task, but neither are you free to evade it" (Avot 2:21). And so we begin.[23]

Defining Community

RACHEL LEV

To understand the role of community, we must first define community. What beliefs, values, and actions are present in a caring community? What denotes a noncaring community? How is community important to survivors? Through story, commentary, and discussions with survivors and activists for nonviolence, this chapter begins to answer these questions. Together we will have to find the rest of the answers, for it is in creating community that we create peace.

When I use the word *community* I mean a place to belong, a place of safety, a center of resources, kindness, warmth, and human connection. In true community, members find a place of caring, hope, and shared life-affirming values. While there is conflict, people are committed to resolve those conflicts without violence. In addition, as discussed by Robert N. Bellah in *Habits of the Heart: Individualism and Commitment in American Life*,[1] communities remember their past and share stories of their successes and failures. They speak of shared suffering and the suffering they've inflicted. In community we can laugh and cry with others and not be shamed for being who we are.

Dr. Judith Herman explains that trauma survivors need the community to (1) acknowledge they've been harmed and to (2) take some form of action that assigns responsibility for the harm and helps repair the injury.[2] This latter is explored more fully in chapters 13, 15, and the appendices.

Elements of True Community
ﾔ

The following elements of community were described by Emunah; Esta Soler, executive director of the Family Violence Prevention Fund (FVPF);[3] and Barbara Engel, activist for nonviolence. "When you ask, 'What is community,' I think about the best time I was in community, living in Israel, in the Orthodox community," said Emunah, a thirty-three-year-old survivor:

Everyone knew you. You could not live in anonymity, and for me that was good. It brought me out of isolation. You walk down the street and people know you. They talk about you. They want to get in your business, but it's a way of interacting. You can't go drifting into nowhere Emunah land, which I can do so easily here in the States. I think there is a richness in that community way of living—a real richness.

The community Emunah describes is one with shared geography. Esta Soler sees that, for many of us, today's community is about shared feelings and values rather than shared geography. While it may have been a literal place in our childhoods, Esta observes that today most of us work in a community that is different from where we live, where our children go to school, or where we worship. The community Esta's daughter knows is a community of friends and activists who are involved in a variety of different occupations. Whether geographic or shared feelings and values, in community there is a sense that we are not alone. It's not just that we have our families. It is a connection to other people as well. We know that "our" community will be there for us in sickness and in health. That can exist whether or not people are geographically close.

Shared Values
↝

When you feel part of a community, Esta explains,

> You want to take care of people in that community. When somebody is in pain or hurting or has been wronged, you know it's important to step up to the plate and help that person. Or when somebody has done something wrong, you support sanctioning that person. Being part of a community means both being there for somebody who is in need and taking a stand when somebody is an actor of violence or violation. Members of a community don't turn their backs.

Emunah described a situation in which members of the community did turn their backs. She could not remember if the Israeli man in the story was a teacher or a rabbi but does remember that he was "booted" from a community in America because he was molesting children. Emunah told me, "He snuck back to Israel and started molesting kids again. Sometimes it would get found out. When I heard about it, I'd say something. I was not a popular person. I would say something and people would say, *Why are you ruining his name? He's trying to get a chance.*" This is not a caring community.

As Esta pointed out, "A community that tries to keep something evil from exploding into the public eye is not a community. It may be a network of friends, but it's not a community." She defines a community as a group of people who recognize that good and evil exist and who commit to work to make sure that their community values what is good. It passionately commits to doing everything it can to make sure its kids are safe and protected from bad things happening to them. Esta said that genuine communities emphatically assert, "We are not going to say that because it doesn't happen in my house, things are OK. We are not going to say that because it happens in somebody else's house and I don't really like that person that it's OK that bad things happen. That is *not* community. It may be a neighborhood and a geographic assignment, a collection of houses, but it's *not* community."

Esta concluded our discussion by saying,

> I grew up in a household where we were taught that the greatest good we could do was to do good for others and in the community. That's how our family measured whether or not we were successful. Whether it comes from religious doctrine or from your own internal sense of what's important, it's the right thing to do. It's something that I try to pass on to my daughter. *You are here to be a member of the community and to care about being a member of the community. When somebody is in trouble, you have to step up to the plate. Do something about it.*

Stepping Up to the Plate
✄

How do we apply these ideas about community to our individual lives? The following is a description of something a colleague witnessed at Kol Nidrei services in the year 5760 (2000). As you read it, ask yourself how you might feel and what you might do, if you saw something like this.

Yom Kippur 5760
by Alice Brody

My friend and I sat in the balcony of the sanctuary, gazing down on the silver-doored ark. The *chasan* (cantor) sang beautifully, and the congregants read responsively with the rhythm of people who have prayed together for a long time. We stood as they opened the ark, sat as it was closed. Up. Down. Up. Down. Pray together. Pray silently. *Daven* (pray). Sermon. Up. Down. Kol

Nidrei[4]—an ancient rhythm—a soothing ritual interrupted over and over and over again by that family in the front row.

How can I think about God and my sins when her hands are all over her sons—*gletting* (stroking) their hair, running her fingers through the hair at the base of their necks, sliding her hand down her teenage son's back, not leaving until she cups his buttocks. There was a rhythmic and erotic feel to it. People across the aisle stared surreptitiously. The couple in the row behind them was angry and moved over at the first opportunity. The couple in the row behind that was disgusted.

My friend said it has always bothered her. Though this is my first year at these services, others have watched this scene for years. It's not just the mother with her sons. The father returns the favor by stroking his wife's back—reaching out to hand wrestle one son, rubbing the back of another—slowly, erotically. One couple said, last year this couple couldn't get up to go to the bathroom without kissing. Now she's deeply massaging the tops of her husband's shoulders with one hand. Done with that, she leans as much of her body as she can onto his, laying her chest on his back, while draping her arms around him.

At first I told myself to just ignore it, so I turned my head in a different direction. But, you see, in that direction I heard the reverberation of an old man's hearing aid. I could handle, actually rather enjoy, his gruff and atonal *davening*, but the static from his hearing aid was a bit much.

I tried to think of reasons this family might be touching each other in this way. Perhaps they were in deep grief over someone's death, or maybe they were physically ill and needed to be connected in this way. Nah.

I prayed to God to bless these people and to lift my reactivity, but as I noticed it was bothering a lot of people, I started thinking—Wait a minute. Why should I pretend this isn't bothering me? I thought about talking to the couple myself, then decided to go talk to the ushers. I said, "You don't know me and this is going to sound strange, but there's something going on upstairs that's very disturbing." I told them, and while we all smiled awkwardly, an usher came to see what I was talking about. After watching a little while, he agreed that this behavior was totally inappropriate and agreed to follow up.

The service was almost over. The mother sat on the aisle, her husband next to her, her son's friend next, and then her son. As she reached behind her husband's back, she stretched to stroke her son and then his friend. The son's friend leaned forward as far as he could to get away from her touch. That seemed healthy. It frightens me that her sons stayed absolutely still, exhibiting neither pleasure nor discomfort as she had full access to touch them in whatever way she wanted. Something is wrong there—in that family and in that congregation.

For years, people watched this inappropriate behavior and did nothing but be miserable and complain. One woman said she was angry, asking, "Why don't they just go get a room?" I told her I spoke to the ushers and they said this was wrong and they'd do something. "You did?" she said, sounding surprised and a bit uncomfortable. Another woman was upset that I mentioned anything to anyone. This is not a caring community.

Conscious Community Members "Step Up to the Plate"
ꜣ

At the synagogue on Yom Kippur 5760, community members committed to the welfare of the community and its members would have said or done something. They might have said, "I'm uncomfortable with the way you're touching each other during these services. I'd appreciate it if you'd stop." If they couldn't confront the couple directly, they could have told someone else who perhaps could. Alice told the ushers. She also suggested the ushers tell the rabbi. I believe the rabbi has an obligation to check into this. Are these children involved in education at the synagogue? How could this be respectfully and directly addressed? Alice said she may send this story to the rabbi. What would you do?

Situations like the above arise in our daily lives providing opportunities to "step up to the plate." Here's an example of a situation I faced.

Monday, Monday
by Rachel Lev

I got on the bus after a very long day. I was not happy to see that it was standing room only. I moved toward the back, looking for a place I could at least be able to hold on. The bus pulled back into traffic, and I settled in for the stop-and-go ride home. I looked around at my fellow passengers and noticed, in the row right beneath me, a sweet-looking little boy, about three years old, sitting by the window. His mother was sitting closest to me, and she was very tightly wound. I could see her rapid pulse pounding in her temple. The little boy was moving around a bit in his seat and asked her something. She exploded, even though I don't think anyone else could have heard her. She grabbed his arm and yanked him, giving him a loud "sit still" look. His lower lip quivered as tears silently started to fall. As I watched—only inches away—she began unconsciously to fold the strap of her shoulder bag. I realized she was going to use it to hit him. I was horrified. I had to do something. As she folded the strap one more time, I looked down at her and smiled and said something about how cute her son was, but how hard it is sometimes to be a mom of a small child. Her eyes began to focus. Her grip on the folded strap loosened. I continued to talk with her, in a calm voice (not the one that was shouting in my head), occasionally talking to the little boy, asking his name and how old he was. Within a few minutes the strap fell from her hand and became just a part of her purse. I told her how lucky she was to have such a lovely boy. Will that scene happen again between them? Probably. I still believe that each time we act for peace, we change the world.

There is always something we can do. Even if it isn't in that moment. We can talk about what we see and brainstorm about what actions we can take the next time we see children (or adults) being harmed. We can recognize that somewhere this mother learned that what she was about to do was an answer, was OK. She'll need education and support to do things differently. We must hold her responsible *and* help. We can find out if our community has a drop-in center for stressed parents to come with their kids. If not, we can help one get established. We can sponsor seminars and bring in experts on conflict resolution, choosing nonviolence and the things we can do—at home and in the larger world. In true community, we pay attention to what goes on around us and intervene when needed.

Men and Women: Essential Partners for Peaceful Communities
✌

As Jews we believe we have a responsibility to repair the world, to bring *tikkun olam*. Part of that repair must include ending violence. In a discussion with Barbara Engel, an activist in the movement to end violence against women for twenty-five years, she pointed out that while much has been accomplished by women of all races, ethnicities, and religions to bring the issues of domestic violence and child abuse to public attention, more is needed. Barbara said, "We could celebrate all that we've done, but women are still being battered, children damaged by experiencing and witnessing violence. Girls are learning that victimization is to be expected;

boys are learning that using force and threats resolves conflicts and makes them feel powerful. We have not ended the violence."

Listening to Barbara, I thought of the times within the Jewish community when I heard rabbis or therapists talk about what girls and women need to do to avoid danger and the importance of teaching them how. That's not enough to end violence and puts the responsibility for violent acts on the potential target. As Gloria Steinem noted, the only time in U.S. history that the rate of abuse against women and children went down was during World War II.[5]

Barbara Engel believes "we need to do more than teach young women self-respect and their right to live free of fear. We must teach young boys the respect, empathy, mutuality, and equality that will prevent them from being abusive. We must hold men and women who abuse accountable for their crimes."

It is only with the help of "compassionate and caring men of conscience" that we can change men and women who molest, Barbara said. With more men joining in this work, becoming leaders in this work, she believes we can change the climate of denial and minimization. Without men and women's active and creative assistance, we cannot.

Barbara described some of what men and women need to do to end violence against women, including: (1) teaching our sons and daughters that being masculine does not mean the domination of others, (2) challenging coworkers, colleagues, friends, and relatives about abusive and controlling behaviors, (3) refusing to laugh about rape and abuse jokes and being willing to explain why they are not funny, (4) creating speakers' bureaus of men and women to talk about these issues with the seriousness and importance they deserve, and (5) stopping the marginalizing of sexual assault and abuse or labeling it as only a "women's issue" because, Barbara underscored, "If we care about creating loving Jewish homes, we need every one of us to be involved in this *tikkun olam*, this repair of our world."

My conversation with Barbara reinforced my belief that until this world is repaired, until there are no abused children, no battered women, men and women need to stop telling and/or laughing at jokes about Jewish women—whether characterized as Jewish American Princesses, high maintenance, or the guilt-tripping Jewish mother. They feed the notion that Jewish women need to be put in their place, that we ask a lot and often too much. These lead to the right to violate. If there is no negative bias in these "jokes," why don't Jewish father jokes abound? Or Jewish Prince jokes?

The sense of entitlement with which many Jewish men are raised needs also to change. This is a responsibility of their fathers and mothers, teachers and rabbis. If entitlement isn't a problem, how do we have members of a Jewish fraternity wearing "Slap-a-JAP" T-shirts? How do we have the daughter of a rabbi being told to keep quiet by her parents about having been gang-raped by members of a local Jewish fraternity? The boys were never held accountable for what they did. No one wanted to hurt their futures. Teen girls on "supervised" trips to Israel have had similar experiences. The problem is not just that these boys and young men feel entitled to take what they want. The problem is also the community's tendency to protect them and judge, isolate, and shame the girls they assault. This is not a healthy community.

I cannot leave this section without mentioning the fact that violence occurs not only in heterosexual relationships, but also in same-sexed couples, that women and men, boys and girls, can be victims and perpetrators. This is even more of a reason for men and women to join together to stop violence in our intimate relationships.

Listening to Survivors:
Interview with Esta Soler
ॐ

Esta discussed the fact that the violations of sexual abuse and incest are so privatized that it's really hard to be a leader and take a stand on these issues. She observed that the voices of survivors have been silenced, that they are not the primary voices in any of the nonviolence movements. She believes that to create communities of peace, we must listen to survivors. We must hear the voices of people who have real experiences, she said. I asked her why she thinks this is so important. She responded:

> I believe violence can be prevented. I don't think it takes magic to prevent violence, to help people heal, to create true community. It doesn't require degrees. It's common sense. When people who have been victims of sexual abuse, who have suffered in that way, speak out, they put a face to the issues. It's very hard to say it doesn't happen in my community when there are faces and voices saying it does.
>
> When you tell a story that's a personal story, it moves people. It also moves the person telling her story. The more people who tell, the

better we will be. If more people tell their stories, more kids will feel protected and able to come forward when something is not right. Once you get past the denial and silence, more and more people will be talking in their communities about these problems and wanting to make sure every home is a safe home. That's what community is all about—and where safety and healing happen.

Informed and Compassionate Leaders
⤳

Esta highlighted the critical role that rabbis, cantors, and educators must play in violence prevention and intervention. She emphasized the importance of reaching all of them because they are often in positions to hear about people who need help. In order to recognize what they're hearing and know what to ask, specialized training is necessary. "They need to know about the kinds of abuses happening in families and what they can do. We need to give them ways to talk about these problems," said Esta, emphasizing, "They are difficult problems to talk about. It's easier for most rabbis to talk about scriptures and *halacha* than about something having to do with child sexual assault or child sexual abuse. Once it's scripted for them, it is important that they bring what they learn into the liturgy." While not every rabbi, cantor, or educator is going to want to go to this kind of training, it seems to Esta that there should be a core group of rabbis, educators, and cantors willing to be trained—people who really care about these crimes of violence, these violations, that are happening in the home, in synagogues, and in schools. These core groups would then develop programs for their constituents. FVPF research has found that young people coming into a field are most receptive to learning about these issues. That is certainly a great place to increase our efforts.

Support Your Local Leaders
⤳

If children are to be safe, religious and lay leaders must know about domestic violence, sexual assault, and child abuse so that they are able to listen and inquire compassionately and speak openly with adults and children who may be in danger or who have been violated. What are we doing to educate those in training to be rabbis, cantors, and Jewish educators (and those who have completed their training)?

As the many stories in this book testify, much more is needed—*now*. What are we doing to help religious leaders and educators integrate teachings that build healthy relationships of mutual respect and honoring? And what are they doing to participate in this process? One rabbi told me he didn't do more because he feared becoming a "Johnny one note." He believed that each rabbi's effectiveness is hampered when he or she gets identified with a particular issue. He spoke about violence in Jewish lives in other states, but not in his congregation.

More rabbis and lay and religious leaders must initiate learning about these issues and put the safety of their congregants—from dangers *within* the Jewish community—on the top of their priority list. Community members must require, support, and applaud their doing so. We cannot let it be risky for them to do the right thing. As activists reach out to religious leaders and religious leaders reach out to activists, peace becomes ever-more possible.

Examples of True Communities in Action
᠊ᢌ

The following examples of communities in action are presented with the hope that they will inspire you to help expand or refine what is being done in your community.

In Baltimore, materials for teaching parents, rabbis, teachers, and children about the spectrum of family violence safety, including good and bad touch, were developed by Jewish Family Services beginning in the early 1990s. At that time, Dr. Lucy Steinitz reported that Jewish Family Services in Baltimore found that 25 percent of counseling cases had issues of family violence. At the same time, one in three of those in their children's unit identified abuse problems in their initial contact with the agency. According to Dr. Steinitz, one-fourth to one-third of all Jewish families are affected by child abuse.[6] When Dr. Steinitz and her colleague Susan Goldstein told lay members what they were finding, they weren't believed. Rabbis and lay leaders "poo poo'd that happening in their congregation or branch," said Steinitz. Knowing they had to get the community to own that it had this problem, Steinitz and Goldstein organized a task force of some of the most powerful community players and brought in experts who knew the facts. From that came a multilevel plan for awareness raising and intervention.[7]

In 2001 Jewish Family Services in Baltimore found that the placement of social workers in schools enables earlier identification of problems and effective intervention. Clinical staff receives ongoing training and consultation to help identify, treat, and/or refer people appropriately. A federal grant to the CHANA domestic violence program enabled rabbinic training sessions on abuse and the role of rabbis in prevention and intervention.[8]

In September 2000 in New York, a program was coordinated by OHEL, a local Jewish social service agency. At this program, "Let's Talk About What Never Happened . . . But It Did," open to the community, local rabbis and OHEL's executive director, David Mandel,[9] spoke compassionately about the pain of survivors and acknowledged that these abuses happen. While some survivors were disappointed at not having the opportunity to speak, the evening was seen by Mandel as a first step in shaping the way the community deals with this issue and a commitment to respond to the needs of victims and increase awareness. A letter from David Mandel dated April 18, 2001, indicates that more than two thousand tapes of this event had been mailed out to twelve hundred Rabbonim (rabbis) and seven hundred yeshiva and day school principals around the United States. Requests continued to come in from around the world.

In a Chicago community, news of a child molester in their midst led to publicity in the local Jewish press and a call to action. Response by the community has been strong and proactive. Rabbis, educators, experts in domestic violence, and lay leaders have begun a process of learning about the problem, identifying what is needed, pulling together appropriate resources, and politicking where needed. Curricula for schoolchildren, aimed at prevention, are being developed as are training programs for educators and rabbis.[10]

A therapist spoke with me about how unique this process continues to be:

> A special bastion of Orthodox rabbis, who span a broad range of the Orthodox community, was able to convene and continues to sit and deliberate how best to handle this. They work in consortium with mental health professionals and social service agencies within the broad range of the Jewish community as well as within a specific Orthodox community. Together we pool resources, experience, offer reality checking, validation, and support. It feels almost as if the power of denial and fear of the shame is thwarted by the strength of the community working together. Denial is still there. We struggle with it every day. It'll come up, and someone says, "Are we into denial today?" There is a continuous checking and rechecking. This is not an

ideal system. There have been politics, power plays, the usual community stuff, but people continue to rise above that. I believe the politicking and other stuff is denial dressed differently.

In another city, a cantor helps rape victims find their voices again while teaching them to sing. In northern California, members of a committee working with the Kehilla Community Synagogue have developed abuse prevention protocols in order to help Jewish (and other) congregations best create environments of safety and healing for all community members. The protocols are designed to be useful for prevention of, healing from, and response to situations of abuse in Jewish congregations.[11]

Their Kavanah (statement of intention) begins:

> As Jews we know that if one of us is enslaved or endangered, none of us is free. As a congregation we want to affirm that the safety and healing of every member of the community is one of our highest priorities. Therefore, it is incumbent upon us to eliminate abuse that occurs within our congregation, for abuse within any relationship jeopardizes the safety and healing of our members as well as of the community. We want to provide reliable and effective resources and support for personal and community healing and justice at all times. . . .
>
> Our responsibility is to promote the end of abuse, to prevent future abuse, and to give people the skills and resources to help themselves and each other. In particular, we want to create community structures that promote safety, help individuals learn how not to be abusive in interpersonal and organizational relationships, and support those who are abused.
>
> Therefore, we commit to establishing abuse prevention policies and procedures in all program areas. We set forth the following policies and procedures to provide healing and safety for past, present, and future situations of abuse. It is our hope that by instituting these policies and procedures, we will set in place a firm mechanism of prevention for us and future generations.

And much more is needed. Even in these proactive communities, Jewish adult survivors usually must create their own resources, their own rituals, because even where the topic of incest is on the table, few services or resources are available within Jewish organizations.

I am sure there is other good work being done that I have not heard about. In addition to those referenced throughout this book, I contacted a number of rabbis, therapists, organizations, and universities across the

United States and Israel that I'd been told were working with issues of sexual abuse and incest in their Jewish communities. For whatever reason, they didn't respond. The good news is, they're out there somewhere. The challenge is to find a way to share what we know across our diverse community so that those in need of help can find it and those providing help can have more resources to support them and those in need. I would love to see a central location of Jewish resources related to prevention and intervention of issues of interpersonal violence—an 800 number perhaps, or a website, reflective of our diverse Jewish community. I encourage rabbis, cantors, educators, and therapists who know Jewish sexual abuse and incest survivors to seek their input about what is needed and actively involve them in whatever they develop. (See *Shine the Light* website information in Appendix G.)

I believe child sexual abuse and incest happen because we let them. They will stop when enough of us assert, as the Kehilla committee has: "Abusive behavior is contrary to Jewish values and is unacceptable in this community. Such behavior will not be tolerated."

Who Serves the Best Interests of the Child?
⁊

In this chapter we have spoken about the responsibilities of individuals, rabbis, educators, cantors, men, and women to create communities of peace. I cannot leave this discussion without underscoring the responsibility of parents and the need to advocate for children in the larger community.

Most of the survivor voices in this book speak of having been molested by relatives, many by our fathers. Parents are accountable for what happens in their homes. All parents need and deserve the support of community to be able to create *shalom bayit*—peace in the home. Some ideas about what this takes are mentioned in chapter 15, "Building Communities of Hope," and in the appendices.

Remembering that we are each systems whose survival and well-being are dependent on the other systems with which we interact, we must look at individuals, families, religious institutions, schools, health care services, and the legal system as we work to build safety and tranquillity into our lives and the infrastructures of our communities. We must work to prevent child sexual abuse and to intervene to assure that community systems respond in the best interests of the child when abuse may be happening.

When children aren't safe in their homes, healthy communities have systems that serve the children's best interests. These systems include child protective services, enlightened legal systems, schools, physical and mental health services, and other resources. Too often, a child's worst nightmare is played out as courts award an abusing parent custody of the child.

In 1993, Gloria Steinem reported to an audience of trauma experts that, statistically, the most likely way for a woman to *lose* her child was for her to accuse a father or stepfather of sexually abusing that child. She went on to say that the more horrendous the abuse, the more likely she is to lose custody. This is despite expert testimony and evidence. This is despite the fact that sometimes there has been a conviction for sexual abuse. Those who testify on behalf of the child are often facing harassment charges themselves. Steinem suggested separating charges of sexual abuse from custody charges so that at least they can be looked at as separate events. The law in Los Angeles separates the two. Steinem concluded, "The future patients who will remember the abuse they experience not only by the parent, but also by the system are already in the making."[12] Judges and guardian ad litem especially need to be better educated.

Whatever we do in our individual networks that are closest to us, we must also attend to the larger world. One social worker pointed out that she and her colleagues are trying to figure out what can and needs to happen when someone found to be molesting children in their community decides to move. What obligation, what right do they have to tell the next school or synagogue of what has happened? And what happens if they do nothing?

The best solutions come when people within each community come together to say, "Yes, these abuses happen. We're committed to finding solutions and willing to take the time and dedicate the resources needed to create peace and safety in our lives and the lives of our children—at home, school, synagogue, and neighborhood. We are committed to helping those who've been abused to heal within our community, if they so desire. We are willing to see, to listen, to help." "The longer we refuse to pay attention to this issue, the more kids go through our synagogues who don't get help," said *Rabbi Carla*.

"As a teenager I lived in a car for a while," said Shauna Green.

> I was certain my parents were going to kill me. I wish there had been a safe house to go to—to get away from my parents. I wish there had

been some way to force them into treatment. It was my word against theirs. No one did anything. The schools made it into a behavioral problem. Family decided I was a discipline problem. I was molested in my temple by the rabbi and others. What do I want the Jewish community to do now? Instead of belittling, educate. Learn the symptoms of abuse. Learn what to do. Learn how you can reach out. Learn how you can provide support. People say they don't want to get involved because they'll make it messy. It's already messy. When we reach out to people in need, we can help.

Let's make it safe to speak about what happens so we can create healing solutions and healthy communities.

THIRTEEN

The Role of Rabbis, Cantors, and Educators in Preventing Abuse and Repairing Its Consequences

RABBI ELLIOT N. DORFF

The Challenge and Duty
๛

Sexual abuse is a complicated reality, causing harm to its victims and to those who know and care about them. To stop sexual abuse and incest in the Jewish community, we must look at the needs of child victims and adult survivors. We must develop ways to prevent future abuses and to confront and hold accountable those who molest. At the same time, we must also provide molesters with an opportunity to make amends for their past sins and to learn how to stop such behavior.

Sexual abuse and incest are bald exercises of physical might for purposes of exerting power over someone and/or expressing one's own frustration and aggression on innocent victims. Judaism unequivocally condemns acts of sexual abuse, whatever the excuse. Jewish law specifies punishments for those who strike others and demands that victims of such attacks do everything in their power to escape such situations in the future, even if it means defaming the assailant or embarrassing oneself and the perpetrator. Judaism also prohibits verbal abuse of all kinds.

Such an attitude on Judaism's part is deeply rooted in its theology and its overarching conception of the human being. In secular systems of thought, abuse is problematic because it violates the Golden Rule and more generous, humanitarian concerns. When the topic is abuse within the family, further matters arise, including the inherent violation of the sanctity of the family and the resultant inability of the family to provide the safety, warmth, and education on which society depends. Judaism shares all of these concerns, but it has more, for abuse of another represents a denial of God's image in every human being.

In this way, Judaism can provide a real source of strength for abused people struggling to escape from their situation and to rebuild their lives. No matter how much someone else has diminished our self-image, Judaism tells us, we must recognize that ultimately we are created in the image of God. Among other things, that means that like God, we have inherent worth, regardless of what anyone else says or does. That divine value represents a challenge to us, for we must each strive throughout our lives to realize the divine within us. It is also a source of comfort in trying times, for it gives life meaning and hope.

While rabbis, cantors, and Jewish educators may agree wholeheartedly with the above, many would probably ask what they can and should do to prevent sexual abuse, where possible, and what they can do to alleviate its consequences when it has occurred. The Clergy Advisory Board of the California Department of Social Services produced a brief pamphlet that was distributed to all members of the Board of Rabbis of Southern California as well as members of the clergy of all religions throughout the state.[1] The pamphlet focuses on child abuse, but its recommendations can easily be adapted to spousal or parental abuse as well. In the paragraphs below, I generalize and paraphrase the pamphlet's instructions to apply to jurisdictions outside California and to specifically Jewish concerns and contexts.

Two preliminary comments should be made before we begin with the specific recommendations. First, in all discussions of violence, we must be careful to distinguish acceptable forms of physical contact from those that are abusive. Our commitment to creating safety must distinguish supportive and loving touch from boundary violations that involve coercive, intimidating, or inappropriate touch, language, or actions. Even with supporting and loving touch, if a child or adult does not want to be touched, we must honor that person's wishes.

Second, prevention is far more effective than cure. Parents fully expect rabbis, cantors, and educators to help them make the Jewish tradition live in their own lives and those of their children; indeed, they join synagogues and enroll themselves and their children in a variety of Jewish activities precisely so that that will happen. Rabbis, cantors, and educators therefore have many golden opportunities to influence parents on all aspects of the Jewish tradition, including its lessons about sexual abuse. Because sexual abuse is so damaging, it is critical that rabbis, cantors, and educators take advantage of their opportunities to teach about proper and improper touch in any way and in any setting they can. The commandments requiring children to honor and respect their parents are very important, but the parents themselves must be taught that proper parenting demands that they refrain from sexually abusing their children while yet physically giving them love and affection.

What We Can Do
ᔓ

Learn to recognize abuse.   If rabbis, cantors, and Jewish educators fail to recognize the signs of abuse in their congregation, school, camp, or youth group, the abuse will undoubtedly continue. The opportunity to protect people from future abuse is often lost because of ignorance, denial, or fear of interference. Our professional schools and organizations should provide training for their students and members in how to discern potentially abusive situations, take family histories that include instances of abuse, provide religious counseling for abusers and their victims, and know which other professionals within the community should be called upon to help in both preventive and curative actions.

Do not assume that you can handle the situation alone.   Clergy, educators, and others who work with youth must learn how best to inquire about the possibility of abuse as well as what to do when they detect or suspect it. While such people can be critically important in helping victims and perpetrators of abuse, they should not try to do this alone. One clergy member is quoted in the pamphlet as saying: "A father divulged to me that he was molesting his daughter. He was repentant. I prayed with him, but did not seek further help to protect the victim. She later made a serious attempt on her life because, even after repentance and prayer, the father had continued to molest. It shook me."

As religious leaders, unless we are trained to understand and intervene in the areas of child sexual abuse, incest, and adult survivors, we should not do therapy with victims or perpetrators. Even volunteers working in domestic violence agencies are required to go through extensive training before they can answer phones or have contact with clients. In our role as spiritual counselors, our interaction with victims and perpetrators should focus on confirming that we believe the victim and that neither Judaism nor the Jewish community countenances the abuser's behavior. An essential part of our role is also putting the victim in touch with trained therapists and volunteers who can help. Working in partnership, we can provide what is best and right.

Know and obey your government's requirements to report abuse to legal authorities. Many states, provinces, and cities have enacted laws that require not only health care personnel, but also clergy and teachers to report abuse to legal authorities. Reporting requirements vary. California, for instance, wants rabbis and teachers to err on the side of overreporting abuse rather than under-reporting it: California law specifies that educational and religious professionals must report *suspicions* of abuse and leave it to legal authorities to determine whether those suspicions are founded. The laws in other places may be different, going further in the direction of protecting the accused. In cases of spousal abuse, reports are generally made to the police, and in some locations that is true for child abuse as well; in other places instances of child abuse are to be reported to the Office of Children's Protective Services (or the equivalent agency of state or local government).

Sometimes clergy or teachers become aware of abuse through the confession of a congregant in a private counseling setting, and that raises questions of confidentiality. California law specifically requires professionals to break professional-client confidentiality when the safety or physical welfare of a child or adult is involved, and it protects professionals from lawsuits complaining of such a breach of confidentiality. Jewish professionals should check whether the laws and/or judicial rulings in their legal jurisdiction follow suit.

In any case, rabbis and teachers almost everywhere have a legal responsibility to be on the alert for instances of family violence and to report such cases to legal authorities when civil law requires it. Failure to do so may subject rabbis or teachers personally, as well as the religious or educational institution for which they work, to both civil and criminal prosecution. Insurance companies are increasingly restricting their coverage so that they can avoid liability for such suits, thus making the rabbis and educators and their institutions all the more legally exposed.

Even if the laws in a particular location do not demand that clergy and educators report abuse to authorities, and even if local law does not clearly protect clergy and teachers when they break confidences to alert authorities to abuse, Jews should do all that is legally allowed to get help for those in abusive situations. Our tradition demands that we protect not only our own lives and health, but also that of others—even to the point of killing a pursuer (*rodef*). While contemporary law may not sanction going that far in protecting someone from abuse, we must do all that is legally allowed to get help for victims of abuse.

Protect your congregation or school from potential abusers. People who prey on children often seek positions that will give them access to, and authority over, children. Since potential molesters cannot be identified by mere appearance, synagogues, schools, youth groups, and camps should, as part of their hiring policies and procedures, take measures to screen out those likely to molest the children under their care. This is important not only for the institutions and their charges, but also for the molester, for we are mandated not to "put a stumbling block before the blind" (Lev. 19:14)—in this case, the morally blind who would be tempted to use their position of authority to abuse those in their care.[2]

As much as institutions must prevent molesters from being part of their staff, they also must avoid making unfair and unwarranted judgments of applicants. They must not base their decisions on prejudices—say, against males, or against homosexuals (the overwhelming majority of convicted child molesters are heterosexual). At the same time, though, background checks should include attention to this aspect of a person's history.

We must remove another stumbling block. Too often known perpetrators of sexual abuse manage to move to other congregations or Jewish schools. Authorities in the former settings are often reluctant to divulge their finding of abuse to those seeking information as part of the hiring process. In some cases, a misplaced sense of compassion for the abuser—and insufficient attention to the plight of current and future victims—motivates this silence. In other cases, fear of a lawsuit for defamation of character is behind the reticence to divulge past abusive behavior. If the abuse has been clearly evidenced and documented, that fear is unfounded. Some administrators understandably want to avoid any potential for a lawsuit by the abuser, even if they will almost surely win in court, because they do not want the expense of time and money involved in defending oneself in court. *If future students are likely to be abused by the person in question, however, Jewish law would require that administrators take on that risk and bother.*

Finally, some clergy and school principals do not disclose evidence of abuse in order to protect the reputation of their own institutions or professions. The truth, though, is that both professions and institutions are much better served when they openly admit their problems and take steps to correct them so that they do not happen again in the future. Nobody can reasonably expect that any human institution or profession will manifest only ideal behavior; after all, Jewish liturgy has us ask for God's forgiveness three times each day! What people can reasonably demand, though, is honesty in disclosing problems and responsibility in confronting them.

Religious and educational professionals are not beyond suspicion in matters of child sexual abuse. Due process must be applied in any investigation of such allegations, and the presumption of innocence must be preserved. If child or spousal abuse by a rabbi or educator is confirmed, however, other Jewish professionals on the staff and in the vicinity must be prepared to respond to the scandal and the public outrage. As the California pamphlet puts it, "While the needs of the victim are primary, compassion needs to be extended to the injured religious community and the perpetrator as well." We would undoubtedly add that steps must be taken to heal the community, help it avoid such incidents in the future, and bring the perpetrator both to justice and to the process of *teshuvah*.

Demanding and Accepting *Teshuvah*
⤳

When a fair hearing determines that there is sufficient evidence that a given person has abused another, in addition to whatever civil or criminal penalties apply, Jewish families and communities must first take steps to protect themselves and avoid any further abuse. This may mean, for a family, forcing the abuser to move out of shared quarters or, if that is impossible, moving out themselves. For a Jewish school, youth group, or camp, it may mean dismissing the person from his/her job and perhaps even ostracizing the abuser from the community.

At the same time, the Jewish tradition puts great faith in the ability of those who do wrong to make amends and correct their behavior. Judaism never expects us to be perfect but does impose a positive obligation on us to do *teshuvah*, to take steps to return to the proper path. It assumes we can do that if we really try.

The steps of *teshuvah* require the perpetrator to: (1) acknowledge that he or she committed a wrong, (2) feel remorse, (3) confess publicly, (4) ask for forgiveness from the aggrieved party, (5) make restitution to the extent that that is possible, and (6) refrain from committing the wrongful act the next time the opportunity arises.[3]

Teshuvah is very difficult, especially when it involves deeply rooted behavior patterns. No wonder, then, that the Talmud says that fully righteous people (*zaddikm*) cannot stand in the same place as those who have repented, for the strength needed to repent is much greater than the strength needed to be good in the first place.[4]

If one succeeds in reversing a history of abuse, one attains the status of a person who has returned (*ba'al teshuvah*). American law makes convicts who have served their sentence indicate their criminal past on all sorts of documents, and such people often continue to be denied voting privileges, the right to apply for a government job, and so on. Jewish law requires us to trust the process of return (*teshuvah*) much more strongly. It mandates that Jews not even mention the person's past violations, let alone bar him or her from participation in society. Recounting the person's wrongful deeds is categorized as verbal abuse (*ona'at devarim*) itself. Moreover, it puts obstacles in the way of those who try to do better, a violation of the biblical command, "Before a blind person you may not put an obstacle."[5] One of the specific examples of *ona'at devarim* given in B. *Bava Mezia* 58a is reminding a person of past violations of the law. Thus the Jewish tradition strongly encourages abusers to seek help to control their abusive drives, promising full restitution in legal, social, and theological status if they succeed.

The abuser, however, *must* go through all these steps to be accorded the renewed status of being in good standing with the community. Being punished by the civil authorities is not sufficient. For example, in one congregation a man who for years was head of the synagogue's Cub Scout troop was later accused by a number of his former charges of sexual abuse. On the strength of the testimony of a number of these teenagers, he was sent to prison. When he was released, he wanted to join the synagogue once again. He refused, however, to admit that he had ever done anything wrong. He therefore failed to fulfill the very first requirement of *teshuvah*—acknowledging that he had done wrong—and so the congregation was right in refusing to readmit him to membership.

If the man in this example (which actually occurred) had fulfilled the requirements of *teshuvah*, the congregation would be duty-bound to readmit him to membership but would not be obligated to reinstate him as its Cub Scout leader. While one may not routinely remind the offender or anyone else of his or her past offense, one may, and probably should, invoke that information in making decisions regarding the ways in which that person is permitted to interact with others. People may do full *teshuvah* and yet continue to be sorely tempted to repeat their offenses if the opportunity arises. For such people, it is a favor neither to the offender nor to the people he/she may harm to put the culprit in the position where such temptation exists; that would be "putting an obstacle before the blind."[6] The past offense is enough of a ground to suspect that the offender may remain weak-willed in this area and likely to harm others once again. This is especially true for child abusers, whose behavior is so deeply rooted in their psyche that it is often impossible to undo. Often the only way to prevent future abuse is for the perpetrators to avoid situations in which they will be tempted to engage in such acts. Therefore, even though we may not gratuitously mention the offense or bar the person from activities irrelevant to the offense, we may, and probably should, use that knowledge to help the offender avoid tempting situations and to protect others at the same time.

Rabbi Mayer Rabbinowitz has pointed out to me that if the process of *teshuvah* works to its fullest extent, the abuser should not even be tempted to abuse others when confronted with situations similar to the ones that led him/her to abuse people in the past. In a similar situation, we do not tell recovering alcoholics to avoid going to a *Kiddush* after Saturday morning services altogether; we ask them, instead, to participate in the *Kiddush* and to take grape juice instead of wine. Following this model, abusers who have gone through full *teshuvah* might be trusted, at least under supervision, to resume their former tasks with children.

While I understand this line of reasoning, and while I can imagine situations in which that may be appropriate, I hesitate to recommend it because in cases of abuse, more than in cases of alcoholism, the welfare of others is directly affected. Moreover, a significant percentage of alcoholics have managed to achieve and sustain a state of recovery, but those who commit incest and sexual abuse have much greater difficulty stopping their behavior. It is therefore better for all concerned for them simply to avoid situations in which they may be tempted. We must trust the process of *teshuvah* while being realistic of its limits—and of the need to protect those who would be victims if it fails.

Thus, for some people, full *teshuvah* may not be possible. For its own protection and for the sake of the abuser, too, the community may not afford the abuser the opportunity to complete the last stage of *teshuvah*, where the sinner confronts the same situation in which she/he previously sinned and acts differently. In such cases, the community, recognizing that that is the case not because of a failure in the abuser's resolve to do *teshuvah* but rather because of its own decision, may reinstate the abuser into membership, despite his/her

failure to complete the process of *teshuvah,* for all purposes except for functioning in situations where he/she was previously abusive. The full process of
teshuvah, as described in the sources, may not be possible or appropriate for all
cases, and the community's norms must respond accordingly.[7]

May an abused party refuse to forgive the abuser even when she/he
completes the process of *teshuvah*? The Mishnah says that if someone who
inflicted injuries on someone else acknowledges the wrong, makes restitution
according to law, and then asks forgiveness, a victim who refuses to accept the
apology under those circumstances is considered "cruel."[8] Normally, then, we
are duty-bound to accept a perpetrator's full *teshuvah* as fulfilling whatever
could be expected of the perpetrator.

That does not mean, though, that the victim needs to resume friendly relations with that person. That is, one may forgive a person without reestablish-
ing a relationship. Conversely, just as forgiveness can come without reconciliation, sometimes reconciliation can come without forgiveness. That, for
example, is what Jews are now trying to do with Christians in general and
with Germans and Poles in particular with regard to their complicity in the
Holocaust. The current generation of Jews does not have the moral standing
to forgive those who perpetrated the Holocaust; only those who suffered
through it can forgive. Moreover, those not yet born or only children during
the Holocaust cannot really ask for forgiveness either, for they were not the
ones who committed the wrong. Still, while forgiveness cannot happen,
reconciliation among the descendants of the generation of the Holocaust can.
Similarly, victims of child abuse may reconcile with their abusers without
forgiving them, or may forgive them without reconciling with them. They may
also refuse to do either one, for some sins are indeed unforgivable. In doing
that, they may be acting cruelly, as the Mishnah asserts, but sometimes even
that is appropriate.[9]

Further Specific Steps to Prevent and Alleviate Sexual Abuse of Children
✧

**Provide child and spousal abuse services and support other communal
efforts to do the same.** In addition to the steps just described, the California
booklet mentions the need to provide services to strengthen families:
"Anything that your community of faith does to strengthen families is child
abuse prevention. For some at-risk families, participation in religious services is

their only real support system. . . . You can reach out to families . . . by addressing parenting issues through sermons, study groups, or by sponsoring public forums."

Such discussions may center on the Rabbinical Assembly's new *Rabbinic Letter on Intimate Relations*[10] because that provides a safe forum for opening up on all issues of human intimacy, including these troubling ones, and it does so in the context of Jewish conceptions, laws, and values. In addition, Mother's Day or Father's Day, or the story of the binding of Isaac read on Rosh Hashanah or during the year, may be used as the occasion for a worship service, forum, sermon, or readings on these subjects.

Work with your network of experts to identify the most effective resources in your community and to determine how your synagogue can support those services and groups. This might mean sponsoring a speaker, creating a workshop, or providing meeting space for a self-help group.

While the California pamphlet refers to at-risk families, we must realize that most families where abuse happens will not appear to be at-risk. Abusers may be those who appear most successful, charming, intelligent, refined, and observant. Children who are being molested may be high achievers and leaders. Therefore, our greatest hope of prevention and intervention will come from teaching everyone the basics of respect and honoring each other including why we should honor others, what we should do to express that honor, and what we should refrain from doing. We can also call upon experts in these areas from Jewish Family Service, from other community agencies, and in private practice for preventive and educational programs within our synagogues and educational institutions.

Use the power of the religion and the community to deter abuse.   Where there is a reasonable expectation that continued membership within the community will more likely bring a change in behavior, the synagogue can and should still express its disgust for such behavior by, for example, refusing to give honors or positions of leadership to those known to be physically or verbally abusive to others. Rabbis should not hesitate to use theological language in explaining to abusers that such behavior is not only a violation of a Jewish communal norm, but a transgression of God's will as embedded in Jewish law and lore.

Counsel adult survivors of abuse.   Adults who abuse others were often abused themselves as children or witnesses to abuse in their homes. Most children who were sexually abused do not sexually abuse others, but they suffer a range of problems, as evidenced in the stories throughout this book. Many have trouble in relationships. Many feel unworthy. Many have trouble believing in God, and, as Marcia Cohn Spiegel writes (chap. 11), many women who were sexually abused or incested cannot seek guidance or comfort from a patriarchal "Lord." If we are to fulfill our obligations to protect and save lives, we must make our community a place where it is safe to discuss these problems and get help. Synagogues can, for example, form support groups for adult children of abuse, with opportunities to express their feelings about having been abused as well as to learn how to create healthy relationships and families. Jewish Family Service agencies may be of aid in establishing and staffing such groups.

Address the spiritual aspects of healing.   We rabbis all too often underestimate the role of religious conviction in aiding the healing process. Twelve Step programs place heavy reliance on faith in God, not only because historically such programs emerged from Christian faith communities, but also because healing is assisted greatly when a person feels that he/she is being aided both by others who have the same problem and by God. We need to cease to be embarrassed by such religious language. We should unselfconsciously invoke the religious tenets of our tradition to help people who have been abused heal the wounds of the past and reconstruct and redirect their lives.[11] With the help of survivors of abuse, and experts in healing trauma, we can provide healing services.

Reconnecting with God's Image within Us
৵

Judaism can provide a real source of strength for abused people struggling to escape from their situation and to rebuild their lives. Recognizing that we are all ultimately created in the image of God helps those who have been violated to heal and reclaim their place in their lives and communities. As Jews, we must accept and fulfill our responsibilities in this area: the abused, abuser, witness, friend, family, rabbi, teacher, and neighbor all have a role to play and a duty to perform in building a community that is safe for all.

The following High Holy Day Message of the Jewish Theological Seminary of America for 1992, published in *Newsweek*, the *New York Times*, and the *Wall Street Journal*,[12] summarizes these themes nicely.

Know whom you put to shame, for in the likeness of God is (s)he made.
(GENESIS RABBAH 24:8)

Some people who are reading this were beaten yesterday, or terrorized, or kept in isolation.
Some who tormented them are reading this now.
And they are not strangers to each other; they are family. Intimates.
People like us. Us.
Home should be a haven, the place where you can count on being valued and protected.
If instead it is a place where the people closest to you beat you up, or keep you on edge with threats, or isolate and demean you—then what is safe?

Violence in the family is not love; it is not discipline; it is not deserved.
It is an abuse of power, and it is wrong—
    because decent people don't behave that way;
    because it is against the law, and for one more reason:
    we are all made in the image of God.
    To lash out in violence—
    especially against someone whose life is linked with yours—
    is to violate a likeness of God, and to degrade that likeness in yourself.
Are you being hurt or humiliated by the person you are closest to?
Believe that you do not deserve the abuse.
No one has the right to tell you that you are worthless: your worth comes from God.

Have you been taking out your anger and frustration against the people who depend on you?
Know that you are better than that; you are made in the image of God.
You have the power to stop hurting and belittling them. God gives it to you.
To all who read this, we ask:

• Look at yourself, at your partner, at your elderly parents, at your children, as images of God. Treat each of them with the respect which that demands.
• Make your home a haven. Instead of raising your hand or your voice, raise your own dignity and the self-esteem of the people who turn to you for love. You may not be able to perfect the world, but this much you can do.
• Help your religious community to face the fact of domestic violence and to offer active support to those who have been enduring abuse, threats,

and humiliation. A house of God should be a place for teaching restraint, decency, and reverence; make yours that place.

• Behave as though God made you worthy; it is true. Behave as though the world depends on your humanity and decency. It does.

"for the sin which we have committed before Thee, openly and in secret"

High Holy Day Liturgy

FOURTEEN ‑⟩

Hope
Creating Day, Living in the Light

HADIYAH C.,
LAURIE SUZANNE REICHE,
ELIZABETH, AND
ELLEN BASS,
WITH RACHEL LEV ·

Those of us who are lucky and have worked hard are neither victims nor survivors. We are multifaceted human beings. We are alive. We are awake. We are aware. We are whole, a living testimony to the healing we forged for ourselves, with help. We grieve. We learn to accept what has been and what is. As we work on ourselves we discover our beauty and resiliency, as reflected in Hadiyah C.'s story, "A Woman Welding," Laurie Suzanne Reiche's biographical statement, and the poems "Putting Out Fires" and "Choices" by Elizabeth.

In the following story by Hadiyah C., her work in the shipyards forms a metaphor for her personal journey from darkness to light.

A Woman Welding: The Underground Part of Me
by Hadiyah C.

In 1973, I wrote in my diary: That's me looking out from the bow of the *Provider*. I can see the steel piled up in the shipyard, Fairhaven Shipyard. I'm wearing a scarf, my helmet beside me.

Hope lays the first weld, connects two pieces of lonely steel. And then a boat. In between a story, a story of people making a boat. A story of me, the only woman in the shipyard.

Feeling the stick, making the fire burn. Feeling my power. The beauty of the yard and the cold shining steel against the Puget Sound bay. Icy steel blue water. Stick a stick, make fire, and make a boat. A beautiful 120' boat that could catch sockeye fish in Alaska.

A Jewish girl from New Jersey, working on the waterfront. A certified welder.

190

The outside. History.

The women's movement.

Women searching to find their way. Women pounding the pavement, setting feet in new doorways: women in law school, women in medical school, women on Wall Street.

Going out into the workforce. College for me, become a teacher or a nurse. Armed with a B.A., a social worker in war-torn Newark. Responsible for sixty welfare families in a one-block radius. Then, a single mother, swaying with the winds of West Coast communes. More. Working for the U.S. Navy, the first woman hired since World War II, a result of the 1963 Civil Rights Act.

Running a tool room in Hunts Point, San Francisco, for three thousand navy men making aircraft carriers. Saw welding. Drawn to the fire. Pursued training at Laney Community College in Oakland, California. Again, the only woman. Several of my fellow students go north to Bellingham, Washington, where they are hired to make Alaskan king crab fishing boats. I follow, but it takes a year's worth of weekly visits to the shipyard to get hired. My fellow classmates threaten to walk out, and finally the foreman, Leonard, puts me to work.

As a single mother, it is a way to support us. But it is more. A way out of my past, a way to escape the well-dressed women of the suburbs keeping house for their upwardly mobile husbands. The life I was pulled to and the life I would never have. I learned how to operate in the male world. Fighting through nasty jokes, crude comments, pinup girls.

There was always something beautiful about that raw steel. I remember the first time I became aware of its awesomeness. I had just moved to California from the East Coast. I came to a spot along the expressway. It was covered with compacted steel—mostly cars. The steel was piled high, car upon car. Something about seeing the crushed steel moved me. I wanted to get inside of it. I wanted to touch it. Layer upon layer of steel reaching to the sky. I could feel its icy smoothness. I could feel its burning. Looking at that steel. The electricity between the steel and me. The connection, the stirring of feelings.

On that same road toward San Francisco were welded sculptures, twisted tortured pieces made into a soul—made into a life. That's how I felt about the shipyards—Hunts Point and Fairhaven. I came to life. I came to the shipyards where a sleeping part of me awoke. It took me back. Crawling around and around, I could feel the wires. The shipyard, the basement. The dark world where no light comes in. A three-year-old that hits against another part of life, skirt in the air.

Now, twenty-five years later, I know. There was something familiar in the electricity, in the connection to that steel, my body encased in leather overalls, my hands holding the torched rod to make the fire. It was the underground part of me. I had spent an early part of my childhood crawling through the underground space of my father's basement in his grocery store. A three-year-old.

This has been my world. Finding a home for the darkness. Crawling through that inner world that so wanted to be acknowledged, to be seen. The fire burning through forging a boat, the fire reshaping a life, a life that couldn't be snuffed out.

Hadiyah's story above and Laurie Suzanne Reiche's biographical statement below exemplify how they each put together the facts of their lives into a coherent story. Their paths are similar to other survivors who, as they heal, weave their stories and qualities into an integrated "Self."

"Who Exactly Am I?"
by Laurie Suzanne Reiche

Who exactly am I? I am many things: a woman who was once a child brutalized who became a wild, sex-crazed, drug-taking maniac teen who became an exploited young adult who became a stripper who became a groupie who became a wanderer who became a wife to a musician, a woman who was exploited by all those around her to a divorced young woman to a single mother to a wife, again, and then—finally therapy, that turned my life around and I became a mother for a second time and a housebound wife and a student of feminism and women's studies in my own school in my own house and I became a good mother and created a good family where we all live in unconditional love and my son is now eighteen and a miracle-wonder of a boy and my daughter is now fourteen and a miracle-wonder of a young woman. And all through my life I've written. All through my life I have kept journals. All through my life I have read and studied psychology, philosophy, religion, literature, poetry, etc. And I have become a photographer recently, which brings me another level of joy, and I keep on writing and writing and writing because my life absolutely depends on it. And I am no longer in touch with any of my remaining family-of-birth, as they will not speak to me unless I never talk about "you know what!" And I consider the fact that I am alive a miracle and every day, every day I am grateful that I was born and survived the brutality of my childhood and I just don't know what else to say at the top of my head like this except that life is astounding. What else is there?

Rachel Lev
ꙩ

We learn about life and ourselves and the choices we have. We learn to write, to cut off relationships that hurt and keep the ones that nurture. We stop taking care of everyone else first and become aware of our own needs. We recognize that the childhood traumas are *over* and start to identify our present life choices, as Elizabeth discusses in "Putting Out Fires" and "Choices." As we are able to heal, we are able to grab the reins of responsibility for our lives.

Putting Out Fires
by Elizabeth

My memory does not grow
Calla lilies or tea roses—
Just thorns.

What little I do remember
Has to do with fetching water
From that deep, dark well
Within my soul; carrying water
Up ten flights of stairs
Always the first one at the scene
Putting out other people's fires
While my own house is burning
Out of control.

Always other people's fires
Always too busy saving
My next door neighbor's
Priceless Tiffany lamp
Or a Chippendale Chair
Too busy to notice
That there is a halo
Of ash gray smoke
Hugging my roof
And the fire is burning
In earnest
With its skeletal arms

Wrapped in red diaphanous gauze
Frantically waving at me
Begging me to come home.

I am home at last
These days I carry water
To put out my own fires
Drenching the garden with sweat
Making the tea roses grow.

Choices
by Elizabeth

1.
You may choose
To stand still
In the eye
Of the hurricane
Not swaying with the wind
Not uttering a sound
Hardly moving
Or not moving at all

You may choose
To spend the night
Among the stars
And in the morning
You may choose
To come down again
Or you may not

2.
You may choose
To remain closed
To life's joys and sorrows
Protected by bolts of lightning
Of your own making
You may choose
To burn down the house
Of those who hurt you

You may choose
To live in an open field
You may choose
To use those lightning bolts
To strike down a dead tree
And make it live again
By building a sturdy house
For a needy child
Not unlike yourself

Triumphs—and Choices
ॐ

For much of my life I couldn't see that I had choices. I felt besieged, beleaguered, put upon by the normal expectations of life and relationships. My range of comfort was pretty narrow. My energy was limited. I didn't want to negotiate. It felt hard enough to know what I felt, let alone tell someone. The fact that they might disagree and we'd have to work it out was just too much. And for decades, I didn't know any of this.

I don't want to ever have to go through another tragedy or trauma; yet I'm beginning to understand that there are no guarantees in life. None. Nope, not for anybody. No matter how much I've suffered, I could go through something horrible again. I hope not. I don't expect that it is inevitable. I just know now that life is what it is. I'm committed to living with joy, love, and hope (with a little crabbiness on the side).

I am editing this chapter in the days after the September 11, 2001, terrorist attacks on the World Trade Center and the Pentagon. I see parallels in the tragic events caused by terrorists and those caused by terrorists in our homes. I see parallels in the courage and wisdom of survivors who can grieve *and* affirm life. The following poem by Ellen Bass describes what it means to be true to our experiences *and* choose life, accept life, on life's terms.[1]

The thing is
by Ellen Bass

The thing is
to love life, to love it even
when you have no stomach for it
and everything you've held dear

crumbles like burnt paper in your hands,
your throat filled with the silt of it.
When grief sits with you, its tropical heat
thickening the air, heavy as water
more fit for gills than lungs;
when grief weights you like your own flesh
only more of it, an obesity of grief,
you think, *how can a body withstand this?*
Then you hold life like a face
between your palms, a plain face,
no charming smile, no violet eyes,
and you say, yes, I will take you
I will love you, again.

As the story and poems in this chapter demonstrate, we survivors rediscover the ability to live. We discover the benefits of looking for the good in life and ourselves, of acknowledging the blessings in each day. It is not about denying pain or being a Pollyanna. It is a combination of knowing we are OK, no matter what the circumstances, of being present and knowing we have choices. Life *is* difficult *and* it's wonderful. For me it is also knowing I am not alone and have never been. Being molested stole our ability to be present to the iridescent, sometimes muddy spectrum of our lives and ourselves. We are taking it back.

Building Communities of Hope

RACHEL LEV

In many schools across the United States, students honor Martin Luther King by completing assignments based on his "I Have a Dream" speech. In one school, the assignment was to draw a picture and write their "dream" for people. Julie wrote, "I have a dream that people should be treated how they want to be treated."

I have a dream, too. I dream that no more children will be molested and that those who have will be helped to heal by a compassionate, informed, and proactive community. This is my dream, my hope. Hope to me means the desire and search for a future good—difficult but not impossible to attain with God's help. This is what it might look like as my dream comes true.

Making the World Safe for Children: Part I
ᠵ

Family gathers round the dinner table. Heads bowed, a sacred stillness falls for a split second, then there are calls to pass the bread. Who wants chicken? Beef? What do you want to drink? Did you wash your hands? Stories fly about the day's events, plans for the weekend. Siblings tease each other, at times looking to a parent to referee, but mostly having fun, enjoying themselves and each other. Some of the food tastes great, but some. . . . For sure, mom's gefilte fish will stay right where it started—a solid mass, perhaps best used to demonstrate things that have weight and take up space.

A brother reaches out to pinch his sister's breast. The girl shouts, "Hey! Cut that out!" Dad says, "Stop that. What makes you think there's any chance that's an OK thing to do?" The boy pulls his hand back. Dad stores the incident away as something to think some more about and figure out, with his wife, how to handle. They're in a class at the local Jewish community center on surviving your kids' adolescence. This might be a good incident to bring up there. In last week's class the discussion

197

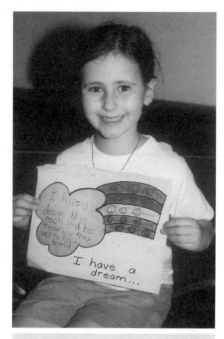

"*I have a dream that people should be treated how they want to be treated.*"
Julie, age seven

centered on the sexual harassment going on in the high school by teen boys against teen girls. The conversation was lively and helpful. Discussion often centered on teaching your kids values and living those values yourself. Often they were asked to think about "what do you stand for?" Talking about respecting and honoring each other turns out to be very different from doing it.

Different local rabbis joined the class each week. They brought their knowledge of Jewish law and tradition, but what Dad liked best was they were there as human beings, parents themselves. As the rabbis talked about the challenges they faced as human beings, parents, teachers, and religious leaders, the discussion in the class broadened and deepened. The rabbis liked participating in the class for lots of reasons. It helped them know more of what was going on in the lives of their congregants and, because they got to be themselves, true partnerships/community developed including their receiving support. Those new to the area met their neighbors and a number of rabbis, easing the strain of living some-place new.

As a result of the last class series, a proposal was made to schools to do a program on healthy relationships. Parents and teachers were going to go through an abbreviated version of the series first, and then kids in their classrooms would talk about problems that come up in all relationships and ways to resolve them with respect. Experts would come in and facili-tate the program. Dad remembered the agony his daughter experienced when she'd become the target of verbal taunting or silent treatment from a bunch of kids the year before.

They were starting to talk about very serious and painful things at the synagogue and community center. Stories of children being abused, of adults who'd been molested as children, were being told. A recent story of a child being molested by a man they all knew had many of them reeling. Others said, but of course this happens. We're no different from anyone else. The rabbi was networking with local experts on sexual abuse and incest as well as with the National Jewish Support line (recently estab-lished to provide resource information for religious and lay leaders, educa-tors, victims of abuse, and their families). And down the hall, a group of all kinds of trauma survivors was putting the finishing touches on a heal-ing service to be held as part of next Friday night's regular services.

It was all quite something, Dad thought to himself. Something quite good.

Making the World Safe for Children: Part II
✧

> *For every complex question there is a simple answer. And, it is wrong.*
> H. L. Mencken

A woman walked along the side of a swiftly running river on a beauti-ful autumn day. Suddenly she heard someone screaming, "Help! Help! Help me!" The woman kicked off her shoes, dove in, and saved this person. As she caught her breath she heard someone else screaming, "Help! Help! Help me!" Again she dove into the water and saved another person. And so it went. As soon as she returned to shore with someone she'd rescued, another cry for help would be heard.

After awhile, the woman could do no more. Heartbroken, she lay by the side of the river, continuing to hear the cries of people drowning in the river. "What is going on here?" she wondered. Walking to the head of the river, she discovered the people were being thrown in.

The end of violence begins with prevention, with identifying when and how these violations can be prevented. We need to do much more than provide services to people after the damage has been done. We must look at what's going on at the head of the river and intervene there.

Many years ago, I was impressed by a gynecologist who offered parenting classes to his pregnant patients and their partners. He believed entirely too much time and energy went into marveling at the miracle of the evolution of the fetus and not enough time was spent on what you do with a baby when you're sleep deprived and nothing you do can stop the child from crying. One child's molestation began in infancy because his mother found "massaging" his penis stopped his crying.

How do we make the world safe for children? By learning to listen better. By creating programs that teach what babies and children need. By attending programs where we explore and learn: What is appropriate touch? What are healthy boundaries? How can we intervene when a relative or friend is touching or holding a child in a way that doesn't seem right? How and when can children be taught they have the right to say, "Stop. I don't like that," to expect others to honor their request, and to tell someone when there's a problem. Where can a child get help when a parent is abusive and home is not a safe place? Early childhood parenting education can continue with discussions about how to create a relationship with your children where they feel comfortable speaking with you, or someone, about anything. Doctors, rabbis, mental health workers, religious educators, and parents working together can make this happen. Parents need to value and be supported to take care of themselves, to have time alone, time together, and support in taking care of their children. Quality, affordable child care is essential for most families.

When molestation happens, we need to stop pulling children from their homes, families, schools, and communities. If anyone should be removed, it is the perpetrator. Too many children so removed (for their safety) get further victimized in a system that often cannot protect them. One teenage girl I know was taken from her suburban home because she was being molested by her brother. She was put in a "safe" home with six eighteen-year-old boys. They all raped her.

Creating a Healing Paradigm
⟿

Before I could write about my healing, I had to accept that I was healing—that what was done to me didn't kill me or my spirit. I had to choose to let go of bitterness and pain as a way of living. For much of my life I lived numb while acting as if I wasn't. For years I was tormented by chronic illness, loneliness, and confusion. I asked, why aren't things turning out better? I was bright, caring, fun, a hard worker. What was wrong? As I looked deeply, I began to feel a cascade of pain. Pain was good—freeing—real. Finally, I felt real. Now, healing the wounds is almost complete. At least, I *hope* so. Now, as I begin to believe that great good is possible for me, there is much I have to learn.

It would be easier to be bitter and angry, to blame. But honestly, I don't know what caused what. Knowing direct cause and effect is not possible. I was sick as a child. I was molested. I was bright. I grew up in an ever-changing, declining neighborhood where I was the only Jewish child in my school. My parents grew up during the depression. Their families had their own blend of problems. My parents loved me. They introduced me to the wonders of travel, history, nature, art, music, and more. I always had a good roof over my head, food in my belly, and lovely clothes to wear. What caused what? I don't know.

To heal I have to let go of causality—let go of using pain as proof of what happened—let go of suffering as a way of punishing "them."

My parents were human. I understand how my father did what he did to me—and it is incomprehensible. Both are true. I know how denial protects us. When my mother's sister died, my mom told me, "She was good to me. When my brother would come at me to sock me, she would stand between us and get socked in the stomach." Yet my mother would never describe her brother as abusive. I would.

To heal our world we have to stop hating, stop blaming, and look to love as the answer. It's not easy. But hate and getting even aren't easy roads either—and ultimately they're not very productive.

When I say I understand how my father did what he did to me it is because as I have looked at him and others who've molested, I see deep wounds. While causality cannot be certain here, I believe he was influenced by what he experienced in his early years.

My father told me of many of the challenges and hardships he had faced. His stories of his family made light of their poverty and struggles during his childhood. He spoke of the delicious delicacy of a dinner of sour cream and rye bread rather than the nights there was nothing to eat. Some of the dismissal was because so many families had those struggles. Some because making light of things was a way to handle them.

My father idealized his mother. While he never wore a wedding band, he always wore a ring that had been hers. He almost never spoke of his father. When he did, it was without respect for this Talmudic scholar who couldn't earn a living. It has been strange, in an extended family so filled with stories about my grandmother, that no one spoke about my grandfather. And then one day came the story, from a cousin, of my grandfather having raped his eight-year-old granddaughter. She was in her seventies when she first told. I have wondered what abuse my father might have witnessed or experienced himself.

Does this background excuse my father's molesting me? Absolutely not. However, I believe, deep in my soul, that the only solution for stopping the violence by one human being of another, is to see the whole picture. While holding those who molest, those who violate, those who abuse, accountable, we must also see them as human beings. When we demonize the abusers, we say somehow we are different from them. I believe this builds the ether of denial. The truth is, each of us is capable of harming others. We each do harm others. While I have never molested a child, I fear I could. I fear you could, too.

Anyone who has known the terror of having been violated and who has done a lot of personal healing work knows that the rage inside, the sense of injustice, the feelings of powerlessness can make you want to *kill*, to *maim*, to *hurt somebody*. It feels like if I can make you hurt the way I do, I won't feel so alone. In most survivors these feelings cause incredible shame and horror. Bottling up our rage can be a major stumbling block to healing. We do it to assure ourselves that we are different from our abusers. What a relief, if survivor and nonsurvivor could acknowledge that we each have the capacity to do monstrous things. Anyone who has fought in a war or witnessed one knows this. Anyone who experienced the Holocaust knows this.

Those who abuse are wounded, scarred, scared. Saying this does not relieve them of responsibility for their actions. It doesn't mean that survivors need to have compassion for their abusers or to forgive them. In order to have communities of hope, we must understand where a penchant to molest comes from and discover what we can do to prevent the incestuous seeds from being planted.

A tale about the heart of evil as told by Rebbe Zalman Schachter-Shalomi, and relayed by David Cooper in his book *God Is a Verb*, teaches, "even the heart of Satan has a divine spark; even the heart of evil yearns to be redeemed." The Rebbe continues, "Our job is not to set up a battle-ground to eradicate evil, but to search out its spark of holiness. Our task is not to destroy but to build; not to hate but to find a place of yielding; not to polarize but to discover the points of commonality so that we can work together."[1]

When we work together on "points of commonality" such as peace in our lives, we build communities of hope. We accomplish this by teaching children and adults how to treat each other with honor, respect, and kind-ness and expecting them to do so. We accomplish this when we open our doors and hearts to those who have suffered from any trauma and help them heal. We accomplish this when we say, "Abuse is never OK," and our actions match our words—that is, we hold those who abuse account-able. We expect abusers to change. We offer to help them change. And when those who abuse say, "I'm fine the way I am. I'm not changing," we hold them accountable. We keep them away from our children and others they might harm. Then, there is hope.

This book bears witness to the fact that incest happens in the Jewish community. That the molestation of a single child impacts that child, the adult she becomes, and all those who meet her. That denial of incest and sexual abuse in our community hurts us all. That Jewish law and tradition clearly state that incest is wrong and that we are each responsible to "save a life," and to "not stand idly by."

Survivor stories bear witness to our incredible strength, courage, creativity, and honor. They bear witness to the importance of community in healing—to the incredible positive impact of the acts of kindness and generosity by a grade school teacher, a nurse, a rabbi, friend, therapist, and others. They whisper to us. They shout at us. "What *you* do matters!"

Most survivors whose work is included here chose to publish under a pen name or first name. For some who used their own names, their parents or perpetrators are dead. For others, the name they use now is not their given or family name. While using a pen name may protect the writer, that is not the primary reason for using one. Most survivors chose pen names because too many people have been hurt already by what was done to us. This proves to me that love is stronger than hate.

The art, poetry, and prose demonstrate the healing power of creative expression for many of us. Whether or not we consider ourselves artists, "concretizing" our process helps us heal.

Not all children who are molested survive. Some who survive do not survive intact. These people never recover the full potential of their lives. Many survivors can and do heal—moving from victim to survivor to vitally alive human being. None of us does this alone. While only we can do the inner work, we reclaim our lives, as the Beatles wrote, "with a little help from our friends." For some of us, we do it with a *lot* of help from our friends.

And so, I end where I began, grateful for that loving connection to God that I felt so many years ago in my grandmother's shul. While I have yet to find that connection within Jewish organizations or religion, I have found it in the way I feel when I write, when I see the splendor of a blue sky, or in the miracle of a chickadee. I find that rhythm in the company of good-hearted people, in movement, in dance. I find it in meditation as I surrender to my higher self, the God within me. My personal journey as a Jew is in process. The writing of this book was part of that process. I don't know what is next. The blessing is that "not knowing" no longer terrifies me. The even greater blessing is that I sometimes experience joy.

Appendices

Never doubt that a small group of committed
individuals can change the world; indeed, it is
the only thing that ever has.

Margaret Mead

Helping Repair Our World (*tikkun olam*)

Suggestions for Rabbis, Educators, Cantors, Parents, and Health Care Professionals

Where to Begin?

Read through these appendices. If you'd like your synagogue, community center, or Jewish family agency to be doing more and you're not sure where to start, think about who else could help. Talk with that person, then someone else. Brainstorm. Network. Learn about the issues and possible solutions. Contact some of the resources listed in Appendix G. See Appendix F for a chart of recommendations developed in 1993 by the Jewish Community Task Force on Child Abuse in Baltimore, Maryland.

Bring your desire to "repair the world" to a rabbi or to a representative of an organization that also wants to take action. Bring the following information, suggestions, and your questions to your rabbis, educators, and cantors and discuss what can be done. Start with the people who are easiest to persuade. That is the way most major transformations occur—one person at a time, linking with another around a common cause. Find something in the following ideas that you'd like to do. Then do it or something else.

Healing ourselves facilitates healing our world. If you were abused as a child, teen, or adult, ask yourself if you have healed those wounds. You deserve to heal and be whole. If there are unresolved remnants from those experiences, talk with someone about them. Get support.

Know that whatever you do makes a difference. Thank you.

APPENDIX B ⌁

When an Adult Says, "I've Been Abused"

Suggestions for Medical and Clinical Professionals,
Rabbis, Teachers, and Other Helpers

The role of rabbis, Jewish educators, and counselors is to respond to reports of abuse based on Jewish values and ethics *and* the best practices in the field of violence prevention. As Rabbi Dorff wrote,

> Do not assume that you can handle the situation alone. . . . If abuse is to be stopped and its effects ameliorated, professionals of various sorts must be called upon.
>
> As religious leaders, unless we are trained to understand and intervene in the areas of child sexual abuse, incest and adult survivors, we should not do therapy with victims or perpetrators. . . . Certainly we have a role as spiritual counselors. In that role, our interaction with victims and perpetrators should focus on confirming that we believe the victim and that neither Judaism nor the Jewish community countenances the abuser's behavior. We should also put the victim in touch with trained therapists and volunteers who can help. Creating a network of experts who help victims and perpetrators of abuse is an essential part of our role. Working in partnership, we can provide what is best and right.

Once someone starts to speak with you about having been molested, remember that listening compassionately is a great gift. Create a safe environment in which survivors can describe what has or is happening to them without fear of disbelief, victim blaming, or retaliation. How?

- Listen. Listen. Listen. Don't debate the facts. Don't ask, "Are you sure?" Don't say, "Oh, but it was so long ago." Avoid saying, "I can't stand hearing this" or "I can't believe it, not _____."
- Be conscious of issues of physical space. Don't crowd the person. Unless you already have a relationship in which putting your arm around the person would be OK, don't touch the person unless you ask if it's OK.

In addition, possible "do's" include the following:

- Say, "I'm so sorry this happened to you."
- Say, "Thank you for trusting me enough to tell me."
- Ask, "How can I help?"
- Sit quietly and patiently with the survivor. Sometimes there is nothing to "do."
- It's OK to feel whatever you feel as you listen. If tears come, let them (yours or theirs). If you get angry, feel that; just be thoughtful about how you express it. Remember, this happened to *them*. Sometimes a survivor will open the door on the subject and then want to leave it alone and talk about something else. That's OK. In order to feel safe, the survivor has to be in control of the pace of her/his disclosure.
- And, of course, anyone listening has every right (and the responsibility) to take care of her/himself. Get support for yourself. Speak to a therapist who knows about sexual abuse and adult survivors.

When a Friend or Family Member Says, "I've Been Abused"

Advice from incest survivor Hillary:

All of those whose reactions I found helpful responded to my sharing with gratitude for my openness, trust in my inner strength, faith in the veracity of my reports, and sympathy for the pain I'd known. They hugged me, they cried with me, they prayed with me—and they even made me laugh when I thought I'd forgotten how. They never failed to include me in social activities, even when they knew I might dampen the mood. They listened. They cared. They loved. And they mended my wounds.

I'm grateful to my father for his reaction to my telling him of the molestation. He sustained his shocked reaction for only a moment before his concern moved to me. He held me and cried with me—and I could tell his tears were for me, not for him. He came with me to therapy and helped me work through some unanswered questions.

In stark contrast was my mother's reaction. Once she got past her denial, she still failed to recognize or acknowledge the magnitude of what had happened. Eventually, I wrote a lengthy detailed letter and I read it to her face-to-face. She held me and cried, but she was crying for herself, for her failure as a mother to protect her young child, and for her inadequacy to face what was going on. Instead of comforting me, she needed me to comfort her.

Educators, School Administrators, Counseling Staff, and Nurses

Many survivors' lives can be altered by a teacher, school principal, or nurse who notices and explores chronic illnesses, falling asleep in class, learning problems, school and other phobias, excessive absences, eating problems, and the like during childhood. To do this most effectively, these helpers need to know and address the following:

- Learn about sexual abuse and incest.
- Look at what can be done in schools to teach children the components of healthy relating, to provide a safe environment for all and a place where children and families in pain can find resources that can help. Help children be compassionate and empathic. This is best done by modeling. Be kind. Studies of altruism with those who helped Jews during World War II found that they had one thing in common—they had not been abused as children.
- Children and adults often begin to talk about what happened to them in a disguised way. When counseling a child who says, "I'm angry/sad/scared," ask them to tell you with or of what, or whom or how they are angry, sad, scared. Listen some more. Remind them it is normal to have these feelings. Ask if there's anything you can do. Most important is establishing a relationship with them in which they feel safe. As you learn about abuse and how to help a child talk to you, you may find it appropriate to ask, "Did somebody hurt you? Do something you didn't like?"
- Teach children the names of their body parts and that their body is private and not supposed to be touched without their permission. (Parents, teachers, and religious leaders all need to do this.)
- Give children unconditional permission to say "No" even to a family member's unwanted touch. Ask them to tell you what is making them feel that way.
- Support them in saying "No" and "Don't" and "I don't want you to do that" to anyone who is talking with them or touching them in ways that they don't like or understand.
- Talk with children about what they can do if someone does something they don't want.

211

- Tell them it is all right to "tell" on someone when that person does something they don't like. Make it clear that you are available, open, and on their side if anyone ever touches them or talks with them in such a way that they feel uncomfortable.
- Let them know you will protect them.

Sukkoth of Healing from Domestic Violence

ADRIENNE AFFLECK

This service was the result of a small committee called together by the social worker that heads up our local *shalom bayit* group at Jewish Family and Career Services (JF&CS). The group was made up of women who had participated in a support group for domestic violence survivors. A slightly larger group of women drawn from the survivors counseled by JF&CS gathered for the actual ritual.

The ritual revolves around Sukkoth. Sukkoth is a thanksgiving celebration held after the fall harvest. It takes place five days after Yom Kippur, the Day of Atonement, which occurs on the tenth day of the Hebrew month of Tishri. The day after Yom Kippur the Jews begin to build wooden huts or booths called *sukkahs*. A *sukkah* is a temporary structure with at least two walls and a roof covered with branches. The *sukkah* represents the dwellings that the Jews lived in while they were in the desert after leaving slavery in Egypt. It is a mitzvah, or good deed, to eat in the *sukkah* during this seven-day holiday.

There are special services held in the synagogue and in the *sukkah*. The particular rituals observed are written in the Torah, or five books of Moses. The Torah tells us to use fruit, palm, myrtle, and willow in rejoicing before G-d. These four kinds of plants are symbols that remind us of everything that grows from the earth.

The fruit we use is a citron, which is a cousin of the lemon, and is known as an *etrog* in Hebrew. The palm branches are *lulav*, the myrtle is *hadasim*, and the willow is *aravot*. The three tree branches are bound together and are waved three times in each direction (north, south, east, west, up, and down) during the Sukkoth service.

Sukkoth generally falls during October, which is domestic violence awareness month. The *sukkah* represents the temporary shelter sought by many battered women fleeing from violence in their home. It is frequently referred to as the *sukkah* of peace, and as such it replaces the *shalom bayit*, the peace that should reside in a Jewish home.

Materials: paper, candles, kindling for fire, matches, vessel, water, shovel(s), tree, *tallises* (prayer shawls), *etrog* (citron), *lulav* (palm branches), purple ribbons, Mi Shebeirach music tape.

Opening

People gather together at the site of a hole that is prepared for the planting of a tree.

Reader: Today we shall begin by listening to the silence of our absence in Jewish history and ritual. To do this, I invite each of us to take a few deep, cleansing breaths.

Reader: Stay connected to your body. Engage each of your five senses. Sway; move to the tune we hum as we begin to gather together.

The leader begins to hum a *niggun* (wordless melody). Toward the end of the melody, she sings, "Let us slowly form a circle; a circle that is broken; a circle that is open; a circle of support."

Reader: Let us greet each other. To the one on our right, we ask, "How is your wholeness?" This question may be answered or not, as you please. (Wait until all have been greeted.)

The Beginning

Reader: Candles are an integral part of many new beginnings. Their light is the light of hope, the flicker of faith, and the flame of strength. They are the spark of the divine that rests deep within our soul.

Leader: Join me now as we thank Our Creator for bringing us safely to this season, that we might experience the First Sukkoth of Healing from domestic violence.

Together: Blessed is The One, The Creator, for giving us life, for sustaining us, and for enabling us to reach this season.

Leader: And now we join in the blessing of the candles whose light shall guide us as we seek to support and comfort ourselves.

Together: Blessed is The One, Our Creator, by whose *mitzvoth* (good deeds) we are hallowed, who commands us to kindle the lights of Sukkoth.

Together: Rabbi Tarfon once said, "You are not required to finish the task of creation and repair. However, neither are you permitted to desist from beginning it."

Leader: All beginnings are difficult; so too is this beginning. We begin by tearing off a section of paper.

Reader: Each of us is "stealing" a piece for ourselves. We are acknowledging that we lost our being, our separate self, in our family, in our own home, in our community. We do this to honor the secrets we have hidden from ourselves, our family, and our community. We tear away that we might save ourselves and our children.

Leader: If you wish, you may write the name of your abuser on your slip of
            paper. You may write about whatever feelings or memories you are
            ready to cast off and leave behind.

The Casting Off

Reader: Our broken relationships, our abuse, have caused us to hide our
            feelings of pain. Our anger brews inside us, corroding our hearts.
            We, who have lived in fear of others, now fear the depths of our
            emotions. In our compassion for ourselves, and for our weaknesses,
            we use the light of our candles to kindle a fire. (Start fire in the
            bottom of the pit for the tree.)
Together: Here we stand, each on our way to healing and on our way
            to becoming unafraid. We come together to offer support and
            comfort, now knowing that there are those who can protect us
            on our journey. We engage in ritual so that each of us might
            experience a moment of freedom, a moment of peace, and a
            moment of safety.
                As each participant who wishes to do so casts her piece of paper
            into the flame, she may say the following, or she may ask the group
            to recite it for her:
Participant: I, who have experienced terror and rage, shall no longer live in
            fear.
Participant: I, who have been humiliated, shall no longer live with shame.
Participant: I, who have known violation, shall know strength.
Participant: I, a woman of compassion, shall not be hardened or immobilized
            by my struggle.
Together: Today I add my rage to this flame that I might reclaim my dignity,
            accept my goodness, and affirm the value and sacredness of my
            individual self.
Leader: Just as it is proper to express our righteous anger, so also may we
            express our sorrows. Here, in this vessel, are the tears of our
            sorrows, and the anguish of our broken-ness and pain.
                As each participant who wishes to do so casts her piece of paper
            into a large bowl of water, she may say the following, or she may
            ask the group to recite it for her:
Participant: In these waters, I drown betrayal.
Participant: Here I drown the voices that taught me that I had no value, that
            made excuses for my abuser, and that were silent during my
            suffering.
Participant: I drown abandonment and secrecy.
Participant: I cast out self-denial and doubt.

Participant:	I cast out feelings of defeat and helplessness.
Together:	(After everyone has finished whichever ritual they wish.) This is the vessel into which we have placed our most profound feelings. And this is the fire that burned so that we might survive. Now, we pour out a portion of our feelings, and drown some piece of our pain that we are ready to let loose. (Each may cup their hands to take some water from the vessel and pour it upon the fire, extinguishing it.)
Together:	These are the ashes from a bitter part of our life. We offer them to this young sapling to use as a foundation for its life. These are the waters of survival and rebirth, use them, young one, to grow. (Place the tree in the hole, and cover the hole with dirt.)
Together:	May you, the tree of our hope, be undefeated by storms and drought. May the resources of this sacred place give you life. And, may your branches serve as shelters of peace. Amen.
Leader:	Today, we have planted a beautiful Vitex bush. Its name comes from the Latin word for life. Long after other plants have stopped blooming, the Vitex is festooned with lavender blooms, the same color that represents the movement dedicated to the elimination of domestic violence. It grows tall and strong in spite of adversity, and provides nectar to the bees. It is a fitting reminder of our gathering here, as it stands for our strength and courage. May this tree of life grow as our hope grows, free and beautifully adorned.
Leader:	We must now force ourselves to move along. Let's walk together to the *sukkah*. Let's walk the healing journey to shelter with courage and resolve.

The In-Gathering

While still outside the *sukkah:*

Leader:	Once, during a festival such as this, a musician, a stranger, appeared in the midst of the crowd. Nobody knew her; she claimed to have traveled long distances, endured hardships, and barely survived by living day to day. She was accepted into their town and joined in their celebration. On the final day of the festival, she wished to repay the village for their kindness and for the hospitality she had received. She played a melody on her flute, one which sounded of hatred and fear, of toil and pain, and yet all over it, of unity and peace. It was impossible to tell how long the haunting melody continued; but, when she was finished, the last note rang in the hearts of the villagers. That was many years ago, but those who still

want to remember can hear that last inspiring note: the sweet sound of hope.

Reader: This is the *etrog* (citron), symbol of my heart, full of longing. This is the *lulav* (palm branches), the backbone forged from my courage and strength. This is the willow, the voice of my inner wisdom, the mouth of my dreams. This is the myrtle, the blind eyes of others, and the eyes of a victim no longer open to beauty. Here are the eyes of those who sleep in the dust, who finally rest in peace.

Reader: I shake these entwined reminders of life. I shake them to the east, where the dawn of hope is rising. I shake them to the west, where the days of fear end. I shake them to the north, towards the winter of my desperation. I shake them to the south, where there is the warmth of community.

I shake them for our foremothers, that the rattling wakes them to join us, to add their wisdom to our in-gathering. Sarah, you are the backbone of our faith; renew our strength and the faith within us. Rebecca, give us your heart of gold, the full measure of your tenderness. Leah, give us eyes to see the needy, and eyes that can stare into a bright, unknowable future. Rachel, guide us when we are lost; bring your powerful voice to us.

Together: Oh venerable ancestors tell us your stories that you might not die twice.

Together: (Sing "Hinei Ma Tov")[1]

Hinei mah-tov uma-naim
Shevet achim gam-yachad

Leader: This is the *sukkah* of hope. This is the *sukkah* of peace. This is the *sukkah* that ends the wandering and the struggling.

Within the *Sukkah*

Leader: This is a *tallis*, a prayer shawl. It is wrapped around the worshiper like a blanket around a baby, to provide security and warmth. It encloses the worshiper in a sacred space that cannot be violated. It is a shelter from the din of wrath, and from sights no eyes can bear to see.

Reader: The *tallis* (prayer shawl) helps us make the transition from the outside world to this special place and time. Wrap yourself within it, if you wish, and then pass it on to another. This is how we shall share our hope, by the giving and the taking of this communal shield of strength.

Each participant may be silent, or may say:

> I am trying on this cloth of honor.
> I am putting on this shawl of dignity.
> I am using this sacred fabric, which has held the hope of generations.
> I am surrounding myself with courage.
> I am wrapping myself in this cloak of respect.
> I am enclosing myself within the support of Israel.
> I am sheltering myself with this banner of peace.
> I am sampling the sweet foretaste of triumph.
> I am comforted by my community, and am swaddled in their colors.

Leader: "Oh Shield of Abraham, who may abide in Your house? Who may dwell in Your holy mountain?

Participants: Those who are upright; who do justly; who speak the truth within their hearts.

Reader: Who do not slander others, or wrong them, or bring shame upon them.

Participants: Who scorn the lawless, but honor those who revere Our Creator.

Reader: Who give their word, and, come what may, do not retract.

Participants: Who do not exploit others, who never take bribes.

Reader: Those who live in this way shall never be shaken."[2]

Leader: Each of you was asked to bring three pieces of ribbon with you today. One ribbon is your past, which brought you here today. One ribbon is the present, and the last is the future.

Reader: These are the colors, the very fabric, of our lives; the joys and sorrows of our days. We bring them here that there might at last be witnesses to all that formed us.

Together: While within this shelter of peace, we are going to weave together shreds and pieces of our lives, and entwine them to make a whole. For no matter how many adversities have come our way, no matter which events came along to break us, we have arrived in one piece, still whole. Halleluyah!

(Each participant who wishes may now braid her three ribbons together. When everyone is finished, the group should be gathered together again.)

Leader: Everything that we create is a metaphor of reality. These braids are formed from our separate realities. Now, our lives are linked one with the other in solidarity and compassion.

(Pick up a purple ribbon and use it to link the leader's braid with another participant's braid.)

Participants:	Today we have given birth to a new community, a community that recognizes the value of every human being and that reflects the potential of each one of us. Now we can go forward to form a new life, free to discover the who and what of our individuality. Our lives can have a new meaning and purpose. Each day can be fully experienced as we risk respecting our needs, using our talents, and completing our destiny.
Leader:	In our tradition, there is a prayer for healing called the Mi Shebeirach,[3] which is generally said, or sung, in support of those with physical illnesses. Let us gather together now to ask that our hearts might be mended, that we might be more fully present to effect our own healing.
Reader:	May this time together help each of us to move forward to create a bolder, fuller life.
Together:	May our ritual bring closure to our past, and healing to our present.
Reader:	May we become messengers of support and compassion, partners in the healing and repair of all who have been, are, and will be abused and neglected.
Leader:	Go forth with renewed peace and wholeness.

Respectfully, and lovingly, submitted by Adrienne Affleck to the Atlanta JF& CS's *shalom bayit* program, and in honor of Wendy Lipshutz.

I wish to thank all those who participated in the "brainstorming" sessions that gave me so many great ideas, and to the following works that inspired me:

Old Symbols, New Rituals by Marcia Cohn Spiegel.

Shalom Bayit: Peace in the Home, A Service of Healing with Justice.

Sukkat Shalom: A Healing in the Sukkah for Battered Women and their Allies by Rebecca Schwartz and Naomi Tucker.

"Our Silent Seasons," a ceremony of healing from sexual abuse, by Leila Gal Berner, in *Lifecycles: Jewish Women on Life Passages and Personal Milestones* by Debra Orenstein, ed. (Woodstock, Vt.: Jewish Lights, 1994), 121–36.

Notes

1. Hinei Ma Tov comes from a prophesy in the Torah which has also been set to a tune. The essence of the passage is: how good and how pleasant it is that brothers and sisters can live peacefully together.

2. *Gates of the House: The New Union Home Prayerbook* (New York: Central Conference of American Rabbis, 1977), 75.

3. The Mi Shebeirach is a traditional prayer said in the synagogue for those unable to attend because of a physical illness. Many congregations use a form of this prayer that has been set to a tune and partly translated by Debbie Friedman. It is offered in support not only to the physically ill, but to all who are in recovery.

A Community Model for Intervention

The following table can be used to brainstorm what is needed in your community. It can also help individuals figure out what they'd like to do to help.

Revised Chart of Recommendations

Whom We Want to Educate[a] (Our Target Populations in Priority Order)	What We Want to Educate Them About (Our Messages)	How We Want to Educate Them (Our Methods)
Top priority: Professionals		
• Jewish nursery school teachers/staff • Jewish day schools • Jewish synagogue-affiliated schools • Jewish camps • Professionals and volunteers affiliated with the associated agency system • Jewish clergy (rabbis, synagogue leaders)	• General awareness (i.e., that child abuse *does* exist in the Jewish community) • How to identify child abuse (signs) • Jewish perspectives on child abuse • Legal requirement to report • How to report • How else to respond (e.g., referral to treatment resources)	• Within the schools' in-service training for teachers and staff • Instructional brochures or booklets, outlining the messages • Development of a policy on child abuse to be distributed and "signed for" by each teacher and staff member (e.g., similar to the Baltimore County Public School Policy)
Second priority: Jewish children (up to eighteen)		
• Pupils in nursery schools and preschools • Pupils in Jewish day schools • Pupils in Jewish synagogue-affiliated schools • Participants in Jewish camps	• Good touch/bad touch • What Judaism has to say about child abuse and victims' rights • What to do if you have been abused or know someone else who has been ("No/Go Tell")	• School curriculum • Children's workbooks • School/camp outreach "road shows"

[a]First-year recommended focus is on children and those who come in direct contact with them (i.e., in the first and second priorities listed in column 1, and tangentially in the third and fourth priorities).

Whom We Want to Educate[a] (Our Target Populations in Priority Order)	What We Want to Educate Them About (Our Messages)	How We Want to Educate Them (Our Methods)
Third priority: Parents		
• JCC parenting programs • Parents of nursery school students • Child study groups • Jewish Lamaze course participants • Refugees from former Soviet Union	• General awareness (child abuse does exist in the Jewish community) • How to identify child abuse (signs) • Jewish perspectives on child abuse • Legal requirement to report • How to report • How else to respond (e.g., referral to treatment resources) • Tips for good parenting, especially at high stress times (e.g., holidays, family transitions, report card time)	• Posters and give-away flyers in selected supermarkets/stores • Speakers' bureau • Brief part of Lamaze curriculum, with instructional brochure/booklet as a handout (same as above) • Written information on acceptable American methods of discipline, presented by resettlement social worker with a handout on good parenting tips, "American style" (in Russian language for refugees) • Adapted version of Baltimore City's Stop/Look/Listen card on how to respond to your child's report card (translated into Russian for immigrants)
Fourth priority: General community[b]		
• Jewish media • Baltimore Jewish Council • Synagogue/rabbinic leaders • Patrons of Jewish stores • Jewish clergy (rabbis, synagogue leaders) • Other professionals in touch with the Jewish community (e.g., doctors, social service professionals) • Overall Jewish community	• General awareness (as above) • How to identify child abuse • Jewish perspectives on child abuse • Legal requirement to report • How to report • How else to respond	• Jewish press feature stories • Posters and give-away flyers in selected supermarkets/stores • Brochures on what to say or do when you see someone abusing his/her child (e.g., in a supermarket)

[b]Steinitz commented that this list should also include judges and lawyers.

Note: "Child abuse" specifically means physical abuse, child neglect, and sexual abuse as defined legally in Maryland. May also address severe emotional abuse.

Source: Jewish Community Task Force on Child Abuse/Subcommittee on Education, Baltimore, Maryland (Lucy Steinitz, March 2, 1993).

Agencies, Resources, and Websites

While there may be Jewish agencies or organizations with programs specifically addressing adult survivors of childhood sexual abuse and/or incest, I have not been able to find them in several years of inquiry. The one self-help group that seemed to focus on Jewish survivors did not respond to phone calls or letters. Letters came back "addressee unknown." Some individuals and community groups are in beginning discussions about how to address the needs of adult survivors.

The following individuals and organizations are listed because I believe they are or could be responsive to efforts to address the needs of adult survivors. The resources listed in this appendix were valid as of October 2001. Not all the resources listed are known to me. Some were recommended by others. The inclusion or exclusion of a resource does not signify either endorsement or rejection. Please evaluate any resource to see if it is right for your purposes. Be sure to ask about specific expertise in working with sexual abuse and/or incest and adult survivors. If they do not have the expertise, are they willing to develop it, or bring in those who do? Trust your instincts. Surf websites with care, remembering that they are rarely monitored or reviewed.

Visit the *Shine the Light* website at www.shine-the-light.com

Jewish Resources Addressing Incest, Sexual Abuse, and Domestic Violence

Center for the Prevention of Sexual and Domestic Violence
Jewish Task Force
936 North 34th St., Suite 200
Seattle, WA 98103
Phone: 206-634-1903
Fax: 206-634-0115 (twenty-four hours)
E-mail: cpsdv@cpsdv.org
Website: http://www.cpsdv.org

The center is an interreligious educational resource addressing issues of sexual and domestic violence. Their goal is to engage religious leaders in the task of ending abuse, and to prepare human services professionals to recognize and attend to the religious questions and issues that may arise in their work with women and children in crisis. Their emphasis is on education and prevention.

The center has a National Clearinghouse on Religion and Abuse. They have a Jewish Task Force and produced a video, *To Save a Life: Ending Domestic Violence in Jewish Families*. While its focus is spouse abuse, the stories told by the women survivors, plus the commentary by five rabbis from different denominations, are powerful.

Shalom Task Force
Phone: 888-883-2323

Hotline providing information on rabbinic, legal, and counseling service for anyone in the Jewish community in an abusive situation.

Jewish Family and Children's Service Organizations

Association of Jewish Family and Children's Agencies (AJFCA)
557 Cranbury Rd., Suite 2
East Brunswick, NJ 08816-5419
Phone: 800-634-7346
Fax: 732-432-7127
E-mail: ajfca@ajfca.org
Website: http://ajfca.org/

The Association of Jewish Family and Children's Agencies is the membership organization of over 145 Jewish family and children's agencies and specialized human service agencies throughout the United States and Canada. AJFCA can refer you to local agencies.

Jewish Family Services (Baltimore)
Joan Grayson Cohen, Esq., L.C.S.W.-C, Manager, Child/Adolescent Outreach, provides consultation about child abuse and domestic violence outreach and prevention programs in the Jewish community.
Phone: 410-542-6300, ext. 203

Mimi Kraus, L.C.S.W.-C, District Office Manager, Baltimore Jewish Family Services, heads the family violence division.
Phone: 410-356-8383, ext. 308

Ohel Children's Home and Family Services
Phone: 718-851-6300 or 800-603-OHEL

Ohel is a social service agency that serves the Jewish community and provides counseling and crisis intervention for children and families experiencing marital conflict, emotional problems, and abuse and neglect. Ohel also operates a program for victims of domestic violence. Housing and outpatient services are available for people with developmental, emotional, and mental disabilities. Referrals are available: for housing, legal assistance, and rabbinic consultations.

Union of American Hebrew Congregations
Department of Jewish Family Concerns
633 Third Ave.
New York, NY 10017
Phone: 212-650-4294
Fax: 212-650-4239
E-mail: deptjewfamcon@uahc.org

Additional Resources for Community Information and Action

Bibliography of Sources on Sexual and Domestic Violence in the Jewish Community
Marcia Cohn Spiegel
Website: http://www.mincava.umn.edu/center.asp.

Jewish Women International (JWI)
1828 L St., NW, Suite 250
Washington, D.C. 20036
Phone: 202-857-1300
Fax: 202-857-1380
E-mail: info@jwi.org
Website: http://www.jewishwomen.org

JWI strives to break the cycle of violence through education, advocacy, and action—locally, nationally, and around the world. They have developed a *Resource Guide for Rabbis on Domestic Violence* that includes a directory of Jewish organizations working with issues of violence and violence prevention (by states).

While most of these agencies focus on battered women, many are also involved in prevention work. Talk with them about what they're doing in the area of child sexual abuse and incest for children and adults. Ask them what they think is needed. If possible, work with them to meet those needs.

Lilith Magazine
E-mail: Lilithmag@aol.com
Website: www.Lilith.org
Phone: 1-888-2-LILITH

National Council of Jewish Women (NCJW), Inc.
53 West 23d St.
New York, NY 10010
Phone: 212-645-4048
Website: http://www.ncjw.org

NCJW is a volunteer organization, inspired by Jewish values, that works through a program of research, education, advocacy, and community service to improve the quality of life for women, children, and families, and strives to ensure individual rights and freedoms for all.

StoP (Strategies to Prevent) Domestic Violence is a multipronged national initiative incorporating education, community action, advocacy, and training to curtail violence in the home. *StoP Watch* is a national newsletter that highlights the hundreds of grassroots activities of NCJW volunteers and coalition partners.

Rabbi Zev Cohen
Phone: 773-465-2282

Rabbi Cohen is available to discuss community development issues regarding child sexual abuse.

Resources for Survivors (also see all other resource listings)

BAMM/Impact Self-Defense classes
For a national referral, please call 800-345-KICK.

For your healing website: http://www.foryourhealing.com

This site is run by Margot Silk Forrest, a survivor, longtime supporter of survivors, and founding editor of *The Healing Woman* newsletter (which closed in 2000). The site includes some of Margot's practical and helpful articles about recovery from childhood sexual abuse. It also contains writing from other survivors on a variety of topics, inspirational quotations, resources, and a page where survivors can request information or advice on some aspects of healing (and where site visitors can respond).

Heroes Great and Small, Inc.
P.O. Box 705
Armuchee, GA 30105
Phone: 706-235-4463
E-mail: heroesgreatandsmall@yahoo.com
Website: http://www.heroesgreatandsmall.org

Free education and support groups for sexually abused children, adolescents, and *nonoffending* family members. Referrals for areas with groups; assistance in starting local groups nationwide.

Incest Awareness Foundation
P.O. Box 1338
New York, NY 10156
Phone: 888-547-3222 or 212-995-2589

The Incest Awareness Foundation offers workshops and readings. Once a year they have a "To Tell the Truth" weekend conference in Manhattan and a survivor art show.

Incest Survivors Anonymous (ISA)
National office: 213-428-5599

A self-help peer program for incest survivors. "We meet to share our experience, strength and hope, so that we may recover from our incest experiences and no longer allow ourselves to be revictimized by our past. As survivors, we strive to recognize the negative behavior patterns developed as children and break free to a new understanding and a new peace of mind. Living and working the twelve steps and twelve traditions of ISA, we find a healing solution to our root causes."

Kempe National Center for the Prevention and Treatment of Child Abuse and Neglect
Denver, CO
Phone: 303-321-3963

Established in 1972 to improve educational, clinical, and research materials for professionals in the field. The center promotes a multidisciplinary approach to prevention and treatment, involving, whenever possible, the entire family.

Making Daughters Safe Again
E-mail: mdsasupport@mail.com
Website: http://mdsasupport.homestead.com/index.html

Resources for mother-daughter incest survivors, including on-line self-help, info, chat, public forums, info for students, researchers, loved ones, general research on female offenders, links.

National Organization on Male Sexual Victimization
P.O. Box 4055
St. Paul, MN 55104
Phone: 800-738-4181

The National Organization on Male Sexual Victimization (NOMSV) began as a single conference in 1988. It was clear that this gathering was a needed resource, and the energy generated by the first conference helped fuel the second conference a year later. In November 1994 a group began the process of creating a permanent organization focused on the issue of male sexual victimization.

Survivors Healing Center
2301 Mission St., Suite C-1
Santa Cruz, CA 95060
Phone: 831-423-7601

Provides education, information, referrals, high-quality services, and support to adult survivors of childhood sexual abuse and to other concerned individuals. "Our primary goals are to empower those victimized by sexual abuse through a healing process and to prevent sexual abuse of children."

VOICES in Action (Victims of Incest Can Emerge Survivors)
P.O. Box 148309
Chicago, IL 60614
Phone: 800-786-4238; 773-327-1500; 800-7-VOICE-8
Website: http://www.voices-action.org

National network of incest survivors. They have more than one hundred special interest support groups who correspond with each other in a systematic way. They run on membership fees, but no one is turned away for lack of funds. VOICES in Action, Inc., an international nonprofit organization, was founded by Diana Carson in 1980. Diana, along with several other women, formed a self-help group working to provide support for victims of incest and child sexual abuse. They named their group VOICE, Inc. In 1984 the headquarters of the organization was moved from Grand Junction, Colorado, to Chicago, Illinois, and they changed their name to VOICES in Action, Inc.

General Resources Addressing Child Abuse and Domestic Violence (Hotlines)

International Domestic Violence Crisis Line (for abused American women in foreign countries): 866-USWOMEN

National Child Abuse Hotline: 800-4-A-CHILD

National Domestic Violence Hotline: 800-799-SAFE (7233)

National Elder Abuse Hotline: 800-992-1660

National Hotline for Child Abusers: Parents Anonymous: 800-421-0353

National Organization for Victim Assistance: 800-TRY-NOVA

National Victim Center: 800-FYI-CALL

Rape, Abuse, and Incest National Network (RAINN): 800-656-HOPE
Website: http://www.rainn.org

RAINN is a twenty-four-hour national hotline for victims of sexual assault. Calls to the hotline are instantly computer-routed to the twenty-four-hour rape crisis center nearest the caller.

Organizations Involved in Prevention, Treatment, Training, and Research

American Professional Society on the Abuse of Children (APSAC)
Website: http://www.apsac.org

Children's Defense Fund
25 E St., NW
Washington, D.C. 20001
Phone: 202-628-8787

Family Violence Prevention Fund
Building One, Suite 200
1001 Potrero Ave.
San Francisco, CA 94110
Phone: 415-821-4553
Fax: 415-824-3873

The Family Violence Prevention Fund (FVPF) works to end domestic violence and help women and children whose lives are devastated by abuse, because every person has the right to live in a home free of violence. The FVPF challenges lawmakers to take domestic violence seriously, educates judges to protect all victims of abuse, and advocates for laws to help battered immigrant women. The FVPF works with health care providers and employers to identify and aid victims of abuse, helps communities support children from violent homes, and shows Americans how to help end domestic violence. FVPF programs and policies have won countless awards and been replicated around the world.

Good-Touch/Bad-Touch
Prevention and Motivation Programs, Inc.
P.O. Box 1960
659 Henderson Dr., Suite H
Cartersville, GA 30120
Phone: 800-245-1527
Fax: 770-607-9600
E-mail: GTBT1@aol.com
Website: http://www.goodtouchbadtouch.com/

Good-Touch/Bad-Touch® is a comprehensive child abuse prevention curriculum designed for preschool and kindergarten through sixth grade students that works as a tool to teach children the skills they need to play a significant role in prevention or interruption of child abuse/sexual abuse in their own lives. Children are taught what abuse is, are given prevention skills including personal body safety rules, and are motivated into action if threatened. They learn to distinguish between touches that feel good, touches that hurt, and touches that are sexual abuse—a forced or tricked touch to private body parts. Private body parts are those covered by a two-piece bathing suit for girls and by swim trunks for little boys. Anatomical language is not used.

Although the program focuses on sexual abuse prevention beginning in the third grade, the program expands into physical abuse and bullying. In the fifth and sixth grades Good-Touch/Bad-Touch® gets even more specific, addressing sexual harassment, physical abuse, emotional abuse, and neglect.

Justice for Children
Kimberly Stabler, Executive Director
2600 Southwest Freeway, Suite 806
Houston, TX 77098
Phone: 713-225-4357; 800-733-0098
Fax: 713-225-2818
E-mail: info@jfcadvocacy.org

Justice for Children-D.C.
Eileen King, Regional Director
733 15th St., NW, Suite 214
Washington, D.C. 20005
Phone: 202-462-4688
Fax: 202-462-4689

Justice for Children is a national nonprofit organization of citizens concerned about children's rights and their protection from abuse. Their mission is to raise the consciousness of our society about the failure of our governmental agencies to protect victims of child abuse, to provide legal advocacy for abused children, and to develop and implement, on a collaborative basis where possible, a full range of solutions that enhance the quality of life for these children.

Programs include Court Watch, Case Advocacy, Resources for Children's Therapy, Legislative Advocacy, Information and Community Resource Referrals, Community Presentations, Legal Advocacy, Assistance with Navigating Public Systems, and Research and Training.

One Voice is a project of Justice for Children, housed in D.C., that provides programs and services, such as legal referrals, semi-annual newsletter reporting on relevant legal decisions, trends in the backlash against sexual abuse survivors, new research and statistics on abuse, trauma and memory, legislative initiatives, new publications, and upcoming conferences.

Healing and Recovery Video Series: One Voice offers three educational videos produced by Marilyn Van Derbur, former Miss America and incest survivor. *Once Can Hurt a Lifetime* is used extensively in sex offender treatment programs across the country and has been found very helpful in engendering empathy for the victims. *The Invisible Link* and *An Invaluable Tool* are two videos developed with health care professionals in mind. They encourage all health care personnel who have contact with patients to be mindful that survivors of child sexual abuse may have unpleasant reactions to some medical procedures and that there may be links between their current symptoms and complaints and childhood abuse. These videos are now used in cancer hospitals and in private practices. The organization is piloting a program for making this information part of medical school education.

There are two information lists that give out legislative alerts, research/ publications news, and announcements.

E-mail: eking@jfcadvocacy.org

Minnesota Center Against Violence and Abuse (MINCAVA)
School of Social Work
University of Minnesota, 105 Peters Hall
1404 Gortner Ave.
St. Paul, MN 55108-6142
Phone: 612-624-0721; in Minnesota: 800-646-2282
Fax: 612-625-4288
Website: http://www.mincava.umn.edu/center.asp

MINCAVA's mission is to support research, education, and access to information related to violence. *Bibliography of Sources on Sexual and Domestic Violence in the Jewish Community* by Marcia Cohn Spiegel is available here.

Clinical Training and Resources for Therapists

Association for Comprehensive Energy Psychology (ACEP)
P.O. Box 910244
San Diego, CA 92191-0244
Voice mail: 858-748-5963
E-mail: acep@energypscyh.org
Website: http://www.energypsych.org

ACEP is an international nonprofit charitable membership organization founded in 1998 to promote professionally responsible energy psychology treatments, and facilitate collaboration among practitioners, researchers, and licensing bodies. ACEP was founded by licensed psychologists David Grudermeyer, Ph.D., Rebecca Grudermeyer, Psy.D., and Dorothea Hover-Kramer, Ed.D., R.N.

EMDR Institute, Inc.
P.O. Box 51010
Pacific Grove, CA 93950-6010
Phone: 831-372-3900
Website: http://www.emdr.com

From the EMDR website: EMDR is an acronym for Eye Movement Desensitization and Reprocessing. It is an innovative clinical treatment that has successfully helped over a million individuals who have survived trauma, including sexual abuse, domestic violence, combat, crime, and those suffering from a number of other complaints including depressions, addictions, phobias, and a variety of self-esteem issues. EMDR is a complex method of psychotherapy that integrates many of the successful elements of a range of therapeutic approaches in combination with eye movements or other forms of rhythmical stimulation in ways that stimulate the brain's information processing system. With EMDR therapy it is unnecessary to delve into decades-old psychological material, but rather, by activating the information-processing system of the brain, people can achieve their therapeutic goals at a rapid rate, with recognizable changes that don't disappear over time. Fourteen controlled studies support the efficacy of EMDR, making it the most thoroughly researched method ever used in the treatment of trauma.

Emotional Freedom Techniques
Gary H. Craig
P.O. Box 1393
Gualala, CA 95445
Phone: 707-785-2848
Website: http://www.emofree.com

From Gary Craig's website: In simplest terms, EFT is an emotional form of acupuncture, except that we don't use needles. Instead, we tap with the fingertips to stimulate certain meridian points while the client is "tuned in" to the problem. We are still learning why EFT (and its many cousins) works so well. The existing theory is that *"the cause of all negative emotions is a disruption in the body's energy system."* EFT has been proven clinically effective (over 80 percent) for trauma, abuse, stress, anxiety, fears, phobias, depression, grief, addictive cravings, children's issues, and hundreds of physical symptoms including headaches, body pains, and breathing difficulties.

Family Violence and Sexual Assault Institute
Texas Office:
7120 Herman Jared Dr.
Fort Worth, TX 76180
Phone: 817-485-2244
Fax: 817-485-0660
E-mail: dwforkids@earthlink.net

California Office:
6160 Cornerstone Ct. East
San Diego, CA 92121
Phone: 858-623-2777, ext. 406
Fax: 858-646-0761
E-mail: fvsai@mail.cspp.edu
Website: http://www.fvsai.org

Guidelines for the Psychosocial Treatment of Intrafamilial Child Physical and Sexual Abuse
Website: http://www.musc.edu/cvc/guide1.htm
Draft Report, April 2001.

HeartMath
14700 West Park Ave.
Boulder Creek, CA 95006
Phone: 800-450-9111
E-mail: info@heartmath.com
Website: http://www.heartmath.com

HeartMath offers techniques that use the transforming power of the heart to release stress, access higher levels of intelligence, establish emotional balance, and stimulate higher brain functioning. HeartMath trains individuals and organizations.

National Committee to Prevent Child Abuse
Phone: 312-663-3520 (voice); 800-835-2671 (publication orders)

The National Committee to Prevent Child Abuse (NCPCA), founded in 1972, is an advocacy organization dedicated to involving concerned citizens in actions to prevent child abuse. NCPCA's programs consist of public awareness and education, national volunteer networks, technical and consultative services, primary prevention, and advocacy. Public awareness and education involve national media campaigns, publications, conferences, and workshops.

Selected Bibliography
For Survivors and Those Who Care about Them

Professional Literature: Sexual Abuse and Incest

Starred items are for survivors as well.

Briere, John. *Child Abuse Trauma: Theory and Treatment of the Lasting Effects.* Newbury Park: Sage Publications, 1992.

———. *Therapy for Adults Molested as Children: Beyond Survival.* New York: Springer Publishing, 1989.

Briere, John, and Diana Elliott. "Immediate and Long-Term Impacts of Child Sexual Abuse." *The Future of Children* 4, no. 2 (1994): 54–69.

*Butler, Sandra. *Conspiracy of Silence: The Trauma of Incest.* San Francisco: Volcano Press, 1985.

*Caldwell, Christine. *Getting Our Bodies Back: Recovery, Healing, and Transformation through Body-Centered Psychotherapy.* Boston: Shambhala Publications, 1996.

*DeBecker, Gavin. *The Gift of Fear: Survival Signals that Protect Us from Violence.* New York: Bantam Doubleday Dell, 1998.

*Elliott, Michelle, ed. *Female Sexual Abuse of Children.* New York: Guilford Press, 1994.

Elliott, D. M., and J. Briere. "Posttraumatic Stress Associated with Delayed Recall of Sexual Abuse: A General Population Study." *Journal of Traumatic Stress* 8 (1995): 629–47.

Everstine, D., and L. Everstine. *Sexual Trauma in Children and Adolescents: Dynamics of Treatment.* New York: Brunner/Mazel, 1989.

Finkelhor, D., G. Hotaling, I. A. Lewis, and C. Smith. "Sexual Abuse in a National Survey of Adult Men and Women: Prevalence, Characteristics, and Risk Factors." *Child Abuse and Neglect* 14 (1990): 19–28.

Gallo, Fred P. *Energy Psychology: Explorations at the Interface of Energy, Cognition, Behavior, and Health.* Boca Raton: CRC Press, 1998.

Gallo, Fred P., and Harry Vincenzi. *Energy Tapping: How to Rapidly Eliminate Anxiety, Depression, Cravings, and More Using Energy Psychology.* Oakland, Calif.: New Harbinger Publications, 2000.

Harvey, M. R., and J. L. Herman. "Amnesia, Partial Amnesia, and Delayed Recall among Adult Survivors of Childhood Trauma." *Consciousness and Cognition* 4 (1994): 295–306.

*Herman, J. L. *Father-Daughter Incest.* Cambridge: Harvard University Press, 2000.

————. *Trauma and Recovery: The Aftermath of Violence—From Domestic Abuse to Political Terror.* New York: Basic Books, 1992.

Herman, J. L., and M. R. Harvey. "Adult Memories of Childhood Trauma: A Naturalistic Clinical Study." *Journal of Traumatic Stress* 10 (1997): 557–71.

Herman, J. L., and E. Schatzow. "Recovery and Verification of Memories of Childhood Sexual Trauma." *Psychoanalytic Psychology* 4 (1987): 1–14.

Holmes, G. R., L. Offen, and G. Waller. "See No Evil, Hear No Evil, Speak No Evil: Why Do Relatively Few Male Victims of Childhood Sexual Abuse Receive Help for Abuse-Related Issues in Adulthood?" *Clinical Psychology Review* 17 (1997): 69–88.

*Hunter, M. *Abused Boys: The Neglected Victims of Sexual Abuse.* New York: Fawcett Columbine, 1990.

Jordan, Judith V., Alexandra G. Kaplan, Jean Baker Miller, Irene P. Stiver, and Janet L. Surrey. *Women's Growth in Connection: Writings from the Stone Center.* New York: Guilford Press, 1991.

Klein, Ethel, ed., Jacquelyn Campbell, Esta Soler, and Marissa Ghez. *Ending Domestic Violence: Changing Public Perceptions/Halting the Epidemic.* Thousand Oaks, Calif.: Sage Publications, 1997.

Lisak, D. "The Psychological Impact of Sexual Abuse: Content Analysis of Interviews with Male Survivors." *Journal of Traumatic Stress* 7 (1994): 525–48.

Lovett, Joan, and Francine Shapiro. *Small Wonders: Healing Childhood Trauma with EMDR.* New York: Free Press, 1999.

McCann, I. Lisa, and Laurie Ann Pearlman. *Psychological Trauma and the Adult Survivor: Theory, Therapy, and Transformation.* New York: Brunner/Mazel, 1990.

*Miller, Alice. *Banished Knowledge.* New York: Doubleday, 1990.

*————. *The Drama of the Gifted Child.* New York: Basic Books, 1980.

*————. *Thou Shalt Not Be Aware.* New York: Farrar, Straus and Giroux, 1984.

Myers, J. E. B., L. Berliner, J. Briere, C. T. Hendrix, C. Jenny, and T. Reid, eds. *The APSAC Handbook on Child Maltreatment.* Newbury Park: Sage Publications, 2002.

Perry, B. D. "Incubated in Terror: Neurodevelopmental Factors in the 'Cycle of Violence.'" In *Children, Youth, and Violence: The Search for Solutions.* Edited by J. Osofsky. New York: Guilford Press, 1997, 124–48.

Pynoos, R. S. "Post-Traumatic Stress Disorder in Children and Adolescents." In *Psychiatric Disorders in Children and Adolescents.* Edited by B. Garfinkel, G. Carlson, and E. Weller. Philadelphia: W. B. Saunders, 1990, 48–63.

Schwarz, E. D., and B. D. Perry. "The post-traumatic response in children and adolescents." *Psychiatric Clinics of North America* 17, no. 2 (1994): 311–26.

Shapiro, Francine. *Eye Movement Desensitization and Reprocessing.* New York: Guilford Press, 1995.

Shapiro, Francine, and Margot Silk Forrest. *EMDR: The Breakthrough Therapy for Overcoming Anxiety, Stress, and Trauma.* New York: Basic Books, 1998.

Shengold, Leonard. *Soul Murder: The Effects of Childhood Abuse and Deprivation.* New York: Fawcett Columbine/Ballantine Books, 1989.

"Symposium: Science and Politics of Recovered Memories." *Ethics and Behavior* 8, no. 2 (1998).

Terr, Lenore, M.D. *Unchained Memories: True Stories of Traumatic Memories, Lost and Found.* New York: Basic Books, 1995.

Van der Kolk, B. A. "The Body Keeps Score." *Harvard Review of Psychiatry* 1 (1994): 253–65. David Baldwin's Trauma Information Pages: http://www.trauma-pages.com/index.htm.

Van der Kolk, B., and R. Fisler. "Dissociation and the Fragmentary Nature of Traumatic Memories." *Journal of Traumatic Stress* 8 (1995): 505–25. David Baldwin's Trauma Information Pages: http://www.trauma-pages.com/index.htm.

Van der Kolk, B. A., and O. van der Hart. "Pierre Janet and the Breakdown of Adaptation in Psychological Trauma." *American Journal of Psychiatry* 146 (1989): 1,530–40.

Williams, L. M. "Recall of Childhood Trauma: A Prospective Study of Women's Memories of Child Sexual Abuse." *Journal of Consulting and Clinical Psychology* 62 (1994): 1,167–76.

Williams, L. M. "Recovered Memories of Abuse in Women with Documented Child Sexual Victimization Histories." *Journal of Traumatic Stress* 8 (1995): 649–73.

Williams, L. M. "What Does It Mean to Forget Child Sexual Abuse: A Reply to Loftus, Garry, and Feldman." *Journal of Consulting and Clinical Psychology* 62 (1994): 1,182–86.

Survivor Literature: Trauma and Healing

All of the following resources are valuable for clinicians as well. Survivors, please also see the selected bibliography of professional literature.

Bass, Ellen. *I Never Told Anyone: Writings by Women Survivors of Child Sexual Abuse.* Coedited with Louise Thornton. New York: HarperCollins, 1983, 1991.

Bass, Ellen, and Laura Davis. *Beginning to Heal: A First Book for Survivors of Child Sexual Abuse.* New York: HarperCollins, 1993.

———. *The Courage to Heal: A Guide for Women Survivors of Child Sexual Abuse.* New York: HarperCollins, 1988, 1994.

Courtois, Christine. *Healing the Incest Wound.* New York: W. W. Norton, 1988.

Davis, Laura. *The Courage to Heal Workbook for Women and Men Survivors of Child Sexual Abuse.* New York: HarperPerennial, 1990.

Diamond, John, M.D. *Life Energy: Using the Meridians to Unlock the Hidden Power of Your Emotions.* New York: Paragon House, 1990.

Duerk, Judith. *Circle of Stones: Woman's Journey to Herself.* San Diego: LuraMedia, 1989.

Fraser, Sylvia, *My Father's House: A Memoir of Incest and of Healing.* New York: HarperCollins, 1989.

Friends in Recovery. *The Twelve Steps—A Way Out: A Working Guide for Adult Children from Addictive and Other Dysfunctional Families*. San Diego: Recovery Publications, 1987.

Kingsolver, Barbara. *The Bean Trees*. New York: Harper and Row, 1998.

———. *Pigs in Heaven: A Novel*. New York: HarperPerennial, 1992.

Kraus, Sharon. *Generation: Poems*. Farmington, Maine: Alice James Books, 1997.

Landry, Dorothy Beaulieu. *Family Fallout: A Handbook for Families of Adult Sexual Abuse Survivors*. Brandon, Vt.: Safer Society Press, 1992.

Lew, M. *Victims No Longer: Men Recovering from Incest and Other Child Sexual Abuse*. New York: Nevraumont, 1988.

Lew, Mike, and Richard Hoffman. *Leaping upon the Mountains: Men Proclaiming Victory over Sexual Child Abuse*. Berkeley: North Atlantic Books, 2000.

Maltz, Wendy. *The Sexual Healing Journey: A Guide for Survivors of Sexual Abuse*. New York: HarperCollins, 2001.

Martin, Howard, and Doc Childre. *The HeartMath Solution: The Institute of Heart-Math's Revolutionary Program for Engaging the Power of the Heart's Intelligence*. New York: HarperCollins, 1999.

Matas, Carol. *The Primrose Path*. Winnipeg, Canada: Blizzard Publishing, 1998. The story of a young girl who is afraid to reveal the abuse perpetrated on her by her rabbi.

Oliver, Mary. *Dream Work*. New York: Atlantic Monthly Press, 1986.

Remen, Rachel Naomi, M.D. *My Grandfather's Blessings: Stories of Strength, Refuge, and Belonging*. New York: Riverhead Books, 2000.

Ryan, M. J., ed. *The Fabric of the Future: Women Visionaries Illuminate the Path to Tomorrow*. Berkeley: Conari Press, 1998.

Siegel, Bernie. *Love, Medicine, and Miracles: Lessons Learned about Self-Healing from a Surgeon's Experience with Exceptional Cancer Patients*. New York: Harper-Perennial, 1990.

———. *Peace, Love, and Healing: Bodymind Communication and the Path to Self-Healing: An Exploration*. New York: HarperPerennial, 1990.

Silverman, Sue William. *Because I Remember Terror, Father, I Remember You*. Athens: University of Georgia Press, 1999.

Supowit, Sandy. *Halves of Necessity*. Austin: Plain View Press, 1999.

Wisechild, Louise. *The Obsidian Mirror: An Adult Healing from Incest*. Seattle: Seal Press, 1993.

Wood, Wendy Ann, and Julie Livingston, ed. *Triumph over Darkness: Understanding and Healing the Trauma of Childhood Sexual Abuse*. 2d ed. Hillsboro, Ore.: Beyond Words, 1993.

Judaism, Healing, and Abuse

Adler, Rachel. "A Stumbling Block Before the Blind: Sexual Exploitation in Pastoral Counseling." *CCAR Journal: A Reform Jewish Quarterly* (spring 1993):

13–54. See responses by H. Kosovske, in *CCAR Journal* (summer 1994): 5, and Arthur Gross Schaefer (summer 1995): 75–79.

Benjamin, Sophia. "God and Abuse: A Survivor Story." In *Four Centuries of Jewish Women's Spirituality: A Sourcebook.* Edited by Ellen M. Umansky and Dianne Ashton. Boston: Beacon Press, 1992, 326–34. Pages 321–25 describe a woman's use of a *mikveh* to heal after rape.

Berner, Leila Gal. "Our Silent Seasons: A Ceremony of Healing from Sexual Abuse." In *Lifecycles: Jewish Women on Life Passages and Personal Milestones.* Edited by Debra Orenstein. Woodstock, Vt.: Jewish Lights, 1994, 121–36.

Biale, Rachel. *Women and Jewish Law: An Exploration of Women's Issues in Halakhic Sources.* New York: Shocken Books, 1984.

Blumenthal, David. *Facing the Abusing God: A Theology of Protest.* Louisville: Presbyterian Publishing House, 1993.

Blustain, Sarah. "A Paradoxical Legacy: Rabbi Shlomo Carlebach's Shadow Side." *Lilith* 23, no. 1 (spring 1998): 10–17; and "Sex, Power, and Our Rabbis: Readers Respond to 'Rabbi Shlomo Carlebach's Shadow Side.'" *Lilith* (summer 1998): 12–16.

Cohen, Joan Grayson. *Playing It Safe with Your Child: Eli and Ellie Learn about Safety.* Baltimore: Jewish Family Services. To order: Elaine Rosenberg, Jewish Family Services, 5750 Park Heights Avenue, Baltimore, MD 21215-3997.

Cooper, David A. *God Is a Verb: Kabbalah and the Practice of Mystical Judaism.* New York: Riverhead Books, 1997.

Featherman, Joan. "Jews and Sexual Child Abuse." In *Sexual Abuse in Nine North American Cultures: Treatment and Prevention.* Edited by Lisa Fontes. Thousand Oaks, Calif.: Sage Publications, 1995.

Giller, Betsy. "All in the Family: Violence in the Jewish Home." In *Jewish Women in Therapy.* Edited by Rachel Josefowitz Siegel and Ellen Cole. New York: Harrington Park Press, 1991, 101–9.

Goldberg, Lilith. "Surviving Incest in a Holocaust Family." *Lilith* 18, no. 1 (winter 1993): 20–23.

Goldhamer, Douglas, and Melinda Tengel. *This Is for Everyone: Universal Principles of Healing Prayer and the Jewish Mystics.* New York: Larson Publications Bardett, 1999.

Gottlieb, Lynn. "Recovering from the Violence in Our Lives: Mikveh and a Public Recovery Ceremony for Women." In *She Who Dwells Within: A Feminist Vision of a Renewed Judaism.* New York: HarperCollins, 1995, 218.

Green, Lilian. *Ordinary Wonders: Living Recovery from Sexual Abuse.* Toronto: Women's Press. 1992.

"Jewish Women Talk about Surviving Incest." *Bridges* 2, no. 1 (spring 1991): 26–34.

Lipson, Gail Josephson. *Practical Parenting: A Jewish Perspective.* Hoboken, N.J.: KTAV Publishing House, in association with the Association of Jewish Family and Children's Agencies. 1-800-JUDAISM.

Lowenstein, Sharon. "Confronting Sexual Abuse in Jewish Families." *Moment* 15, no. 2 (April 1990): 48–53.

"Religious Education and Child Abuse." *Religious Education* 89, no. 4 (fall 1994).

Resource Guide for Rabbis on Domestic Violence. Washington, D.C.: Jewish Women International, 1996. JWI, 1828 L Street, NW, Suite 250, Washington, D.C. 20036. Website: http://www.jewishwomen.org.

Ribner, Melinda. *New Age Judaism: Ancient Wisdom for the Modern World.* Deerfield Beach, Fla.: Simcha Press, 2000.

Russ, Ian, Sally Weber, and Ellen Ledley. *Shalom Bayit: A Jewish Response to Child Abuse and Domestic Violence.* Los Angeles: Jewish Family Service of Los Angeles, Family Violence Project, 1993.

Siegel, Rachel Josefowitz, and Ellen Cole, eds. *Seen but Not Heard: Jewish Women in Therapy.* New York: Harrington Park Press, 1990.

Spiegel, Marcia Cohn. *Bibliography of Sources on Sexual and Domestic Violence in the Jewish Community.* Available at the Minnesota Center Against Violence and Abuse (MINCAVA). See Appendix G for contact information.

———. "The Last Taboo: Dare We Speak about Incest?" *Lilith* (summer 1988): 10–12.

Twerski, Rabbi Abraham. *The Shame Borne in Silence: Spouse Abuse in the Jewish Community.* Pittsburgh: Mirkov Publications, 1996.

Wegner, Judith Romney. *Chattel or Person? The Status of Women in the Mishnah.* New York: Oxford University Press, 1988.

Spirituality

Anderson, Sherry Ruth, and Patricia Hopkins. *The Feminine Face of God: The Unfolding of the Sacred in Women.* New York: Bantam Books, 1991.

Boorstein, Sylvia. *It's Easier Than You Think: The Buddhist Way to Happiness.* San Francisco: HarperSanFrancisco, 1997.

Boorstein, Sylvia, Sharon Lebell, and Stephen Mitchell. *Funny, You Don't Look Buddhist: On Being a Faithful Jew and a Passionate Buddhist.* San Francisco: HarperSanFrancisco, 1998.

Borysenko, Joan. *Fire in the Soul.* New York: Warner Books, 2001.

———. *A Woman's Journey to God.* New York: Riverhead Books, 2001.

Goldhamer, Douglas, and Melissa Stengel. *Universal Principles of Healing Prayer and the Jewish Mystics.* Burdett, New York: Larson Publications, 1999.

Harvey, Andrew. *The Direct Path: Creating a Journey to the Divine Using the World's Mystical Traditions.* New York: Broadway Books, 2000.

Lamott, Anne. *Traveling Mercies: Some Thoughts on Faith.* New York: Pantheon Books, 1999.

Salzberg, Sharon, and Jon Kabat-Zinn. *Lovingkindness: The Revolutionary Art of Happiness.* Boston: Shambhala Publications, 1997.

Creativity and Healing

Cameron, Julia. *The Artist's Way: A Spiritual Path to Higher Creativity*. New York: J. P. Tarcher, 1992.

Capacchione, Lucia. *The Creative Journal: The Art of Finding Yourself*. North Hollywood, Calif.: Newcastle Publishing, 1989.

Cornell, Judith. *Mandala: Luminous Symbols for Healing*. Wheaton, Ill.: Quest Books, 1994.

Ganim, Barbara. *Art and Healing: Using Expressive Art to Heal Your Body, Mind, and Spirit*. New York: Three Rivers Press, 1999.

Harris, Pat, with Jeannette Batz. *A Child's Story: Recovering through Creativity*. St. Louis, Mo.: Cracom Corporation, 1993.

Lamott, Anne. *Bird by Bird: Some Instructions on Writing and Life*. New York: Anchor, 1995.

Phillips, Jan. *God Is at Eye Level: Photography as a Healing Art*. Wheaton, Ill.: Quest Books, 2000.

Samuels, Michael, and Lane M. Rockwood. *Creative Healing: How to Heal Yourself by Tapping Your Hidden Creativity*. San Francisco: HarperSanFrancisco, 1998.

Books for Children (and Adults, too)

Bass, Ellen. *I Like You to Make Jokes with Me, but I Don't Want You to Touch Me*. Durham, N.C.: Carolina Wren Press, 1993.

Bassett, Susan. *When I Go to Bed at Night: A Modern Tale of Fear, Magic, and Healing*. Redmond, Wash.: Enchanted Swan Productions, 1994.

Freeman, Lory. *It's MY Body*. Seattle: Parenting Press, 1986.

Girard, Linda Walvoord. *My Body Is Private*. Morton Grove, Ill.: Albert Whitman, 1992.

Johnson, Karen. *The Trouble with Secrets*. Seattle: Parenting Press, 1986.

Polese, Carolyn. *Promise Not to Tell*. New York: Human Sciences Press, 1985.

Action Plans and Guides for Teaching Nonviolence

Choosing Nonviolence: The Rainbow House Handbook to a Violence Free Future for Young Children. Also *Take Ten*, an action plan for nonviolence created by Anne Parry. Rainbow House Institute for Choosing Nonviolence, 2313 S. Millard, Chicago, IL 60623.

Creighton, Alan, and Paul Kivel. *Helping Teens Stop Violence: A Practical Guide for Counselors, Educators, and Parents*. Alameda, Calif.: Hunter House, 1992.

———. *Young Men's Work: Stopping Violence and Building Community*. Center City, Minn.: Hazelden, 1995/8.

Kivel, Paul. *Boys Will Be Men: Raising Our Sons for Courage, Caring, and Community.* Gabriola Island, B.C.: New Society Publishers, 1999.

———. *I Can Make My World a Safer Place: A Kid's Book about Stopping Violence.* Alameda, Calif.: Hunter House, 2001.

Kivel, Paul, and Alan Creighton. *Making the Peace: A 15-Session Violence Prevention Curriculum for Young People.* Alameda, Calif.: Hunter House, 1997.

Lewis, Barbara A. *What Do You Stand For? A Kid's Guide to Building Character.* Edited by Pamela Espeland. Minneapolis: Free Spirit Publishing, 1998.

Myhand, M. Nell, and Paul Kivel. *Young Women's Lives: Building Self-Awareness for Life.* Center City, Minn.: Hazelden, 1998.

NOTES ༄

Contributing Authors and Artists

1. Mizrahi refers to Jews indigenous to the Middle East and North Africa, otherwise known as Mizrahim (Hebrew for "Easterners").

Introduction

1. *JUF News*, December 1997, 53.
2. Therapists and survivors use the word "incested" because it places emphasis on the "action" of the perpetrator, the act of molesting a child.
3. "Abusers come from all walks of life. There is no uniform 'profile' or other method to accurately distinguish those who have sexually abused children from those who have not." *Statement on Memories of Sexual Abuse*, American Psychiatric Association, December 12, 1993.
4. Hannah Arendt, *Eichmann in Jerusalem: A Report on the Banality of Evil*, 2d ed. (New York: Penguin Books, 1964), 276. See also Robert Jay Lifton, *The Nazi Doctors: Medical Killing and the Psychology of Genocide* (New York: Basic Books, 2000).
5. Diana Russell, *The Secret Trauma: Incest in the Lives of Girls and Women* (New York: Basic Books, 1986); and David Finkelhor, *Child Sexual Abuse: New Theory and Research* (New York: Free Press, 1984).
6. Michelle Elliott, ed., *Female Sexual Abuse of Children* (New York: Guilford Press, 1994); G. R. Holmes, L. Offen, and G. Waller, "See No Evil, Hear No Evil, Speak No Evil: Why Do Relatively Few Male Victims of Childhood Sexual Abuse Receive Help for Abuse-Related Issues in Adulthood?" *Clinical Psychology Review* 17 (1997): 69–88; and M. Hunter, *Abused Boys: The Neglected Victims of Sexual Abuse* (New York: Fawcett Columbine, 1990).
7. J. L. Herman, *Trauma and Recovery: The Aftermath of Violence—From Domestic Abuse to Political Terror* (New York: Basic Books, 1992), 215.
8. Ibid., 123.
9. American Orthopsychiatric Conference. Panel presentation.
10. Melanie Kaye/Kantrowitz, "The Issue Is Power: Some Notes on Jewish Women and Therapy," in *Jewish Women in Therapy: Seen But Not Heard*, ed. Rachel Josefowitz Siegel and Ellen Cole (Haworth Press, 1991), 13.

11. "Sephardic Jews are descendants of the large Jewish community living in Spain and Portugal in the Middle Ages. Forcibly expelled from those countries in 1492, many settled in The Netherlands. Sephardic Jews never lost their identity and are found living all over the world today." 1997 B'nei Shaare Zion Congregation, www.bsz.org/lsephardichistory.htm.

12. Ashkenazi: of or relating to the Jews of Germany and Eastern Europe.

13. Historically, patriarchy was tied to the rule of the father in the family. Power and control over land, wife, and children lay in the hands of the "patriarch." His wife and children were his property, to do with as he pleased. Within the context of this book, patriarchy refers to the tendency for men to be more valued than women (what happens to them is more important), to have more power than women, and to have unfair advantages just by virtue of being born male.

The pay gap in the United States is one example of an unfair advantage. Full-time women workers earn 73 percent of what full-time working men earn. (These figures are based on information available between 1997 and 1998, from the National Committee on Pay Equity.)

A patriarchal power system operates on assumptions that contribute to violence against women and children, how individuals and communities intervene when violence occurs, and what we do to prevent it. For example, the assumption that women and children are inferior makes what happens to them less important; thus funds are less likely to be available for services. On an individual level, a patriarchy encourages men and women to feel that men have the right to "make" women and children do as they demand and to treat them however they wish. When any group has "preferred" status, they feel entitled to "take" what they want. The needs and rights of those with "nonpreferred" status are generally invisible to those with "preferred" status.

Social structures are always complex and seldom (if ever) reducible to a single factor (class, race, or gender). Patriarchy itself is not enough to explain violence by men, women, and children. Other variables enter in as well.

14. *Bubby* is a Yiddish word for grandmother.

15. A *tallis* (or *tallith*) is a prayer shawl. It is a rectangular piece of silky fabric with knotted fringe on the ends. The fringes are called *tsitsis*.

Chapter One

1. At times debate ensues within professional communities (e.g., psychiatry, psychology, social work) and in the media about the veracity of delayed recall, sometimes referred to as recovered memories. The debate is sometimes very heated. Participants in the debate include clinicians, researchers, lawyers, parents accused of molesting their children, and adults who say they've been molested.

One aspect of the debate centers on the question, "Can someone 'forget' something traumatic and later remember it?" On December 12, 1993, the American Psychiatric Association issued a statement regarding recovered memories, stating, "Children and adolescents who have been abused cope with the trauma by using a variety of psychological mechanisms. In some instances, these coping mechanisms result in a lack of conscious awareness of this abuse for varying periods of time. Conscious thoughts and feelings stemming from the abuse may emerge at a later date."

My hospitalization experience at age three exemplifies delayed recall. An experience "forgotten" for decades was remembered in fragmented ways and verified by someone else and hospital records. While all memory is fallible, research of trauma (combat, the *Challenger* explosion, earthquakes, accidents, rape, incest, etc.) verifies that while details may be inaccurate, there is essential truth to the memory.

A statement from Dr. Cheit Ross's Institute (Brown University) explains that memories are "influenced by feelings, current social context, how the brain functions, and many other factors." A "*Harvard Law Review* article in January 1996 argued that while scientific evidence proves the existence of delayed memories, biased reporting has helped create a social climate in which people, including some judges, have come to believe just the opposite." Mike Stanton, "U-Turn on Memory Lane," *Columbia Journalism Review* (July/August 1997).

For more information on the debate about recovered memories, see "Symposium: Science and Politics of Recovered Memories" and other sources listed in the bibliography (Appendix H).

2. In the late 1980s I visited an inpatient eating disorders unit to learn about their program as a possible referral source. In that week 100 percent of the patients (all women) spoke of having been sexually abused or incested (or both) prior to the age of eighteen. Disorders ranged from anorexia to bulimia and/or compulsive overeating. In a five-region study (CATOR), 40 percent of women in inpatient alcoholism treatment reported having been forced to have genital intercourse before the age of eighteen.

3. At a conference in 1994, John Briere spoke of a range of tension-reducing activities sexual abuse survivors use, including self-mutilation as well as the full range of addictive behaviors (eating, drinking, drugging, shopping, etc.).

4. Biography on *E! True Hollywood Story*, aired August 26, 2001. Premiere April 4, 1999.

5. Over one hundred survivors contacted me via e-mail, letters, and/or phone calls.

6. *Zede* is a Yiddish word for grandfather.

7. "Grandmother's story," similar to "old wives' tale."

8. Alice Walker, "Giving Birth, Finding Form," discussion between Walker, Isabel Allende, and Jean Shinoda-Bolen. *Sounds True Recordings*, 1993.

Chapter Two

1. These figures are based on research in Canada and the United States. The prevalence data are based on research by D. E. H. Russell, *Sexual Exploitation: Rape, Child Sexual Abuse, and Sexual Harassment* (Beverly Hills: Sage, 1984).

Also, *The Secret Trauma: Incest in the Lives of Girls and Women* (New York: Basic Books, 1986). Also, see Lloyd DeMause, "Universality of Incest," *Journal of Psychohistory* 19, no. 2 (fall 1991). Statistics on rates of child abuse and neglect are controversial. Where boys are concerned, research demonstrates a prevalence rate ranging from one in six to one in ten boys. In studies of either gender, different prevalence rates have been found in different samples. Many variables, including the forum and methods in which information is gathered, influence the outcomes. For purposes of this book, I am using figures that are commonly accepted. For discussion of some of the variables impacting the validity of child abuse research, see psychologist Jim Hopper's website: www.jimhopper.com.

2. *Child Maltreatment 1995: Reports from the States to the National Child Abuse and Neglect Data System*, U.S. Department of Health and Human Services, National Center on Child Abuse and Neglect (Washington, D.C.: Government Printing Office, 1997).

"The major setting for violence in America is the home. Intrafamilial abuse, neglect and domestic battery account for the majority of physical and emotional violence suffered by children in this country. Despite this, a majority of our entertainment, media and public policy efforts focus on community or predatory violence. Understanding the roots of community and predatory violence is impossible unless the effects of intrafamilial violence, abuse and neglect on the development of the child are examined." B. D. Perry, "Incubated in Terror: Neurodevelopmental Factors in the Cycle of Violence," in *Children, Youth, and Violence: The Search for Solutions*, ed. J. Osofsky (New York: Guilford Press, 1997), 124–48. See also Carnegie Council on Adolescent Development, *Great Transitions: Preparing Adolescents for a New Century* (New York: Carnegie Corporation of New York, 1995); K. Horowitz, S. Weine, and J. Jekel, "PTSD Symptoms in Urban Adolescent Girls: Compounded Community Trauma," *Journal of the American Academy of Child and Adolescent Psychiatry* 34, no. 10 (1995): 1,353–61; C. E. Koop and G. Lundberg, "Violence in America: A Public Health Emergency," *Journal of the American Medical Association* 22 (1992): 3,075–76; M. Straus, "Cultural and Organizational Influences on Violence between Family Members," in *Configurations: Biological and Cultural Factors in Sexuality and Family*, ed. R. Prince and D. Barrier (Lexington, Mass.: Lexington Books, 1974).

3. David Finkelhor, *Child Sexual Abuse: New Theory and Research* (New York: Free Press, 1984); J. Michael Cupoli, "One Thousand Fifty-Nine Children with a Chief Complaint of Sexual Abuse," *Child Abuse and Neglect* 12 (1988): 158.

4. For example, in the area of domestic violence, Professor Paul H. Ephross completed a study in 1996 of fifteen hundred Jewish women in Baltimore. Twenty percent of these women (Orthodox, Reform, Conservative, and "just Jewish," ranging in age from their twenties to age ninety) reported having been abused by their husbands. All the men and women had always been Jewish. Findings were presented at the General Assembly Council of Jewish Federations and Welfare Funds, Seattle, Washington, November 1996. Personal communication with author, June 2001.

5. Julie R. Spitzer, "The Abused Child: Help and Hope," *Compass* (fall 1989).

6. The Talmud is the record of the rabbis' discussion, application, and amplification of the Mishnah. There are two Talmuds: the Jerusalem (or Palestinian), edited in c. 400 C.E.; and the Babylonian, edited in c. 500 C.E. The word "Talmud" without specification refers to the longer and more authoritative of the two, the Babylonian Talmud.

7. Ian Russ, Sally Weber, and Ellen Ledley, *Shalom Bayit: A Jewish Response to Child Abuse and Domestic Violence* (Panorama City, Calif.: Jewish Family Service, 1993).

8. Panel on domestic violence in the Jewish community, American Jewish Congress, 1994.

9. To be a *mensch* is to be a good person. *Menschen* are good people.

10. Finkelhor, *Child Sexual Abuse*.

11. D. Laub and N. Auerhahn, "Knowing and Not Knowing Massive Psychic Trauma: Forms of Traumatic Memory," *American Journal of Psychoanalysis* 74 (1993): 287–302.

12. Blumenthal first broached this topic in "A Genesis of Faith," which is an extended book review in *Religious Studies Review* 18, no. 3 (July 1992): 209–11. A thorough study of this comparison needs to be done.

Note: The lack of capitalization of the word Holocaust was consciously decided by Blumenthal who, "based on spiritual principle," only capitalized the word God and those terms that refer to God in *Facing the Abusing God, A Theology of Protest* (Louisville: Presbyterian Publishing House, 1993), xxii.

13. Blumenthal writes: "For the holocaust survivor, the pain is not only personal; it is historical and national. The degradation and extermination were intended for all Jews. It was also part of a pattern of Jew-hatred that had existed for centuries and is perceived to continue to exist. For the survivor of family abuse, there was the lack of any support, utter aloneless. There was no underground, no resistance, no other prisoners, no fellow Jews. The non-abusing parent was part of the conspiracy; sometimes so were the siblings. For the holocaust survivor there was real death: emaciated corpses, healthy corpses, mutilated corpses, screaming infants cast onto pyres, excremental attack, the walking dead. And, it was large in scale, all around, all the time. For the survivor of family abuse, the suffering lasted longer, sometimes more than a decade. Family abuse was also interwoven with normal daily living; it was not isolated in a hell-place and a hell-time; it took place at home, not in a prison or camp. For the survivor of family abuse, abuse also came from those who loved, or claimed they did, even as they abused. And it came from those one is supposed to love, from those who love and are loved in other people's homes. Holocaust abuse came from the enemy who was the real sub-human, who could be hated. For the holocaust survivor, recovery was sustained by the Jewish people and embodied by the State of Israel. Family abuse survivors were lucky to find a spouse who would be tolerant, and even luckier to find a therapist who would listen." Blumenthal, *Facing the Abusing God*, 259–66.

14. Ibid., 266.

15. Marcia Cohn Spiegel, "The Last Taboo: Dare We Speak about Incest?" *Lilith* 20 (1987): 12.

16. Bob Gluck, "Domestic Violence: No More Silence," *Reconstructionist* (1989): 8.

17. Lenore Terr, *Unchained Memories: True Stories of Traumatic Memories, Lost and Found* (New York: Basic Books, 1994), 129.

18. "When we, at Emory University in the 1980s, began interviewing American GI's who had liberated the concentration camps, one of the first things we discovered is that they had never talked about the liberation experience, even though they had talked about the war. There was no one to talk to. Jews who had survived or liberated camps, on the other hand, had a community that at first did not want to listen, but, by the late 1960s, was beginning to support this kind of sharing. In addition, Jews haunted by the holocaust could, and did, channel their rage and fear into working for the protection of the surviving remnant of the holocaust by establishing and maintaining the security of the State of Israel." Blumenthal, *Facing the Abusing God*, 261.

19. *Lilith* (winter 1993): 23. Reprinted with permission from *Lilith: The Independent Jewish Women's Magazine*. Subscriptions ($18/year) and sample copies available from Lilithmag@aol.com, www.Lilith.org, or toll free from 1-888-2-LILITH.

20. Ibid.

21. Rachel Yehuda et al., "Phenomenology and Psychobiology of the Inter-generational Response to Trauma," in *International Handbook of Multigenerational Legacies of Trauma*, ed. Y. Danieli (New York: Plenum Press, 1998).

22. Sally Weber, telephone conversation with author, December 6, 1995.

23. *Frum* is a word used to refer to members of the Orthodox community. *Frum* identifies those who have always been Orthodox as distinguished from *ba'al teshuvah*. *Ba'al teshuvah* are Jews who have returned to Orthodoxy or become Orthodox.

24. *Aliyah* is a term used when a Jew is called to say a blessing before and after the Torah is read. It is also a term used for emigrating to Israel. Literal meaning is "going up" or ascension; in that light, emigrating to Israel is seen as a spiritual ascension.

25. Yehuda et al., "Phenomenology and Psychobiology."

26. Rabbi Yehudah Fine, "Ignorance Is Not Bliss: Teens in Crisis Want Answers" is an article from Vachss's website http://www.vachss.com/guest_dispatches/yfine.html. Yehudah Fine, rabbi and family therapist, is author of *Times Square Rabbi: Finding the Hope in Lost Kids' Lives* (Center City, Minn.: Hazelden, 1997), and is a member of the guidance staff at Yeshiva University.

Yehudah is currently featured at Andrew Vachss's child advocacy website. Mr. Vachss is a child advocacy lawyer and author of many best-selling books that speak of the struggles and traumas of children and people in recovery.

27. Melanie Kaye/Kantrowitz, *The Issue Is Power: Essays on Women, Jews, Violence, and Resistance* (San Francisco: Aunt Lute Books, 1992), 89.

Chapter Three

M. = Mishnah (edited by Rabbi Judah, president of the Sanhedrin, c. 200 C.E.);

T. = Tosefta (edited by Rabbi Hiyya and Rabbi Oshaiyah, c. 200 C.E.);

B. = Babylonian Talmud (edited by Ravina and Rav Ashi, c. 500 C.E.);

J. = Jerusalem (Palestinian) Talmud (edited c. 400 C.E.);

M.T. = Maimonides' *Mishneh Torah (Yad Ha-Hazakah)* (1177 C.E.);

S.A. = Joseph Karo's *Shulhan Arukh* (1565 C.E.). A citation to S.A. followed by the word "gloss" indicates the comments of Moses Isserles on the passage in the *Shulhan Arukh*, indicating where Ashkenazic (northern European) practices differed from the Sephardic (Mediterranean) practices Karo recorded.

1. Rabbi Mark Dratch, Proposal to the RCA Roundtable, "The Physical, Sexual, and Emotional Abuse of Children," Nissan 5752.

2. Jewish law is a set of rules and practices known as *halakhah*. *Halakhah* literally translated means "the path that one walks." The word is derived from the Hebrew *Heh-Lamed-Kaf*, meaning to go, to walk, or to travel.

3. The Mishnah is the first officially recognized collection of the Jewish Oral Torah. It was edited by Rabbi Judah, the president of the Sanhedrin, in approximately 200 C.E.

4. The Talmud is the record of the rabbis' discussion, application, and amplification of the Mishnah. There are two Talmuds: the Jerusalem (or Palestinian), edited in c. 400 C.E.; and the Babylonian, edited in c. 500 C.E. The word "Talmud" without specification refers to the longer and more authoritative of the two, the Babylonian Talmud.

5. Marcia Cohn Spiegel, communication with author, October 2001.

6. This chapter is based on my rabbinic ruling (*teshuvah*), "Family Violence," approved unanimously by the Conservative Movement's Committee on Jewish Law and Standards on September 13, 1995. See *Responsa 1991–2000: The Committee on Jewish Law and Standards of the Conservative Movement*, ed. Kassel Abelson and David J. Fine (New York: Rabbinical Assembly, 2002), 773–816. It will also appear in its full form in my forthcoming book on Jewish personal ethics, to be published by the Jewish Publication Society in 2003.

7. The word "Torah," in its narrowest meaning, refers to the five Books of Moses—Genesis, Exodus, Leviticus, Numbers, and Deuteronomy—and that is how it is used here. The root of the word means "instruction," and so in its broader meaning it refers to the entire Jewish tradition that instructs us—the Oral Torah as well as the Written Torah.

8. Genesis 1:26–27; 9:6.

9. The Midrash is the body of Jewish interpretations of biblical passages. Most of those who contributed to the Midrash were and are rabbis, but there is no bar to lay Jews contributing their own interpretations for discussion. While there is no one, authoritative collection of Midrash, the most often quoted is *Midrash Rabbah* (where Rabbah means "big, or extended"), which includes a collection of interpretations on each of the books of the Torah and on the Five Scrolls that are read in the synagogue on specific days—Song of Songs, Ruth, Lamentations, Ecclesiastes, and Esther.

10. M. *Bava Kamma* 8:1.

11. M. *Avot (Ethics of the Fathers)* 2:15.

12. Proverbs 23:13–14; cf. Proverbs 3:11–12, 13:24, 19:18, 20:30, 29:17.

13. The Mishnah (M. *Ketubbot* 5:5) requires a wife to "grind [flour], bake [bread], wash [clothes], cook food, nurse her child, make his [her husband's] bed, and work in wool." If the wife refuses to perform these duties or violates Jewish law in some other way, Maimonides permits the husband to discipline her by hitting her with a rod. See M.T. *Laws of Marriage* 21:10; cf. 21:3. In M.T. *Laws of Injury and Damage* 4:16, however, he makes the husband who beats his wife liable for the usual remedies of assault, and in M.T. *Laws of Marriage* 15:19 he says that a man should honor his wife more than his body and love her as his body. Other medieval rabbis who permit husbands to beat their wives include Rabbi Yehudai Gaon (*Otzar Ha-Geonim* to B. *Ketubbot*, 169–70), and Rabbenu Nissim refers to "the Gaon of blessed memory" who allows a husband to whip (or to refuse to sustain) his wife if she refuses to do the chores delineated for her by law; see Rabbenu Nissim's comments on B. *Ketubbot* 63b. On this topic generally, see Naomi Graetz, *Silence Is Deadly: Judaism Confronts Wifebeating* (Northvale, N.J.: Jason Aronson, 1998).

14. For four approaches to this methodological question, see *Contemporary Jewish Ethics and Morality: A Reader*, ed. Elliot N. Dorff and Louis E. Newman (New York: Oxford University Press, 1995), chap. 9–12. For my own view of the matter, see my book, *Matters of Life and Death: A Jewish Approach to Modern Medical Ethics* (Philadelphia: Jewish Publication Society, 1998), 395–417.

15. Deuteronomy 21:18–21; B. *Sanhedrin* 71a.

16. Seek justice: Deuteronomy 16:20. Love our neighbor: Leviticus 19:18. Use honest weights and measures: Leviticus 19:35–36.

17. Exodus 21:2ff; Leviticus 25:39–46.

18. Leviticus 18:22, 19.

19. One might argue that Jews must avoid family violence because we are bound by civil law under the dictum, "the law of the land is the law" (*dina de'malkhuta dina*). That may well be true, but it is not as clear as one might think, for that dictum was usually restricted to commercial matters. Even during the Middle Ages, though, Jews were forced by the government under which they lived to abide by its laws, and rabbis generally saw that as a Jewish obligation as well as a civil one—at least to protect the Jewish community from expulsion or governmental interference. Certainly, when Jews began living as full citizens

under governments shaped by the philosophy of the Enlightenment, they saw themselves both legally and morally bound to abide by the government's laws and that continues to this day. The operative principle, then, is not so much "the law of the land is the law" as it is (1) the need to avoid the *hillul hashem* (desecration of God's name) involved in Jews breaking just civil law and (2) the requirement in Jewish law that Jews see themselves bound by moral standards beyond those of other nations.

For a discussion of the scope and rationales of "the law of the land is the law," see Elliot N. Dorff and Arthur Rosett, *A Living Tree: The Roots and Growth of Jewish Law* (Albany: State University Press of New York, 1988), 515–23. For a discussion of sanctification of God's name (and avoiding desecration of God's name) and holiness as reasons to obey Jewish law, see Elliot N. Dorff, *Mitzvah Means Commandment* (New York: United Synagogue of America, 1989), 113–34. For the demand that Jews be at least as moral as non-Jews, see, for example, David Novak, *The Image of the Non-Jew in Judaism* (New York: Edwin Mellon, 1983), 90–93; and "Kiddush Ha-Shem," *Encyclopedia Judaica* 10: 979–80.

20. Pat Wingert and Eloise Salholz, "Irreconcilable Differences," *Newsweek*, September 21, 1992, 84–90. The citation appears on 84.

21. The two cited verses are Leviticus 18:6 and 18:29–30.

22. I think that we would all agree that the Torah's use of the words "abomination" and "defilement" aptly apply to the kind of sexual abuse of which we are speaking. Whether we should also endorse this biblical language with regard to its prohibition against homosexual sex is, to put it mildly, a matter of dispute in our time. Even those who would permit homosexual relations, though, would definitely apply that language to coercive sex (be it homosexual or heterosexual), and that is the subject of our discussion here.

23. Deuteronomy 25:11–12.

24. *Sifre* on Deuteronomy 25:12; cf. M. *Bava Kamma* 8:1; B. *Bava Kamma* 83a, 86a–b, 28a, etc.

25. B. *Shabbat* 13a; M.T. *Laws of Forbidden Intercourse* 21:1; Maimonides, *Sefer Ha-Mitzvot*, Prohibition #353; *Sefer Ha-Hinukh* #188; S.A. *Even Ha-Ezer* 20:1. Some, however, maintain that intimacy without penetration is not biblically, but rabbinically prohibited. See, for example, Nahmanides on B. *Shabbat* 13a and on *Sefer Ha-Mitzvot*, ibid.; the Gaon of Vilna, *Biur ha-Gra* on S.A. *Even Ha-Ezer* 20:1.

26. Dr. Ian Russ, a child psychologist and a good friend, has suggested the following on the long-term, serious effects of the sexual abuse of children: John Briere, *Therapy for Adults Molested as Children: Beyond Survival* (New York: Springer Publishing, 1989); John Briere and Diana Elliott, "Immediate and Long-Term Impacts of Child Sexual Abuse," in *The Future of Children*, vol. 4, no. 12 (Los Altos, Calif.: Center for the Future of Children, David and Lucille Packard Foundation, 1994), 54–69; Christine Courtois, *Healing the Incest Wound* (New York: W. W. Norton, 1988); and D. Everstine and L. Everstine, *Sexual Trauma in Children and Adolescents: Dynamics of Treatment* (New York: Brunner/Mazel, 1989). I would like to thank Dr. Russ for supplying this bibliography for our use.

27. B. *Bava Kamma* 56a; S.A. *Hoshen Mishpat* 28:1, gloss. In B. *Pesahim* 113b, Rav Papa has a man named Zigud punished for testifying alone against another man named Tuvya on the ground that the testimony of a single witness is inadmissible, and so Zigud, knowing that he was the only witness, was effectively spreading defamatory information (*motzi shem ra*) about Tuvya. That, however, was when the act had already occurred; the requirement in *Bava Kamma* and in the comment of Isserles to testify even singly in all cases in which there is a benefit, including preventing another person from sinning, refers to a future gain.

28. M.T. *Laws of Murder* 1:14. In 1:15, Maimonides adds both affirmative and negative injunctions to this obligation based on Deuteronomy 25:12, "And you shall cut off her hand [being applied here to the abuser]; your eye shall have no pity." See also Rashi, B. *Sanhedrin* 73a, s.v. *lo ta'amod.*

29. M. *Sanhedrin* 8:7; B. *Sanhedrin* 73a.

30. Tosafot, B. *Sanhedrin* 72b, s.v. *kan be-av al ha-ben*, make this explicit with regard to children's right (obligation?) to defend themselves against abusive parents.

31. B. *Yoma* 85a–b; B. *Sanhedrin* 72a, 74a. On these principles generally, Immanuel Jakobovits, *Jewish Medical Ethics* (New York: Bloch, 1959, 1975), chap. 3–7.

32. Leviticus 19:16. The new translation of the Jewish Publication Society reads, "Do not profit by the blood of your fellow," interpreting this phrase, whose meaning is uncertain, as the note there says, in the context of the civil legislation in the verse immediately before this one. The rabbinic tradition, however, interpreted and applied Leviticus 19:16 to establish a positive obligation to come to the aid of those in danger; cf. M. *Sanhedrin* 8:7; B. *Sanhedrin* 73a.

33. M.T. *Laws of Testimony* 1:1.

34. *Kesef Mishneh* to M.T. *Laws of Testimony* 1:1; *Rosh* to B. *Makkot*, Chapter 1, #11. "Destroy the evil from your midst" occurs a number of times in the Torah as a general purpose of the law: Deuteronomy 13:6, 17:7, 19:19, 21:21, 22:21, 24:7; cf. also 17:12 and 22:22.

35. M.T. *Laws of Testimony* 9:1; S.A. *Hoshen Mishpat* 35:1.

36. B. *Gittin* 88b; M.T. *Laws of Courts* (*Sanhedrin*) 26:7. See Dorff and Rosett, *A Living Tree: The Roots and Growth of Jewish Law* (Albany, N.Y.: State University of New York Press, 1988), 320–24, 515–39. See also Herschel Schachter, "*Dina deMalchusa Dina,*" *Journal of Halacha and Contemporary Society* 1, no. 1, and Simcha Krauss, "Litigation in Secular Courts," *Journal of Halacha and Contemporary Society* 11, no. 1. Sephardic Jews generally have maintained the prohibition, probably because they have not until recently lived in nations governed by Enlightenment principles, but even Sephardic Jews permit going to the non-Jewish courts when the case poses a threat to the Jewish community (*meitzar ha-tzibbur*).

37. "Sephardic Jews are descendants of the large Jewish community living in Spain and Portugal in the Middle Ages. Forcibly expelled from those countries in 1492, many settled in The Netherlands, Turkey, or North Africa. Sephardic Jews

never lost their identity and are found living all over the world today." 1997 B'nei Shaare Zion Congregation, www.bsz.org/lsephardichistory.htm. I mention Sephardic Jews specifically here because it was primarily medieval Sephardic authorities who permitted husbands to beat their wives. See note 13.

38. B. *Hullin* 10a; see S.A. *Orah Hayyim* 173:2; *Yoreh De'ah* 116:5 gloss. The three exceptions—that you must give up your own life rather than commit murder, idolatry, or adultery/incest—are specified in B. *Sanhedrin* 74a. That saving your own life takes precedence over saving the lives of others is established in B. *Bava Mezia* 62a.

39. M. *Bava Kamma* 8:1.

40. The biblical command to honor parents: Exodus 20:12; Deuteronomy 5:16. The command to respect parents: Leviticus 19:3. That daughters as well as sons are commanded to honor and respect their parents: M. *Kiddushin* 1:7; B. *Kiddushin* 29a. The rabbinic exposition of those commands: B. *Kiddushin* 31b, from which this citation comes; M.T. *Laws of Rebels* (*Mamrim*) 6:3; S.A. *Yoreh De'ah* 240:2, 4; cf. also 228:11. For further development of these commandments, see my article, "Honoring Aged Fathers and Mothers," *Reconstructionist* 53, no. 2 (October–November, 1987): 14–20.

41. B. *Kiddushin* 31b–32a; M.T. *Laws of Rebels* 6:3; S.A. *Yoreh De'ah* 240:5. Using one's own resources is, however, preferred: cf. *Kesef Mishneh* to M.T. *Laws of Rebels* 6:7.

42. B. *Kiddushin* 31b–32a; J. *Kiddushin* 1:7 (61b); J. *Pe'ah* 1:1 (15c–d); *Deuteronomy Rabbah* 1:15.

43. Exodus 21:15. Cf. B. *Sanhedrin* 84b. If the child did not cause a bruise while striking his/her parents, however, the child is liable for the damages of assault rather than for the death penalty; cf. M. *Bava Kamma* 8:3.

44. B. *Kiddushin* 30b.

45. The command to love your neighbor as yourself: Leviticus 19:18. Rashi, on B. *Kiddushin* 32a, s.v. *podin u-ma'akhilin*; R. Elazar Azkari, *Sefer Haredim* (Warsaw: 1879), 31; R. Abraham Danzig, *Hayyei Adam* (1810) 67:1. These sources are cited and discussed in Gerald Blidstein, *Honor Thy Father and Mother* (New York: Ktav, 1975), 56–57.

46. Maimonides, *Responsa*, ed. J. Blau, vol. 2, no. 448, 728. Cited in Blidstein, *Honor* (at n. 45), 55.

47. Rashi: B. *Sanhedrin* 47a, s.v. *'al*; B. *Berakhot* 10b, s.v. *girer*. Tosafot: B. *Yevamot* 22b, s.v. *ke-she-asah*; Rabbenu Tam: *Mordecai* to B. *Yevamot*, sec. 13. R. Alfas: B. *Yevamot* 22b. Maimonides: M.T. *Laws of Rebels* (*Mamrim*) 5:12; see also 6:11. Karo and Isserles: S.A. *Yoreh De'ah* 240:18 (with gloss). On this generally, see Blidstein, *Honor* (at n. 45), 130–36; and Benay Lappe, "Does A Child Who Has Been Sexually Abused by a Parent Have the Obligation to Say *Kaddish* for that Parent: A *Teshuvah*," an M.H.L. thesis at the University of Judaism, Los Angeles, 1993.

48. *Exodus Rabbah* 34:3. Note also that one version of the story of the death of Rabbi Judah, president of the Sanhedrin, has it that as he was dying, he specifically

asked for his children to be in attendance; see B. *Ketubbot* 103a. The ideal of giving personal care, however, did not become a legal requirement recorded in the codes—although those legal texts probably assume such care; cf. Blidstein, *Honor* (at n. 45), 113–15.

49. *Sefer Hasidim*, R. Margaliot, ed. (Jerusalem, 1957), sec. 564, 371; cf. sec. 343, 257. R. Eliezer Pappo, *Pele Yo'etz*, part I, "Kaph," 170–72; cited in Blidstein, *Honor* (at n. 45), 115.

Chapter Four

1. From *The Prophet* by Kahlil Gibran, copyright 1923 by Kahlil Gibran and renewed 1951 by Administrators C.T.A. of Kahlil Gibran Estate and Mary G. Gibran. Used by permission of Alfred A. Knopf, a division of Random House, Inc., and by Gibran National Committee in Beirut, Lebanon.

2. Sue Evans and Susan Schaefer, "Incest and Chemically Dependent Women: Treatment Implications," in *Chemical Dependency and Intimacy Dysfunctions*, ed. Eli Coleman (New York: Haworth Press, 1988), 150.

3. Kaye/Kantrowitz, "The Issue Is Power," 13.

4. Dr. John Briere (presentation at Advances in Treating Survivors of Sexual Abuse: Empowering the Healing Process II, San Diego, Calif., March 1994).

5. I am grateful to Alice Miller for her body of work addressing the impact of society's view of children and the impact of neglectful or abusive childhoods, beginning with *The Drama of the Gifted Child*, in which she describes parents' unhealthy reliance on their children, and *Thou Shalt Not Be Aware* and *Banished Knowledge* (see Appendix H), in which she informs and confronts us with the prevalence of abuse of children and our participation in its denial.

Chapter Five

1. Copyright 1980 Ruth Whitman Sacks. First printed in *The Radcliffe Quarterly* and later collected in *Permanent Address: New Poems 1973–1980 by RWS* (Alice James Books). Reprinted with permission of Morton Sacks.

2. Dr. Richard Kluft, "Town Meeting: Delayed Memory Controversy in Abuse Recovery" (panel presented at the Fifth Annual Eastern Regional Conference on Abuse and Multiple Personality, Alexandria, Virginia, June 1993).

3. Nathan Aanseng, *You Are the Juror* (Minneapolis: Oliver Press, 1997); Patricia Campbell Hearst with Alvin Moscow, *Every Secret Thing* (New York: Doubleday, 1982); David Boulton, *The Making of Tania: The Patty Hearst Story* (London: New English Library, 1975); Christopher Castiglia, *Bound and Determined: Captivity, Culture-Crossing, and White Womanhood from Mary Rowlandson to Patty Hearst* (Chicago: University of Chicago Press, 1996); Patricia

C. Hearst with Alvin Moscow, *Patty Hearst: Her Own Story* (New York: Avon Books, 1988, originally published as *Every Secret Thing*).

4. Herman, *Trauma and Recovery*, 115–16.

5. Dr. John Briere (presentation at Advances in Treating Survivors of Sexual Abuse: Empowering the Healing Process II, San Diego, Calif., March 1994). As Dr. Bessel van der Kolk, Boston University psychiatry professor, said, "People who have been abused in childhood cannot change the events, so they spend energy trying to make the feelings go away. They drink, drug, cut themselves, or stuff themselves with food."

6. A. Jacobson and B. Richardson, "Assault Experiences of One Hundred Psychiatric Inpatients: Evidence of the Need for Routine Inquiry," *American Journal of Psychiatry* 144 (1987): 908–13; J. B. Bryer, B. A. Nelson, J. B. Miller, and P. A. Krol, "Childhood Sexual and Physical Abuse as Factors in Adult Psychiatric Illness," *American Journal of Psychiatry* 144 (1987): 1,426–30; A. Jacobson, "Physical and Sexual Assault Histories among Psychiatric Outpatients," *American Journal of Psychiatry* 146 (1989): 755–58; J. Briere and M. Runtz, "Post Sexual Abuse Trauma: Data and Implications for Clinical Practice," *Journal of Interpersonal Violence* 2 (1987): 367–79.

7. J. Briere and L. Y. Zaidi, "Sexual Abuse Histories and Sequelae in Female Psychiatric Emergency Room Patients," *American Journal of Psychiatry* 146 (1989): 1,602–6.

8. Forms requesting medical history need to ask about sexual abuse and other traumas along with questions about heart disease, prior surgeries, diabetes, and so on. The presence of such questions reflects the knowledge and orientation of the practitioner, the institution, or both. Questions about present or past abuse/trauma need to be routinely asked of all patients.

9. *Lilith Goldberg*, "Surviving Incest in a Holocaust Family," *Lilith* (winter 1993): 23.

10. Bessel A. van der Kolk, "Psychobiology of Trauma" (paper presented at the 1993 Eastern Regional Conference of the International Society for the Study of Multiple Personality Disorder, Alexandria, Virginia, June 1993). Also see: Perry, "Incubated in Terror," 124–48.

11. "In 1990, the *New York Times* reported that Dennis Charney, M.D., a Yale psychiatrist and director of clinical neuroscience at the National Center for Post-Traumatic Stress Disorders, had found that even one experience of overwhelming terror, permanently alters the chemistry of the brain. The longer the duration and the more severe the trauma, the more likely it is that a victim will develop PTSD. . . . Researchers following the development of sexually abused kids are now reporting abnormalities in the central nervous system regulation of adrenal cortical, thyroid and reproductive hormones. These neurobiological abnormalities appear to persist long after the abuse has presumably come to an end. Implications of this growing body of research are really quite disturbing because it's appearing that childhood trauma may have a permanent affect on the developing brain, or

hard wire affects." Heidi Vanderbilt, "Incest: A Chilling Report," *Lears*, February 1992, 55.

12. See A. Kardiner and H. Spiegel, *War, Stress, and Neurotic Illness* (New York: Hoeber, 1947), first published in 1941 as *The Traumatic Neuroses of War* by A. Kardiner (cited in Herman, *Trauma and Recovery*, 241, n. 6).

13. Bessel A. van der Kolk, "The Trauma Spectrum: The Interaction of Biological and Social Events in the Genesis of the Trauma Response," *Journal of Traumatic Stress* 1, no. 4 (1985): 273–74. See also Dr. Charles B. Nemeroff et al., "The Pituitary-Adrenal and Autonomic Responses to Stress in Women after Sexual and Physical Abuse in Childhood," *The Journal of the American Medical Association* 284 (August 2, 2000), a study which links trauma, depression, and response to anxiety. "Women who were physically or sexually abused in childhood show exaggerated physiological responses to stressful events." (*New York Times*, August 2, 2000, A14)

14. Van der Kolk, "The Trauma Spectrum," 282.

15. Ibid.

16. According to the American Psychiatric Association in their "Statement on Memories of Sexual Abuse," December 12, 1993: "Implicit and explicit memory are two different forms of memory that have been identified. Explicit memory (also termed declarative memory) refers to the ability to consciously recall facts or events. Implicit memory (also termed procedural memory) refers to behavioral knowledge of an experience without conscious recall. A child who demonstrates knowledge of a skill (e.g., bicycle riding) without recalling how he/she learned it, or an adult who has an affective reaction to an event without understanding the basis for that reaction (e.g., a combat veteran who panics when he hears the sound of a helicopter, but cannot remember that he was in a helicopter crash which killed his best friend) are demonstrating implicit memories in the absence of explicit recall. This distinction . . . is fundamental because they have been shown to be supported by different brain systems, and because their differentiation and identification may have important clinical implications."

17. Complex PTSD is listed in the DSM-IV definition of PTSD and associated features section.

18. Herman, *Trauma and Recovery*, 115–16.

19. Judith Herman, "Trauma: The Challenge of the Enlightened Witness" (presented at Bearing Witness Conference, October 1998).

20. Herman, *Trauma and Recovery*, 53–54.

21. Research in the early 1970s by Dr. Judith Wallerstein on the effects of divorce on children indicated they were more or less "resilient."

22. Judith Herman, "Backtalk," *Mother Jones*, March/April 1993, 3–4.

23. Ibid.

24. A. Stein, *Hidden Children: Forgotten Survivors of the Holocaust* (Harmondsworth, Middlesex: Penguin Books, 1994), 106–7.

25. Ibid., 188.
26. See notes 8–12 and Perry, "Incubated in Terror," 124–48.

Chapter Seven

1. Friends in Recovery, *The 12 Steps—A Way Out: A Working Guide for Adult Children from Addictive and Other Dysfunctional Families*, rev. ed. (San Diego: Recovery Publications, 1989).
2. *Meshuggah* is a Yiddish word that generally refers to someone who is "a little bit crazy."
3. Bessel A. van der Kolk, "Psychobiology of Trauma" (paper presented at the 1993 Eastern Regional Conference of the International Society for the Study of Multiple Personality Disorder, Alexandria, Virginia, June 1993). Also see note 26 for chapter 5.
4. BAMM/Impact Self-Defense. For national referral, please call 800-345-KICK.
5. Alcoholics Anonymous, *The Big Book*, 449.
6. Sylvia Boorstein, Sharon Lebell, and Stephen Mitchell, *Funny, You Don't Look Buddhist: On Being a Faithful Jew and a Passionate Buddhist* (New York: HarperSanFrancisco, 1998), 38.
7. I attended a HeartMath presentation in 2001 and was intrigued to learn that the heart has its own nervous system and its own "brain," and that there is research that demonstrates that focusing on feelings of gratitude, appreciation, compassion, and love make us feel better and improve our health. See resource list in Appendix G for contact information.

Chapter Eight

1. The idea of the artist as healer has become popularized in recent years. In a Bill Moyers special, "Healing and the Mind," people were introduced to Dr. Rachel Naomi Remen, the medical director of Commonweal Cancer Retreat Center. Dr. Remen used poetry and sand play to help people find their images, their voices, and their story of healing. At Shands Hospital, in Gainesville, Florida, artists work with patients and families to develop healing images that surround the patient. Music is being used to heal and comfort the dying.
The arts have become an integral part of the healing process. Dr. Michael Samuels and Mary Rockwood, authors of *Creative Healing: How to Heal Yourself by Tapping Your Hidden Creativity*, remark, "Art and healing is a new medically proven technique that strengthens body, mind, and spirit. It is about honoring yourself and waking up the creative spirit inside you and letting the spirit come forth."
2. To honor the sanctity of God's name, traditional Jews write "G-d."

Chapter Nine

This is an excerpt from a speech delivered by Sue William Silverman at the conference "From Denial to Dialogue: The Jewish Community Confronts Domestic Violence," sponsored by the Jewish Federation and Jewish Family and Career Services of Atlanta. A portion of it appeared in *Because I Remember Terror, Father, I Remember You* by Sue William Silverman, copyright by Sue William Silverman, published by the University of Georgia Press in 1996.

1. Sue William Silverman, *Because I Remember Terror, Father, I Remember You* (Athens, Ga.: University of Georgia Press, 1996), 120–22. This excerpt is reprinted with permission of the University of Georgia Press and the author.

Chapter Ten

1. Kaye/Kantrowitz, "The Issue Is Power," 11.
2. For more discussion of these and other barriers, see chapter 11 by Marcia Cohn Spiegel.
3. Open meetings allow anyone to attend; those that are closed are open only to recovering alcoholics.
4. *Vipassana* is described by its promotional literature as "the ability to see things as they really are, through a process of self-observation." Satya Narayan Goenka, the man responsible for bringing this 2,500-year-old technique back to its land of origin, refines the definition: "It is the development of insight (vipassana means insight in Pali, an ancient Indian language) into one's own nature by which one may recognize and eliminate the causes of suffering."
5. HarperSanFrancisco.
6. A *chavurah* is a prayer or study group functioning with lay leadership.
7. See note 2, chapter 3.

Chapter Eleven

1. My story is told in its entirety in "Growing up Jewish," in *Four Centuries of Jewish Women's Spirituality: A Sourcebook*, ed. Ellen M. Umansky and Dianne Ashton (Boston: Beacon, 1992), 292–98.
2. Marcia Cohn Spiegel and Deborah Lipton Kremsdorf, *Women Speak to God: The Prayers and Poems of Jewish Women* (San Diego: Woman's Institute for Continuing Jewish Education, 1987).
3. Anne Barnard, Steve Ritea, and Ralph Vigoda, "Rabinowitz Admits Killing Wife: A Dream Urged Him to Do the Right Thing," *Philadelphia Inquirer*, October 31, 1997, A1.
4. *Lilith* (March 1998).
5. Adam Fifield and Michael Lesher, "A Child's at Stake: A Custody Fight Becomes a Political Nightmare," *Village Voice*, October 1, 1996, 10.

6. "Rabbi's Aide Gets Twenty-Two Months," *Los Angeles Times*, *Metro*, January 20, 1996, 2.

7. Isaac Metzker, ed., *A Bintel Brief: Sixty Years of Letters from the Lower East Side* (New York: Doubleday, 1972).

8. See Betsy Giller, "All in the Family: Violence in the Jewish Home," in *Jewish Women in Therapy*, ed. Rachel Josefowitz Siegel and Ellen Cole (New York: Harrington Park Press, 1991), 101–9; and Mimi Scarf, *Battered Jewish Wives* (Lewiston, N.Y.: Edwin Mellen, 1988).

9. See David Blumenthal, *Facing the Abusing God: A Theology of Protest* (Louisville: Presbyterian Publishing House, 1993).

10. Marcia Lee Falk, *The Book of Blessings: A Feminist Jewish Reconstruction of Prayer* (San Francisco: HarperSanFrancisco, 1996).

11. Judith Glass and Shoshana Gershenzon, "Rosh Hashonah Service for Shabbat Shenit" (Los Angeles, September 1992).

12. A healing *mikveh* ritual for recovery from rape can be found in Laura Levitt and Sue Ann Wasserman, "Mikvah Ceremony for Laura (1989)," in Ellen M. Umansky and Dianne Ashton, eds., *Four Centuries of Jewish Women's Spirituality: A Sourcebook* (Boston: Beacon Press, 1992), 321–26. A meditation for the *mikveh* is presented by Jane Litman, "Meditation for the Mikveh," in *Lifecycles: Jewish Women on Life Passages and Personal Milestones*, ed. Debra Orenstein (Woodstock, Vt.: Jewish Lights, 1994), 253–54.

13. Matia Angelou, "Kos Miryam: Development of a Women's Ritual," *Neshama* (summer 1990): 1–2. This blessing appears in Penina V. Adelman, "A Drink from Miriam's Cup: Invention of Tradition among Jewish Women," *Journal of Feminist Studies in Religion* 10 (fall 1994): 151–66. For permission to use the blessing, write to Kol Isha, P.O. Box 132, Wayland, MA 01778.

14. Although many such Haggadoth have been created, three that are commercially available are the *San Diego Women's Haggadah* (San Diego: Woman's Institute for Continuing Jewish Education, 1986) and Elaine Moise and Rebecca Schwartz, *The Dancing with Miriam Haggadah* (Palo Alto, Calif.: Rikudei Miriam, 1995), and *The Journey Continues: The Ma'yan Haggadah* (New York: Ma'yan, 1998).

15. See Penina V. Adelman, *Miriam's Well: Rituals for Jewish Women around the Year* (New York: Biblio, 1990); and Susan Berrin, *Celebrating the New Moon: A Rosh Chodesh Anthology* (Northvale, N.J.: Jason Aronson, 1996).

16. See Savina J. Teubal, "Simchat Hochmah," in Umansky and Ashton, *Four Centuries*, 257–65.

17. Music for the song was composed by Deborah Lynn Friedman with lyrics by Debbie Friedman and Drorah O'Donnell Setel.

18. See Falk's *Book of Blessings*, 206.

19. These two rituals and other midlife celebrations are described in Irene Fine, *Midlife, A Rite of Passage, The Wise Woman, A Celebration* (San Diego: Woman's Institute for Continuing Jewish Education, 1988), and *Timbrels and Torahs: Celebrating Women's Wisdom*, a video produced by Joy of Wisdom Productions, Berkeley, Calif., 2000.

20. See Jane Litman, "Women's Folk Judaism," *Lilith* (fall 1991): 6.

21. A complete description of Jewish mourning customs is contained in Anne Brener, *Mourning and Mitzvah: A Guided Journal for Walking the Mourner's Path through Grief to Healing* (Woodstock, Vt.: Jewish Lights, 1993), 217.

22. See Kerry M. Olitzky and Stuart Copens, *Twelve Jewish Steps to Recovery* (Woodstock, Vt.: Jewish Lights, 1991), 52.

23. I thank the women of Bnot Esh, Shabbat Shenit, and the Mikveh Ladies who created some of these rituals and participated in others, and who model creative change in uses of ritual and liturgy.

Chapter Twelve

1. Robert N. Bellah (ed.), Richard Madsen, William M. Sullivan, Ann Swidler, and Steven M. Tipton, *Habits of the Heart: Individualism and Commitment in American Life* (Berkeley, Calif.: University of California Press, 1996).

2. Herman, *Trauma and Recovery*, 70.

3. The Family Violence Prevention Fund is a national and international organization, which, in coalition with a number of groups, develops innovative programs that are advocacy based, public policy based, prevention based, and education based.

4. The Kol Nidrei prayer, recited on the eve of Yom Kippur, is one of the most solemn prayers in Hebrew liturgy. It is chanted three times as Jews ask forgiveness for their transgressions against God.

5. Speech by Gloria Steinem at the Eastern Regional Conference of the International Society for the Study of Multiple Personality Disorder, Alexandria, Virginia, June 1993.

6. The Jewish Child at Risk Conference, Jewish Children's Bureau, Alexandria, Virginia, June 1995.

7. See Appendix F.

8. Per discussions with Joan Cohen and Mimi Kraus.

9. OHEL Children's Home and Family Services, David Mandel, executive director; 718-851-6555. Speakers on September 26, 2000, included (rabbis) HaRav Avraham Pam, shlita; HaRav Shmuel Kamentzky, shlita; and HaRav Yisroel Reisman, shlita.

10. Contact Rabbi Zev Cohen (phone: 773-465-2282) for discussion of community development issues regarding child sexual abuse.

11. For comments, questions, or requests to adapt this to your congregation, write to: Shalom Bayit, 3543-18th St., #10, San Francisco, CA 94110. Phone: 510-451-8874. Website: www.shalom-bayit.org.

12. Speech by Gloria Steinem at the Eastern Regional Conference of the International Society for the Study of Multiple Personality Disorder, Alexandria, Virginia, June 1993.

Chapter Thirteen

1. *Protecting Our Children: Information for Clergy Members about Child Abuse and Neglect*, a publication of the Clergy Advisory Board of the California Consortium to Prevent Child Abuse, in collaboration with the Office of Child Abuse Prevention of the California Department of Social Services.

2. The verse forbidding putting a stumbling block before the blind (Lev. 19:14) is probably talking in its plain meaning about physically blind people and physical stumbling blocks, but the classical rabbis applied it also—indeed, more often—to intellectual and characterological stumbling blocks put before those who are blind in those areas. See the *Sifra* on that verse and a variety of Talmudic passages, including B. *Pesahim* 22b; B. *Mo'ed Katan* 17a; and B. *Kiddushin* 30a.

3. The classic rabbinic statement of these steps is that of Maimonides, *Laws of Repentance* (*Teshuvah*), especially 2:1–2. For a fuller discussion of Jewish approaches to forgiveness, see my article, "The Elements of Forgiveness: A Jewish Approach," in *Dimensions of Forgiveness: Psychological Research and Theological Perspectives*, ed. Everett L. Worthington, Jr. (Philadelphia: Templeton Foundation Press, 1998), 29–55, to be included in my forthcoming book on Jewish social ethics, tentatively entitled *Doing the Right and the Good: A Jewish Approach to Social Ethics* (Philadelphia: Jewish Publication Society, 2002).

4. B. *Sanhedrin* 99a, and see Rashi's comment there. See Naomi Graetz, "The Haftorah Tradition and the Metaphoric Battering of Hosea's Wife," *Conservative Judaism* 45, no. 1 (fall 1992): 29–42, for further discussion of when and how the safety of the synagogue can be helpful for airing matters of human intimacy, including areas of vulnerability such as being a victim or perpetrator of abuse.

5. For explanations of these phrases and sources, see the key before the notes in chapter 3.

6. Leviticus 19:14. See note 2 above for the meaning of that verse in Jewish law.

7. I would like to thank my friend and colleague, Rabbi Joel Rembaum, for pointing out to me the implications of such situations for the process of *teshuvah*.

8. M. *Bava Kamma* 8:7.

9. See my article on forgiveness cited in note 3 above for a fuller treatment of these distinctions.

10. Elliot N. Dorff, *"This Is My Beloved, This Is My Friend": A Rabbinic Letter on Intimate Relations* (New York: Rabbinical Assembly, 1996).

11. The entire fall 1994 issue of *Religious Education* (vol. 89, no. 4) was devoted to the cover topic, "Religious Education and Child Abuse." That issue includes important articles on how religious educators (and presumably rabbis and cantors among them) can recognize child abuse when it happens, help victims to extricate themselves from the abuse, and help to prevent child abuse in the first place. Marion Wright Edelman of the Children's Defense Fund, James Fowler, and Nel Nodings are among the writers.

12. Published in *Newsweek*, September 28, 1992, in selected regions and in the *New York Times*, October 1, 1992, and the *Wall Street Journal* on the same

date. The material first appeared as the High Holy Day Message of the Jewish Theological Seminary for 1992 and is copyrighted by JTS.

Chapter Fourteen

1. "The thing is" from *Mules of Love* (Rochester: BOA Editions, 2002).

Chapter Fifteen

1. David A. Cooper, *God Is a Verb: Kabbalah and the Practice of Mystical Judaism* (New York: Riverhead Books, 1997), 156.

INDEX ❧